EXPLORER'S GUIDES

San Diego

WITHDRAWN

San Diego

A Great Destination

Debbie K. Hardin

The Countryman Press   Woodstock, Vermont

SECOND EDITION

San Diego: A Great Destination
ISBN 978-1-58157-133-2

Interior photos by the author unless otherwise specified
Book design by Bodenweber Design
Page composition by PerfecType, Nashville, TN
Maps by Mapping Specialists, Ltd., Madison, WI © The Countryman Press

Published by The Countryman Press, P.O. Box 748, Woodstock, Vermont 05091
Distributed by W. W. Norton & Company, Inc., 500 Fifth Ave., New York, NY 10110
Printed in the United States of America

*To my mom, Irine Axton, who always told me that I could
travel around the world and never find a better place than San Diego.
She was right—as usual.*

Acknowledgments

I owe a lot to the many experts throughout San Diego with whom I spoke when writing this book, and I am sincerely grateful to all who answered my pleas for advice. Included in this group are several extraordinary public relations professionals who made my work easier and more enjoyable: Judith Adams, Rob Akins, Leslie Araiza, Robert Arends, Malika Baniyahya, Marje Bennetts, Kate Buska, Kurstin Christie, Lauren Clapperton, Marguerite Clark, Lauren Clifford, Sean Curry, Sara DeYoung, Joanne DiBona, Lauren Donoho, Chris Engler, Eva Marie Gutierrez, Vanessa Kanegai, Rana Kay, Ann Kelsey, Linda Kissam, Katherine Lewis, Katherine Los, Helen McClaire, John McClintock, Janel Moncada, Sanjay Parekh, Heather Pimentel, Sarah Prudhomme, Miliña Reeves, Christina Simmons, Joe Timko, Hilary Townsend, Mikel Wadewitz, and Marisa Zafran all went the extra mile for me. A special thanks goes to Joe Timko at the San Diego Convention and Visitors Bureau.

In addition, I called on family and friends to share favorite places. For their willingness to divulge their secrets and for their support, I thank Lori Boechler, Susie Bright, Karen Carriere, Swati Dalvie, Cate DaPron, Nancy Deal, Alyson Earnest, Gilbert Gonzalez, Pat Gonzalez, Donna Johnson, Emilee Legg, Kevin Legg, Stacy Richards, Margie Rogers, Cindy Simpson, and Rosanna and River Weiss. In addition, I owe a special debt of gratitude to two brothers-in-law who gave me insight into their favorite sports: Larry Legg, who helped me make the fishing sections authoritative, and Joe Preimesberger, who shared his expertise on golf.

For entrusting me with this project, I thank Kim Grant and Kermit Hummel of Countryman Press, both of whom have been supportive and exceedingly kind. Thanks also go to the production team: Lisa Sacks, who patiently shepherded the project through production; Justine Rathbun, who copyedited the book; and Doug Yeager, who oversaw typesetting and production.

Finally, I thank my husband, Jon Preimesberger, and my daughter, Juliane, for making the exploration and research of our hometown a family project—and a fun one, at that.

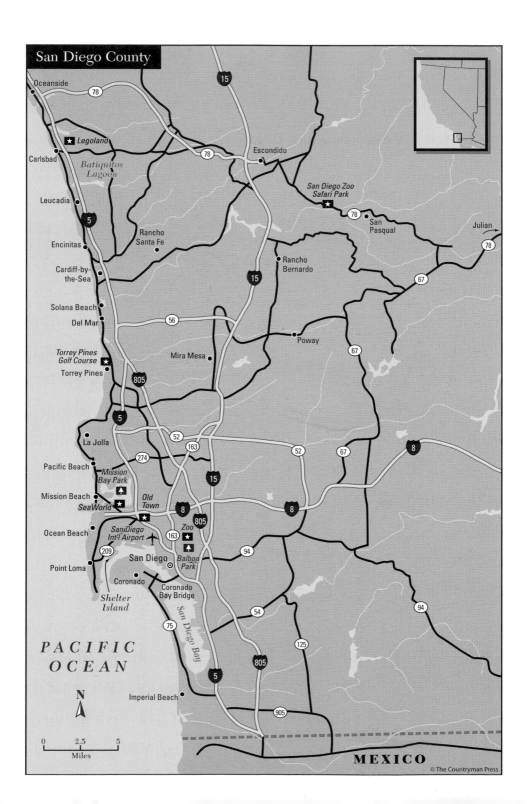

Contents

Introduction

San Diego has long attracted tourists and new residents who are looking for unbeatable weather, miles of pristine shoreline, and a relaxed pace. With a Mediterranean climate and abundance of outdoor attractions, San Diego is often characterized as merely a resort destination—and indeed, this embarrassment of natural riches *does* tend to put one in a holiday frame of mind. But San Diego has grown up over the past few decades and is now the eighth-largest city in the United States, with a population of almost 1.3 million in the city and more than 3 million in the county. San Diego's rich historical heritage, geographical diversity, and blending of cultures make for a thriving city that offers a staggering variety of experiences. Where else can you kayak through ocean-sculpted caves, admire cruise ships and Navy carriers docked side by side, attend world-class theater in a reproduction of Shakespeare's Old Globe Theatre, have a sleepover with lions, tee off at premier oceanfront golf courses in the shadow of local Phil Mickelson, stroll through Roy Lichtenstein's and Christo's work at the foremost contemporary art museum in California, or dive alongside a sunken World War II submarine?

In addition to the variety of activities, it's hard to miss the incredible natural beauty in San Diego: sage-colored mountains rise up close to the sea, the Pacific Ocean glitters in the sun like a rolling blanket of diamonds, and the sun bleaches the landscape and the sky to impressionistic hues. The explosion of flowers year-round, the imported evergreen palm trees, and the relentless sunshine confuse the seasons. It isn't quite endless summer, but it's close. There is barely a day when an outdoor café is out of the question; surfers paddle out seeking the perfect wave year-round; and runners hit the pavement even in the middle of winter.

I was born in San Diego and have lived most of my life here. The sights, sounds, and tastes of the area are intimately connected with my earliest memories: I was on a boat in Mission Bay at just two weeks old; I spent childhood summers at nearby Mission Beach; I attended college at the University of California, San Diego, in beautiful La Jolla. Today I live with my family in North County. My perspective as a longtime native informs everything that I write. In the pages that follow I'll help you discover for yourself the secrets of old-time favorites and delights of new hot spots—and I'll help you plan your days so that the geographical distance (and the traffic that sometimes goes along with exploring the area) doesn't become a nuisance. Once you explore San Diego for yourself, you are sure to join the ranks of the millions of people who call this area their heart's home.

—Debbie K. Hardin

The Way This Book Works

This book is divided into seven sections. The first section provides historical context, and the second explores transportation to and around the area. Chapters 1 through 3 divide the area into three geographical regions (downtown, La Jolla and the beaches, and North County). Following this is a section that explores a half dozen side trips, should you be inclined to extend your visit beyond the borders of San Diego County. The final section offers a useful guide that will help you plan your trip. You can skip from section to section to suit your interests, and you can take this book along with you for handy reference in a given neighborhood or region of the city. Better yet, read the book cover to cover, and then go back and look up your favorites.

Be sure to refer to the maps throughout the book to help you familiarize yourself with the area. Because it is nearly impossible to cover much ground without a car, I've included a freeway map, too, which ought to come in handy when negotiating the large distances that can be involved when touring the many neighborhoods.

If you're searching for places to stay or to eat, I suggest you first check out the listings under "Dining" in the index, which subdivides the entries by locale. Turn to the page references, and you'll find entries that include myriad choices and a wide range of price points. Note that I've included three categories of dining: Fine Dining, which includes upscale restaurants (many of which require reservations); Casual Dining, which includes casual restaurants and take-out joints; and Snacks, which offers suggestions for between-meal treats.

New for this edition, I've included dozens of best-of-the-best lists to alert you to the finest restaurants, lodging options, cultural attractions, historical places, green spaces (including beaches and gardens), outdoor activities (including golf, surfing, boating, and fishing), family-fun attractions, shopping, and nightlife. Also new to this edition, at the end of coverage for each geographical region, I've included five suggested itineraries appropriate for couples, families, outdoors enthusiasts, culture enthusiasts, and those on a tight budget. The itineraries chart 48 hours in the region, starting on Friday night and finishing on Sunday afternoon.

A WORD ABOUT PRICES

Note that hours and prices change regularly; I have endeavored to provide the most up-to-date information possible, but it is always wise to check the Web site or call ahead for specifics. To that end, I've avoided listing specific prices for most entries, preferring instead to indicate a range (from inexpensive to very expensive).

Lodging price categories are based on a standard (nonview) per-room rate, double occupancy, during high season (summer and holiday months). Low-season rates are likely to be as much as 40 to 50 percent less. Prices do not include taxes (hotels tack on a transient occupancy tax that averages to about 15 percent). San Diego has some of the most expensive real estate in the country, and the lodging prices reflect this reality. Many lodging options fall in the expensive to very expensive category (and note that the very expensive category can extend into thousands of dollars a night for premium rooms), but there are exceptions and a few bargains to be had. I've tried to include a range of options within the sections titled *Pick Your Spot*.

Likewise, dining in this region reflects big-city prices, but there are values in this arena as well. I have included many inexpensive options for budget-conscious travelers within the Casual Dining and Snacks portions of the sections titled *Local Flavors*. Restaurant prices indicated throughout the book include the cost of an individual meal, including appetizer, entrée, dessert, tax, and tip but not including beverages. Refer to the following key:

	Lodging	**Dining**
Inexpensive	Up to $150	Up to $15
Moderate	$151–250	$16–30
Expensive	$251–350	$31–75
Very Expensive	More than $351	More than $76

LODGING NOTES

Rates
High-season rates generally apply in San Diego during the summer months, starting on Memorial Day weekend and continuing through the end of September. Higher rates will also apply during the holiday season running from Thanksgiving week through the first of the year and during spring break.

Minimum Stay
During high season, and at some smaller establishments all year long, it isn't unusual for hotels to insist on a minimum stay of two or even three nights for advance bookings. However, if you reserve accommodations at the last minute (which I do not recommend, because this is a recipe for disappointment), you can often bypass these requirements.

Deposit/Cancellation
You'll be expected to provide one night's security deposit, which may be charged to your account at the time of your booking or may be charged the day you are due to arrive. Most hotels will allow cancellations and rescheduling up to 72 hours in advance without penalties, but expect as much as a full night's charge if you cancel within 24 hours.

There are a plethora of national chain restaurants and hotels in San Diego—some of them very fine indeed. But I've chosen to bypass most of these and instead focus on independent establishments that will be less familiar to both the traveler and to newcomers in San Diego. I made some exceptions to this rule (e.g., a Southern California taco chain that got its start in Pacific Beach, and a five-star hotel chain with a landmark property in Carlsbad), but otherwise I've concentrated on those experiences you can't get outside of San Diego.

MORE INFO: SAN DIEGO

The best sources for year-round tourist information are the **San Diego Convention and Visitors Bureau** (619-232-3101; www.sandiego.org/nav/Visitors; 2215 India Street, San Diego), **Carlsbad Convention and Visitors Bureau** (760-434-6093; www.visitcarlsbad.com; 400 Carlsbad Village Drive, Carlsbad), and **Coronado Visitor Center** (619-437-8788; www.coronadovisitorcenter.com; 1100 Orange Avenue, Coronado).

If you need emergency assistance while traveling, consult the **Travelers Aid Society** (619-295-8393; www.travelersaidsandiego.org; 110 W. C Street, Ste. 209, San Diego); there is also a location in the San Diego airport (619-295-1277; San Diego International Airport, Terminal 2).

Overlooking Del Mar Beach

History

FROM MISSIONARIES TO SUN WORSHIPPERS

San Diego has been influenced by a number of disparate cultures: Native Americans called the area home as long ago as 12,000 BC. Nearly 14,000 years later, Spanish missionaries claimed the land—and the souls that inhabited it—as their own. But it wasn't long before Mexican revolutionaries fought for their independence from colonial Spain, only to have U.S. forces take massive tracts of territory soon after for the pioneers who believed it was their divine right to move west. Since that time, immigrants like Chinese workers in the late 19th century, Portuguese fishermen in the early 20th century, and Vietnamese refugees in the 1970s have thronged to San Diego to pursue their own manifest destinies. In addition, throughout the years Hispanic immigrants have come across the border in search of a better life for themselves and their families, and in so doing have infused the whole of Southern California with the rich heritage of Mexico and many other Latin American countries.

The identity of San Diego has been enriched and enlivened with each successive wave of immigration, and this has made for a hospitable social climate. San Diegans are quick to greet visitors with a smile, and longtimers welcome newcomers warmly. Under clear skies and unrelenting sunshine, all San Diego locals congratulate each other on living in what most believe is the best place in the world.

There are a lot of locals to make this argument, because San Diego is the second most populous city in California and the eighth largest in the country. But unlike many East Coast cities that are tightly packed and have had little choice over the years but to grow upward, San Diego has sprawled outward; the county covers more than 4,000 square miles, and it takes hours to drive from one end to the other. Drive we must, however, because the county is actually a collection of neighborhoods strung together amid a spiderweb of freeways and highways. Over the past decades, developers have filled in the spaces between, and now it is nearly impossible to distinguish where one neighborhood begins and the other ends.

The diverse geography around which San Diego is built ranges from miles of dramatic coastline in the west to mountains that rise up east of the city. Beyond the mountains lie vast expanses of desert that extend past the eastern border of the state. The semiarid climate that results from this proximity to the desert is world-famous for its mildness. Average precipitation is less than 10 inches per year—but this sunny outlook has a dark side: the city has been dealing with a serious water shortage and cyclical droughts for decades. Because of the hilly topography punctuated with low-lying valleys, on the rare occasions when it does rain heavily, portions of the city are subject to floods and mudslides.

As any sun worshipper knows, this mostly dry, sun-kissed weather has its upside, too: the region is an outdoor sporting mecca, and the economy is fueled by visitors who want in on the action. Although the growing population and expensive real estate have driven out most agriculture, many parts of the county are still prime for growing flowers, strawberries, citrus, and avocados. With the natural beauty of the region, and the bounty possible with irrigation, it's no wonder people throughout history have felt a primordial pull to settle here.

THE FIRST LOCALS

Long before Europeans "discovered" San Diego, Natives known as the San Dieguito people called San Diego home. Then came the La Jolla people, the Diegueños, and finally the Yuman and Shoshonean peoples. The latter group comprised the Luiseño, who settled in the North County, and the Kumeyaay, who settled in what is now Mission Valley.

The Natives lived in dome-shaped dwellings made from willow-branch frames covered with bark or grasses. The Kumeyaay were hunters and agriculturalists. They planted beans, corn, and squash and hunted bighorn sheep, deer, and rabbits. They were exceptional artisans, crafting coiled grass baskets that were of such fine quality they could hold water. They were peaceful people and initially welcomed the first colonists—although when it became apparent in later years that their lands were being overtaken, the Natives grew distinctly less cooperative.

CONQUISTADORS AND MISSIONARIES

On September 28, 1542, Portuguese explorer Juan Rodriquez Cabrillo, sailing on behalf of Spain, became the first European of record to set foot on the west coast of the United States. He sailed his flagship, the *San Salvador*, into the San Diego Bay, just off the peninsula of Point Loma, in search of a trade route between Mexico and the Spice Islands in Asia. Cabrillo never found the shortcut to riches for which he was looking, but he did claim the newfound area for Spain. Cabrillo named the spot San Miguel and then quickly moved on in search of another discovery.

In 1602, just 60 years after Cabrillo, another Spanish explorer came along: shortly after landing, Sebastian Vizcaíno and his party celebrated the first Christian religious service in California to commemorate the feast day of Saint Diego. Vizcaíno renamed the city San Diego de Alcalá. This time the name stuck.

Explorers didn't come to San Diego again in significant numbers for 150 years. In the mid-18th century, however, Russian colonies started popping up in northern California, and Spain worried that Russia might threaten the Spanish settlements in southern California. So Spain decided to found its own colonies.

Cabrillo National Monument

Father Junípero Serra, a Franciscan friar charged with establishing missions throughout California, and Gaspar de Portolá, a Spanish officer leading the accompanying military force, landed in San Diego in 1769 to begin Spanish colonization. Shortly after arriving, Father Serra chose a site on what is now Presidio Hill to build the first mission in California. Natives living near the mission were not particularly happy to see the Spaniards, but they were soon convinced to cooperate or were subdued, either through sheer force wielded by the soldiers or through the more subtle persuasion of religious conversion wielded by the friars.

In 1771 Father Serra moved on to Mission Carmel, and Father Luis Jayme succeeded him. In 1774, when it became clear that the original site had inadequate supplies of water and poor land for farming, the friars moved 6 miles inland, near the San Diego River, where the mission stands today.

The new mission site was already a Kumeyaay village, however, and the Kumeyaay resisted the missionaries from the beginning. A little more than a year after the move, on November 5, 1775, several Kumeyaay brutally murdered Father Jayme and burned the mission structures to the ground. The Kumeyaay were soon overpowered by Spanish soldiers, and the insurrection came to a quick halt.

In the aftermath of the revolt, Father Serra returned to San Diego to oversee the rebuilding, and soon the mission was back in business. By 1797, almost 600 souls had been baptized into the faith, and more than 1,400 converted to Christianity. Although the Spanish colonists were successful in carrying out their mission, the Natives suffered enormous losses because of the rapid spread of diseases against which they had no natural immunity. In addition to the many who died—some historians estimate as many as half succumbed to European-spread illnesses—Natives who defied the Spaniards or deserted the mission settlement were beaten, jailed, or both. Although the Kumeyaay acquired farming and ranching skills and thereby learned a more sustainable way of life, their native culture was all but wiped out within the colonies.

In 1798, the Mission San Luis Rey de Francia was founded by Padre Fermín de Lasuén about 30 miles north of the San Diego mission, in what is now Oceanside. The Mission San Luis Rey, the 18th in a line of 21 missions in California, is much grander and larger than the first modest mission in San Diego. Although there was

Mission San Luis Rey de Francia, Oceanside

little physical resistance to the missionaries who moved into San Luis Rey, the Natives were again forced to relocate or to become a part of the new mission.

MEXICAN WARS RESHAPE THE BOUNDARIES

The Native Americans were not the only ones to chafe under Spanish rule. Starting in 1810, Mexico fought for independence from colonial Spain. In 1821, revolutionary troops in Mexico overthrew Spain's government. But because Spanish involvement in San Diego at the time didn't extend far beyond the missions, the political handover in the area was nonviolent and relatively anticlimactic.

At the end of the Mexican War of Independence, by Mexican law, the missions were secularized and the goal to convert Natives fell by the wayside. The settlers who'd lived in the shadows of the first mission started to move away. The settlement now known as Old Town—which was founded in 1769—became the favored place to live in San Diego.

In 1845, prominent San Diegan Pio Pico became governor of California. Shortly afterward, the Mexican American War (1846–48) broke out. At that time, Mexico's territory stretched through Texas and included all of California (divided into Alta California—or upper California—and Baja California). But U.S. settlers guided by the tenets of Manifest Destiny moved west into California and other Mexican territories, and it wasn't long before these pioneers looked to make the land their own.

A decade earlier, in 1836, Texas settlers fought for and won independence from Mexico. However, Mexico refused to recognize the loss of Texas, and when the United States admitted Texas into the Union in 1845 (as the 28th state), Mexico fumed. President James Polk fanned the flames when he sent emissaries to Mexico in an effort to buy Alta California and New Mexico and to settle the matter of Texas once and for all. But Mexico announced its intention to take back Texas, and by mid-1846, relations between the countries deteriorated significantly. The United States declared war on Mexico in May, and U.S. forces invaded the Mexican territories.

Mexican governor Pico and Gen. José Castro fled from their headquarters in Los Angeles before the U.S. troops arrived, so by the time the invading forces landed, there was almost no one to fight. This nearly bloodless takeover may have given the United States false confidence, however, because the U.S. generals in charge left a skimpy occupying force. Rebel forces later attacked the remaining U.S. troops in Los Angeles, and several died before the area was once again secured for the United States.

One of the most decisive battles of the war was fought in San Diego County. In 1846, Gen. Stephen Watts Kearny's army marched from Santa Fe to San Diego, along with guide Kit Carson and more than one hundred soldiers. In response, Mexican general Andrés Pico gathered nearly double the number of men, and his forces readied to intercept the U.S. troops before they arrived in the city. On December 6, Kearny countered by attacking the Mexican army at a site near the San Pasqual Valley, about 5 miles from what is now Escondido. At least 18 U.S. soldiers were killed during the Battle of San Pasqual—the largest number of U.S. casualties in California throughout the war.

Kearny and his troops had been outwitted and outnumbered, and it wasn't long before they were surrounded and cut off from food and ammunition. Carson and another soldier managed to sneak away for help. On December 11, more than two hundred Marines and sailors from San Diego arrived to escort the remaining U.S. troops into the city. Pico's army withdrew, and within a few weeks Pico surrendered at Cahuenga Pass north of San Diego. A few weeks later, the Treaty of Guadalupe ended the war completely and established the current U.S. border with Mexico, which put Alta California in U.S. control. Mexicans living in Alta California and other conquered territories (which included Nevada and Utah as well as parts of New Mexico, Arizona, Colorado, and Wyoming) were given the choice to either stay and become citizens of the United States or return to Mexico.

THE ROOTS OF "NEW TOWN"

In the aftermath of the Mexican American War, San Diego was named the seat of newly established San Diego County, and it was incorporated as a city in 1850. Businessman William Heath Davis was one of the first developers in the city, and he invested in 32 square blocks between Broadway and Market streets (now the Gaslamp Quarter). But the citizens of San Diego were by then happily ensconced in Old Town and didn't see the point in moving the city. They watched with amusement as Davis threw up several prefabricated buildings (shipped in from a company in Maine) and began to build a wharf on the waterfront. But Davis was a man ahead of his time, and residents did not flock to his so-called New Town as he'd hoped. The failure was so complete that New Town soon became known as "Davis's Folly."

A few years later, in 1867, businessman Alonzo Horton came along and revived interest in New Town. He bought 800 acres of bay-front property and completed Davis's wharf. Horton and his supporters managed to move the county courthouse from Old Town (housed in the building now known as the Whaley House) to New Town, which effectively ended Old Town's reign as the seat of San Diego government. At the same time, Horton set aside 1,400 acres of the city as parkland—what would eventually become Balboa Park. The new downtown was quickly established as the heart of the city, and Old Town faded from prominence. A few years later, in 1872, a firestorm swept through Old Town and obliterated most of what was left of the original settlement.

THE STINGAREE DISTRICT

The city grew quickly over the next several decades—perhaps too quickly, because downtown soon became a wild and dangerous place. By the late 1880s, there were more than 100 bordellos downtown, as well as more than 70 saloons, dance halls, and gambling parlors, many of which were open all day and night. The Gaslamp Quarter at the time was called the Stingaree District, because it was said that a person could get stung as badly there as she or he could by the stingrays in the San Diego Bay.

During this period, Wyatt Earp rolled into town with his third wife, Josie. It was 1885—a few years after Earp's infamous gunfight at the OK Corral in Tombstone, Arizona—and Earp was looking to make some fast cash in the booming city of San Diego. Earp bought or leased several saloons in the Stingaree—and dropped even more cash gambling in establishments owned by others. But in 1888, the boom in population that San Diego had enjoyed finally went bust, and Earp and his wife moved on as quickly as they came. Several years later, in the first of many revitalization attempts of the area, city law enforcement swept through the Stingaree and shut down most of the bordellos and many of the bars.

WORLD EXPOSITIONS

In 1915, San Diego hosted a spectacular World's Fair to celebrate the completion of the Panama Canal. It was during this period that the ornate Spanish buildings in Balboa Park were built. The structures were originally intended to be temporary buildings to house exhibits, but most of them were left standing after the exposition was over. At the same time, respected nursery owner Kate Sessions was hired to plant trees and gardens throughout the park.

The Panama–California exposition was a major success and attracted the likes of Theodore Roosevelt, William Taft, and Thomas Edison. When it was all over, Harry Wegeforth, a surgeon from Baltimore who'd recently relocated to San

Ornate architecture in Balboa Park

Diego, wondered what would become of the animals brought into Balboa Park for the exposition. It occurred to him that the city needed a zoo, and he persuaded city leaders to help him create and fund the San Diego Zoological Society. In 1921 the park set aside 100 acres as zoo grounds, and cages were erected to house the remaining animals from the exposition. It wasn't long before the zoo started to acquire exotic species from around the world.

Because the first had been so successful, in 1935 San Diego hosted a second World's Fair, this time known as the California–Pacific Exposition. El Prado—the main thoroughfare in Balboa Park—was expanded, and more ornate Spanish buildings were erected to house an even larger collection of exhibits.

SAN DIEGO DURING THE WORLD WARS

The U.S. military looked favorably on San Diego as early as the late 19th century. By World War I, North Island in Coronado was created as a marine base, and the navy built a massive shipyard downtown, as well as a training station and a hospital.

It wasn't until World War II, however, that the military presence in San Diego became prominent.

After the Japanese attack on Pearl Harbor, San Diego became a critical port for the Pacific Fleet, as well as a hub of defense contracts. The population swelled to nearly 400,000 as workers sought employment in the San Diego aircraft plants that worked 24 hours a day to meet Uncle Sam's demands. Military bases already in the city were expanded during the war, and new facilities were built throughout the county. The San Diego Bay was laced with giant netting devices intended to obstruct Japanese submarines, and the beautiful buildings in Balboa Park were converted to hospitals.

Local leaders had to scramble to keep ahead of the demand for housing and adequate water and sewer systems. Linda Vista, just east of Mission Bay, started out life as Defense Housing Project No. 4092. In the largest construction project to date, the government spent $14 million developing nearly 1,500 acres into small homes to house the burgeoning military. More than three thousand houses were built in two hundred days, all of which were immediately rented out to soldiers' families and defense plant employees. Other developments like it filled in the mesas north of downtown in the months that followed.

On February 9, 1942, President Franklin D. Roosevelt signed Executive Order 9066, which gave U.S. authorities the legal right to remove Japanese Americans living in coastal cities in the West from their homes and relocate them to inland camps (like the infamous Manzanar), where they would be forcefully detained. Proponents of the order claimed that by relocating Japanese Americans away from coastal regions, U.S. interests would be protected from possible espionage that would confound the war in the Pacific. Within weeks of the order, the Western Defense Command removed close to two thousand individuals of Japanese descent from San Diego. Most returned after the war to find their homes and property were gone.

SAN DIEGO INTO THE MODERN ERA

The Korean and Vietnam wars continued to fuel the San Diego economy, which was still heavily invested in the defense industry, but with urban sprawl in the late 1960s and early 1970s the city center deteriorated. Longtime businesses folded up shop, and few new businesses dared to relocate in the increasingly dangerous area. The downtown area became a haven for the mentally ill, sleazy businesses, and illicit activity. By the early 1980s, it wasn't safe to walk below Broadway Street— just as it wasn't safe one hundred years before, when the area was known as the Stingaree.

Thanks to the vision of a succession of local politicians, the Centre City Development Corporation, and many deep-pocket investors, downtown San Diego has undergone a remarkable revitalization in the past few decades. Starting with the opening of Seaport Village shopping mall in 1980, Horton Plaza shopping mall in 1985, and subsequent urban renewal efforts by entrepreneurs and city leaders, the downtown corridor now sparkles with a glamorous waterfront, eclectic architecture, fine dining, vibrant clubs, and upscale shopping. The Gaslamp Quarter—16 blocks that stretch from Broadway to Market between Fourth and Sixth streets—is a particularly stunning success. With the 2004 opening of the Petco Park baseball stadium in the East Village, adjacent to the Gaslamp, renewal has spread like wildfire. Old buildings are being renovated and new buildings are going up at an astounding rate to fill the demand for more downtown housing and office space. Although the economic downturn that began in 2008 has rocked San Diego, it has barely touched the increasingly popular downtown corridor, which continues to grow in vibrancy. New condo developments continue to sell well, and new restaurants and hotels seem to pop up monthly.

LOOKING FORWARD

Although the San Diego economy is still dependent on the U.S. military, as well as tourism, defense-related businesses, and commercial shipbuilding, increasingly high-tech industries are moving into the area. World-class research institutes are scattered throughout town, the most prominent among them being the University of California, San Diego (UCSD); The Salk Institute; and the Scripps Research Institute. These brain trusts have spun off hundreds of research and development

Wyatt Earp Building in the Gaslamp Quarter

companies as well. San Diego is now home to dozens of Nobel Prize winners, pre-dominately in the field of science.

Thanks to this burgeoning scientific focus, which helps drive the strong econo-my, and because of the incredible natural beauty of the region and the infamous laid-back attitude of its inhabitants, it's easy to imagine San Diego as an idyllic city that has little to do but bask in the sun and play in the surf. But like every major municipality in the United States, we have our fair share of challenges.

From the very beginning of San Diego's history, the region's most precious—and scarce—natural resource has been water, and it promises to continue to be so. Throughout the early missionary period and beyond, the region fell under cycles of extreme drought conditions followed by catastrophic flooding, when parched lands couldn't absorb intense rainfalls.

To provide an increased water supply for the growing population, early reme-dies in San Diego included major dam construction throughout the county and brokered agreements from neighboring regions to siphon off their water supplies. Despite these efforts to borrow water from other locales, city planners severely underestimated the area's need for water. When the population of San Diego exploded during World War II, President Roosevelt stepped in to authorize the building of the San Diego Aqueduct, which brought in Colorado River water that was hoped to be enough for generations. Thanks to severe droughts and a continu-ally growing population, San Diego's needs exceeded these water rights within a decade.

By the turn of the 21st century, the city was looking for new answers to its water crisis, and within a few years civic leaders instituted yet another stopgap measure. In 2003, the Imperial Irrigation District approved an agreement to share Colorado River water and transfer additional water rights to San Diego County—an unpopular move among Imperial Valley farmers, who were concerned about the adequacy of their own water supply in the future. The controversial agreement will supply San Diego with about a third of its water needs in the coming years. In the meantime, mandatory conservation efforts have been instituted throughout the city, which allow residents to water our landscape and wash our cars only on desig-nated days of the week. Local golf courses have begun to use recycled water to irrigate their greens, and landscaping with native, drought-resistant plants is becoming more popular. Visitors will notice that many restaurants will not auto-matically bring water to the table; this must often be ordered (although tap water is always free). In addition, hotels throughout San Diego use low-flow water fix-tures and ask guests to hang up towels they are willing to reuse, to save the immense water needed to launder linens daily.

Another major problem facing the city is the inadequacy of the international airport. Lindbergh Field was built on dredged land fill from the San Diego Bay in 1928 and now sits surprisingly close to downtown. Jets fly directly over crowded freeways and near high-rises to approach the runways, making an approach to Lindbergh Field thrilling and unbelievably scenic. Lindbergh long ago exceeded its intended capacity, and neighbors in pricey Mission Hills and elsewhere com-plain about the noise. Restrictions have been in place for decades to prevent jets from landing late in the evening to pacify nearby residents.

City planners and business leaders are searching for new sites for a second air-port, but so far nothing has been deemed satisfactory. Choices have included

Revitalized Harbor District

reclaiming military bases for the purpose, building an airport as much as 50 miles outside of the city, and even unlikely scenarios like building a floating airport in the Pacific Ocean. It will take years (and billions of dollars) to investigate each possible site, and likely decades to fund and then build a new facility—and given the economic crisis that has hit California hard, it is unlikely the city or the state will have the funds to tackle the project anytime soon.

Despite these and other challenges the city faces, San Diego remains a vibrant, exciting metropolis that has the ambiance of a much smaller city. The area enjoys a strong economy that has been battered—but not beaten—by the national recession, and leaders are starting to pay attention to managed growth. The most valuable natural resource in the region—the diverse and optimistic group of people who call San Diego home—are sure to keep fighting to improve their communities, for themselves and for those who choose to visit.

Transportation

GETTING FROM THERE TO HERE

Some out-of-towners believe the stereotype that Southern Californians have a love affair with our cars, but for most of us, the thrill is gone. Any lingering passion for the open road has been extinguished by increasing traffic, particularly on freeways, and the expensive cost of fuel (San Diego is often rated as the most expensive place in the nation to buy gasoline).

With that said, it is almost impossible to see much of San Diego without a car. If you arrive by other means, you'll want to rent a vehicle for your stay, if at all possible. San Diego County stretches over 4,269 square miles (roughly the size of Connecticut), and you'll find the city easier to negotiate with your own wheels.

Freeways and major surface streets pile up during rush hours on weekday mornings between 6:30 and 9 AM and in the afternoons starting as early as 3:30 PM and extending as late as 7 PM. On Friday afternoons, the worst of the traffic begins at noon, with folks rushing into and out of town for the weekend. Traffic can be heavy on both sides of a freeway, but typically, north–south freeways are most congested heading south in the mornings and north in the evenings. East–west freeways are generally more congested heading west in the morning and east in the evening. Weekend mornings offer no free rides, either, with heavy traffic coming into the south and west, toward the beaches and downtown, especially during summer months. Interstate 5 and Highway 101 at Del Mar are particular problems from mid-June through early September, when the popular county fair and the racetrack season create additional congestion. Even if you plan well, you are bound to find yourself spending some quality time inhaling exhaust fumes. There are really only two choices: (1) Turn up the radio and roll back the convertible top; or (2) repeat my own personal mantra, "Go early, and allow yourself extra time en route."

PARKING

Once you arrive at your destination, the challenge becomes finding a place to leave your vehicle. Parking is at a premium along the beaches, especially in Pacific Beach and La Jolla, as well as throughout downtown San Diego. When it comes to

29

the beaches, find street parking if you can, but more reliable options are paid parking lots. In La Jolla, most of the better restaurants offer valet parking at dinnertime. You can usually find metered parking on side streets a few blocks off Prospect Street, and at night, some office buildings open their underground parking to guests.

In downtown, it isn't unusual to snag a two-hour metered spot on the street during a weekday, but it is next to impossible in the evenings and on weekends, especially in the trendy Gaslamp Quarter. Take a tip from the locals and park in the expansive **Westfield Horton Plaza Mall** parking garage (324 Horton Plaza, between Broadway and G streets and First and Fourth avenues); if you purchase even a little something in the mall, you're entitled to three free hours of parking (but be sure to get your ticket validated after purchase). There are also dozens of small paid lots scattered throughout downtown, and some underground office parking is available to the public in the evenings and weekends; check the Gaslamp Quarter Association's Web site at www.gaslamp.org for maps and tips on finding "hidden" parking downtown.

> **Insider Tip:** Another good bet for Gaslamp parking is the convention center, which charges $10 for the day (or $20 for special events). Unless a very large convention is in town, you're likely to snag a spot.

GETTING TO SAN DIEGO

By Air
San Diego is served by **Lindbergh Field** (619-400-2400; 3225 N. Harbor Drive, San Diego), an international airport that hosts more than 20 airline carriers; there are three terminals and free transportation between them via a complimentary bus system, which makes a loop between Terminals 1 and 2 and the Commuter Terminal and stops along the way every few minutes. Additional airports outside the city include the **John Wayne Airport** (949-252-5200; 18601 Airport Way, Santa Ana) in Orange County and the **Long Beach Airport** (562-570-2600; 4100 Donald Douglas Drive, Long Beach) in southern Los Angeles.

By Bus
Arrive in San Diego by bus at the **Greyhound Bus Terminal** (619-239-3266; 120 W. Broadway, San Diego), which is within walking distance of most downtown hotels. There are generally taxicabs waiting outside the terminal.

By Car
Visitors arriving in San Diego in their own cars will find that freeways and surface streets are well marked, and most parts of town are pretty easy to navigate. Freeway exits are in the far-right lane, and they are generally announced well in advance. Many freeways have HOV, or high-occupancy vehicle, lanes, which are worth using if you can do so legally—you must have at least two people in the vehicle.

If you arrive by other means, it's easy to rent a car. Most major rental agencies operate out of Lindbergh Field downtown; catch a shuttle from the airport to your

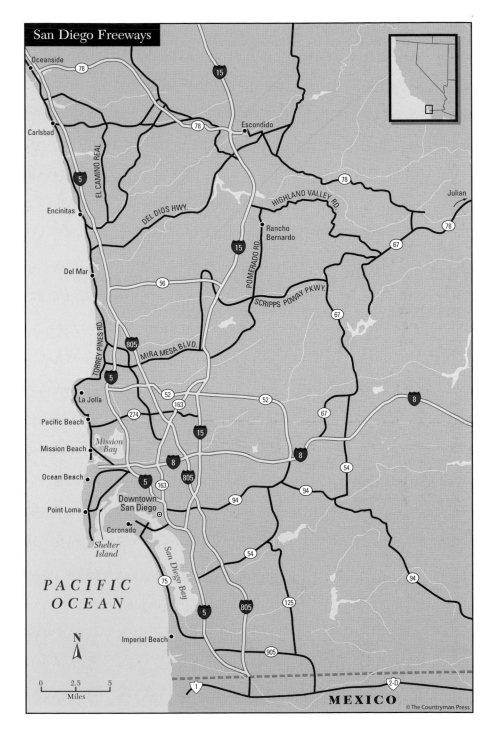

San Diego Freeways

© The Countryman Press

rental car agency at the Transportation Plaza at Terminals 1 and 2. Those arriving via the Commuter Terminal should use the baggage claim transportation phones to contact the rental agencies directly. Agencies are also within walking distance of the cruise ship terminal and the Santa Fe Train Depot downtown. Be sure to reserve ahead to ensure vehicle availability, especially during holidays.

By Cruise Ship

The number of visitors arriving in San Diego via cruise ships that dock at the B Street Pier Cruise Ship Terminal has tripled since 2001. In addition, major carriers such as Carnival and Holland America initiate cruises to the Mexican Riviera (Cabo San Lucas, Puerto Vallarta, and Mazatlan), the Sea of Cortez, and Hawaii from the Port of San Diego, and several other top lines stop in San Diego for the day. Cruise ship guests at the port are ideally situated to explore the Harbor District downtown, including the shopping mecca of Seaport Village, and are within easy walking distance of the lively downtown Gaslamp Quarter.

By Train

You can arrive in San Diego from Los Angeles by train via **AMTRAK**'s *Pacific Surfliner* passenger trains at the Santa Fe Depot downtown (800-872-7245; 1050 Kettner Boulevard, San Diego). Comfortable bi-level cars make the ride along the coast a beautiful, relatively stress-free experience.

GETTING AROUND THE AREA

Freeways and Drive Times

To save yourself headaches when you're on the roads in San Diego, try to travel on freeways during off hours, and if you are held to a timetable, be sure to leave earlier than you think you need to. It's possible to skirt the freeways during the worst traffic periods, especially if you're traveling north to south or vice versa, but the traffic signals and frequent stops on surface roads may be just as frustrating and time-consuming as the freeways. The best advice when traveling significant distances is to invest in a GPS system or a good map, which will enable you to formulate an escape plan, so that if the freeway starts looking like a parking lot, you can take the nearest exit and try to drive around it.

Before you head out, call the 24-hour hotline at the **California Department of Transportation** (800-427-7623) for road-closure information and trouble spots or check the **CalTrans** Web site (www.dot.ca.gov/dist11/d11tmc/sdmap/showmap.html) for continuously updated information and real-time traffic maps.

Metropolitan Transit Service

The **Metropolitan Transit Service (MTS)** is the local body that runs most of the public transportation throughout the city, including bus lines, the *Coaster* train service, and the San Diego Trolley. Specifics on these options follow, but for up-to-date information on routes, schedules, and fees, check with the Information Office of the MTS at 619-233-3004 or check the Web site at www.sdcommute.com. You can also visit the Transit Store downtown (619-234-1060; 102 Broadway, San Diego) to purchase bus and trolley tokens, Day Tripper passes, and monthly passes for MTS buses, the trolley, and the *Coaster.* Note that public transportation runs on an abbreviated schedule on holidays, and the *Coaster* doesn't run at all on Sundays and major holidays.

City Buses

The MTS comprises several bus lines throughout the city proper, and routes are extensive. One-way fares start at $2.50; seniors and disabled guests ride for a discounted rate that starts at $1.10, and there are monthly passes available. For specific information on routes and transfers, access the Web site at www.sd commute.com.

Beyond the city limits, the **North County Transit District** operates a bus system called the Breeze, which serves North County coastal communities such as Del Mar, Carlsbad, and Oceanside, and northern inland communities such as Escondido, Vista, and Ramona. These buses will take you beyond the county limits as well, to San Clemente, Camp Pendleton, and Orange County. To view Breeze routes, go to the Web site at www.gonctd.com. Single-ride passes cost $2 for adults, $1 for children, or an all-day pass is available for $5. Seniors ride for $1, or $2.25 for an all-day pass. Children younger than five years old are free. Tickets can be purchased at NCTD bus pass outlets throughout the North County or by credit card over the phone at 760-966-6500.

Coaster

Once inside the county lines, you can take the commuter train, called the *Coaster,* a clean and enjoyable way to avoid the traffic that runs along the coast; it travels from Oceanside to downtown and passes through some of the loveliest scenery in the county. Ticket costs range from $5 to $6.50 for one-way tickets (free for children five and younger) and can be purchased at any *Coaster* station using simple automated machines. Tickets *cannot* be purchased on the train. Call 800-262-7837 for specific information on routes and fares. Note that the *Coaster* does not run on Sundays or major holidays.

The NCTD also has a commuter rail system in place called the *Sprinter,* which runs 22 miles along the CA 78 corridor from Escondido to Oceanside. Tickets are $2 for single fares, and $1 for senior citizens and disabled individuals. Children five and younger ride free. All-day passes are $5 for adults, $2.50 for senior citizens and disabled individuals. For more information, check the Web site at www.sdmts.com/Tripplanner.asp.

Pedicabs

Downtown is overrun with pedicabs; they are easier to hail on the streets than traditional taxicabs (in fact, the operators can be a nuisance if you aren't interested in a ride), and you can find them near major hotels as well. Costs vary according to time of day and number of passengers, but be sure to ask about fares in advance, and don't be afraid to haggle.

Trolley

The bright red San Diego Trolley system has three easy-to-follow routes that cover downtown and parts of the east county. Please refer to the Trolley Route Map on page 35 for specifics. You can take your bike along with you on the trolley and load it at all trolley stops. Fares begin at $2.50, and all-day passes are available for $5. These

San Diego Trolley in front of the convention center downtown

tickets, which can be purchased at any trolley station, are good for two hours from the time of purchase.

Taxis

Although you will find waiting taxis at the airport (on Transportation Plaza, across from Terminals 1 and 2 and the Commuter Terminal), near the cruise ship terminal when ships are in port, and outside the Greyhound Bus Terminal, San Diego isn't really a taxi-friendly city. Even in downtown it is difficult to hail a cab; better to call ahead for one or walk to the nearest large hotel, where you'll generally find several waiting—or for a small tip you can get a hotel employee to hail one for you. The average fare for one to four people is $2.70 per mile, plus an initial charge of $2.50.

Tours and Organized Sight-Seeing

Old Town Trolley Tours (619-298-8687) offers an on–off tour that loops throughout 10 stops around the city. You can catch the orange and green trolleys at any of the stops and ride all day, visiting Coronado, Old Town, Balboa Park, and the Gaslamp Quarter downtown. Other entertaining tour options offered by this com-

Bargain Passes for Local Attractions

The **Southern California City Pass** allows visitors to buy a customized bundle of attraction passes good for six days' worth of admission (valid if used within 14 days) that includes attractions in San Diego (San Diego Zoo, San Diego Zoo Safari Park, and SeaWorld) as well as Anaheim and Los Angeles (Disneyland, California Adventure, and Universal Studios). Currently the passes sell for $276 for adults ($229 for children)—what would otherwise cost $381 ($340 for children). If you plan to visit most of these attractions, this means big savings. You can purchase tickets online at www.citypass.com/southern-california.

Starting at $69 a day, the **Go San Diego Card** offers one unlimited admission for one to seven days to more than 50 attractions in town, including Legoland, the San Diego Zoo, a whale watching tour, a Petco Park tour, and admission to the Birch Aquarium. Purchase your Go Cards online at www.smartdestinations.com /san-diego-attractions-and-tours/_d_Sdo-p1.html?pass=Sdo_Prod_Go.

If you are an animal lover, you might want to consider the **Three-for-One Pass.** For $121 for adults and $99 for children, you'll receive unlimited admission to the San Diego Zoo, the San Diego Zoo Safari Park, and SeaWorld over the course of five days. Tickets can be purchased at any of the participating parks.

pany include a 90-minute amphibious SEAL Tour onboard a "hydra terra" vehicle that runs on city streets and then heads straight into the water for a tour of the bay.

If you're looking for a more adventurous way to explore the city, consider a bird's-eye view onboard **Corporate Helicopters** (800-345-6737), zip along the boardwalk with **Segway Pacific Beach** (858-270-2881), or float high above the cliffs of Del Mar on a sunset tour with **Skysurfer Balloon Company** (800-660-6809).

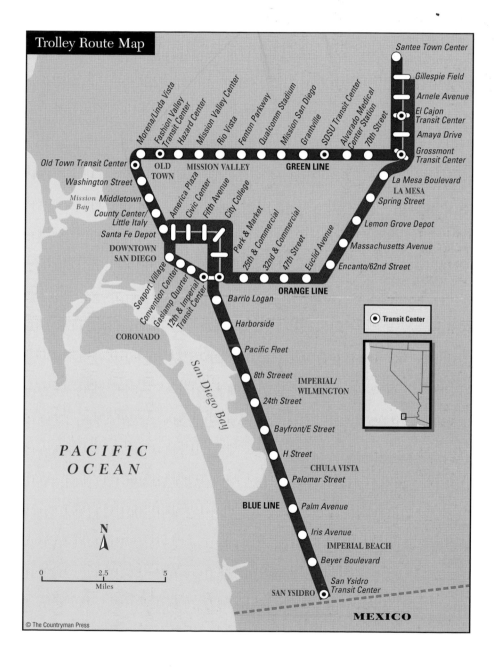

Trolley Route Map

Downtown and Surrounds

BRIGHT LIGHTS, BIG BAY

Downtown is the heart of San Diego and includes the gentrified and restaurant-rich Gaslamp Quarter—16 blocks of 19th- and early-20th-century Victorian architecture restored to maintain the original character of the historic buildings—as well as the Petco Park baseball stadium in the increasingly popular East Village; a wildly successful convention center in the Harbor District on the water; stunning views and fresh seafood restaurants on the harbor; and charming Little Italy, home to new mid-rise condominiums, eclectic boutiques, quaint bistros, and a handful of Italian restaurants and businesses that have been in the city for more than 50 years.

Uptown, which comprises Hillcrest and tony Mission Hills, along with funky North Park and the emerging Adams Avenue district, offers kitschy shopping, plenty of comforting diners, upscale ethnic eateries, and alternative entertainment for the gay community. These cozy neighborhoods are friendly, accessible, and busy every night of the week. Old Town, just north of the city center, is where San Diego began. Visitors can step back in time to glimpse a charming mixture of native Kumeyaay influences, Spanish colonialism, and cowboy chic at the restaurants, shops, and museums of the Old Town State Historic Park, and then do some serious shopping in the specialty stores of the Bazaar del Mundo and the new Fiesta de Reyes.

Just south of downtown and connected to San Diego via the beautiful curving Coronado Bay Bridge, Coronado "island" (actually a peninsula) is the town that time forgot. The ultraexpensive enclave is part relaxing beach resort and part U.S. military base, dominated on one end by North Island and subject to spectacular jet flybys. The homeliness of this "small town" community belies its upscale underpinnings: it feels a lot like Mayberry by the Sea, albeit populated with wealthy locals. Visitors can stroll along the exceptionally wide, dune-riddled beach that fronts the famous Hotel del Coronado, browse the independent shops along Orange Avenue (the main street through town), or relax with a cup of coffee at any number of sidewalk bistros. To the south, Point Loma juts out to the southernmost point of the county, insulated on a natural peninsula that was the first bit of land to be discovered by Europeans. This area has one of the most beautiful old residential districts in the city and, nearby, one of the loveliest beaches in the city: Sunset Cliffs. Shelter Island, a little human-made offshoot of Point Loma, is *the* place to come for great views of the San Diego Bay and the myriad sailboats plying the waters.

Pick Your Spot

Best places to stay in San Diego, and what you'll find nearby . . .

Best Picks for Lodging

Best Family Friendly: Omni San Diego

Best Romantic: Sé San Diego

Best Historical: U.S. Grant Hotel

Best Luxurious: Hotel del Coronado

Best Views: Manchester Grand Hyatt

Best Trendy: Hard Rock Hotel

Best Service: Westgate Hotel

Best Value: Hotel Indigo

DOWNTOWN SAN DIEGO

The revitalized downtown offers a number of beautifully restored historic properties and new, stylish boutique hotels that provide an intimate experience for travelers looking for something a little different, as well as dozens of medium-rise hotels, many of which are offshoots of huge national chains. Staying in downtown offers proximity to the hot Gaslamp Quarter and the cultural attractions at Balboa Park (including the world-renowned San Diego Zoo), as well as endless opportunities for fine dining, gallery crawling, and boutique shopping. An added bonus? If you're looking for

Jacarandas blooming downtown

Courtesy of Joanne DiBona, San Diego CVB

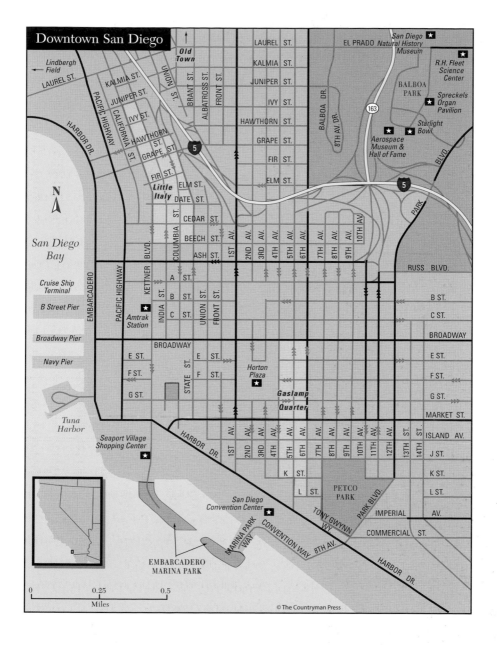

nightlife, downtown is *the* place to be in San Diego. There are dozens of clubs within walking distance of all the best hotels, making it easy—and safe—for those lodging downtown to barhop.

Hard Rock Hotel (619-702-3000; www.hardrockhotelsd.com), 207 Fifth Ave. The Hard Rock Hotel is at the pulse point of the Gaslamp Quarter and right across the street from the convention center downtown—and there's really no place in town that offers this kind of excitement and cool factor. Be sure to explore the sleek hallways of the public spaces, because this property also serves as a rock and roll museum, displaying scribbled notes, cartoons, and telegrams authored by rock gods like Bruce Springsteen, Elvis, and John Lennon, as well as memorabilia like a dress Madonna wore on stage, a microphone stand used by the Ramones, and a jumpsuit that once belonged to Janis Joplin. Standard guest rooms are stylish and modern and offer lots of upscale amenities, but if you really want to party like a rock star, splurge on one of the fabulous suites, which offer room enough to invite your whole posse. On-site are two of the hottest clubs in the area: the sexy, sultry **207** and the rooftop, poolside **Float**, as well as two restaurants: the retro **Maryjane's Coffee Shop** and the wildly popular **Nobu**. Expensive.

> **Insider Tip:** Celebrity watchers would do well to come to Nobu for a late dinner during ComicCon in July, when the city is crawling with Hollywood actors participating in the beloved comic-book and sci-fi convention at the San Diego Convention Center across the street.

Horton Grand Hotel (619-544-1886; www.hortongrand.com), 311 Island Ave. This gingerbread-trimmed Victorian beauty offers a chance to step back into historic San Diego while still providing nearly immediate access to the best restaurants and bars modern-day downtown has to offer. Guest rooms are stuffed with period reproductions, a working gas fireplace in each room, and small bathrooms with classic water closets. Afternoon high tea is served at the hotel, and on the weekends jazz musicians perform in the on-site bar. Moderate.

Hotel Indigo overlooking Petco Park

Courtesy of Hotel Indigo

Hotel Indigo (619-727-4000; www.ichotelsgroup.com/h/d/in/1/en/hotel/sanis), 509 Ninth Ave. One of the newest lodging options downtown, the hip Hotel Indigo offers 100 percent smoke-free accommodations and a youthful vibe. The chic hotel is located in East Village downtown, easy walking distance from the Padres' Petco ballpark. Guest rooms feature hardwood floors, plush bedding, wall murals, and spacious spalike bathrooms. The rooftop **Phi Terrace** bar and lounge is small but welcoming, thanks to inviting fire pits and nice skyline views. Frequent visitors will notice that the hotel undergoes seasonal transformations, so that music, artwork, murals, and even scents correlate with the time of year. Moderate.

Hotel Solamar (877-230-0300; www.hotelsolamar.com), 435 Sixth Ave. This energetic midsized hotel is part of the eclectic Kimpton chain, and in addition to high-style décor and an edgy ambiance, this hotel offers a premium location: near both the hot Gaslamp Quarter and the artsy East Village. Guests are treated to unusual in-room amenities like beach flip-flops, zany bathrobes in zebra and leopard prints, and fuzzy socks. At the water's edge of a fourth-floor rooftop pool you'll find the trendy **Jbar Lounge** (619-531-8744), accented with three cozy fire pits and offering inspiring views of the skyline. Downstairs is the fabulous **Jsix** restaurant. Expensive.

The Keating Hotel (619-814-5700; www.thekeating.com), 432 F St. The Keating sets the bar for hip elegance downtown. The ruby red lobby and the clean lines and upscale amenities are reminiscent of what you'll find in Milan and Rome—and for good reason. The hotel was the brainchild of famed Italian design firm Pininfarina, responsible for designing the Maserati and Ferrari lines. Suites are housed in the Keating Building, an 1890s Victorian whose historic facade has been painstakingly restored. Each guest accommodation has the latest in audio equipment, plasma TVs that carry 150 channels, and gleaming espresso machines. Stainless-steel vanities and large rain-shower fixtures in the baths are sleek and modern—although they offer very little privacy (there are no solid walls to separate the bathing area from the sleeping area). Very expensive.

> **Insider Tip:** If you are a light sleeper, request a room at The Keating away from the busy corner of Fifth and F streets, which is cluttered with nightclubs and usually rowdy until dawn. Whichever room you occupy, the hotel management wisely provides earplugs and white-noise machines to drown out the worst of the din.

Manchester Grand Hyatt (619-232-1234; www.manchestergrand.hyatt.com), 1 Market Pl. At 40 stories tall, the luxurious Manchester Grand Hyatt is the tallest waterfront hotel on the U.S. West Coast—and offers incomparable views overlooking the lovely San Diego Bay, the vibrant harbor front, and the sparkling downtown skyline. The large waterfront hotel is adjacent to the lively Seaport Village shopping and entertainment center and within

> **Insider Tip:** There is no better vantage point in town to watch Independence Day fireworks than the Manchester Grand Hyatt. In addition to the great views of the fireworks, the San Diego Pops Orchestra plays an annual Fourth of July concert at nearby South Harbor Island, which can be heard from the pool deck and from most of the guest room windows.

easy walking distance of the convention center and the popular Gaslamp Quarter. But you don't have to leave the property to have fun: On-site you'll find a 24-hour gym with state-of-the-art equipment; a full-service spa that specializes in reflexology and Swedish massage; a 25,000-foot fourth-floor deck that offers a huge pool, whirlpools nestled beneath curving pergolas, a festive outdoor bar, ample lounge space, and a fire pit—all with views over the harbor. Also on-site are tennis, volleyball, and basketball courts; seasonal children's programs, including popular "dive-in" movies at the pool; several in-house boutiques; and a handful of exceptional restaurants and lounges. Grab a cocktail at the **Top of the Hyatt** bar on the top floor at sunset and enjoy the most expansive views in San Diego. Expensive.

Omni San Diego (619-231-6664; www.omnihotels.com/FindAHotel/SanDiego .aspx), 675 L St. For baseball lovers, there ought to be no other choice for lodging in downtown San Diego. The high-rise Omni is part luxury hotel, part baseball shrine, with displays dedicated to the most famous boys of summer in history: here you can see baseball artifacts like Joe DiMaggio's spikes, worn during his 56-game hitting streak in 1941; a rare 1850 "lemon peel" baseball, one of the first baseballs ever made; and a game ball signed by Willie Mays— among dozens of other artifacts that are displayed behind glass throughout the property. In addition to premier views of the nearby harbor and the convention center (which is just across the street), the hotel is adjacent to the San Diego Padres' Petco Park; there's even a sky bridge from the hotel that will take guests directly into the park on game day. Moderate to expensive.

View from the harbor-side Marriott

San Diego Marriott Hotel and Marina (619-234-1500; www.marriott .com/hotels/travel/sandt-san-diego -marriott-hotel-and-marina), 333 W. Harbor Dr. The San Diego Marriott has one of the prettiest pool complexes in downtown San Diego—a series of lagoons and a spa that wind free-form through the lush tropical landscape, which is punctuated by dramatic waterfalls and peaceful koi ponds. Within walking distance of the convention center, the mirrored 25-story twin towers of this iconic structure right on the harbor are reminiscent of billowing sails. Views are to die for—either the sparkling San Diego Bay or the glittering downtown skyline. There are a number of on-site dining options, including the amazing **Roy's**, and there are dozens of other options at nearby Seaport Village and the Gaslamp Quarter (which is within easy walking distance). Moderate to expensive.

Sé San Diego (619-515-3000; www.sesandiego.com), 1047 Fifth Ave. Formerly known as the Setai San Diego, this property has a Zen-chic aesthetic with sultry Asian design. Accommodations range from basic, small guest rooms to the most exclusive three-story penthouse on the U.S. west coast. There are also residential condominiums on the property. Service is top-shelf, and amenities are wide ranging, including the impeccable **Sé Spa**, state-of-the-art workout facilities, an exclusive movie-screening room, and a rooftop pool and nightclub. On-site dining is at **Suite and Tender**, a fine-dining establishment that prides itself on impeccable presentation and includes a "create your own" raw bar. Expensive.

U.S. Grant Hotel (619-232-3121; www.usgrant.net), 326 Broadway. The most luxurious historic property downtown, this hotel was built in 1910 by Ulysses Grant Jr. in memory of his father, President Grant, and reigned as one of the finest hotels in the city for decades. It recently underwent massive renovation that has brought it back to the opulence of its heyday. This sumptuous 270-room hotel is just across the street from the Horton Plaza shopping mall and a few blocks from the trendy Gaslamp Quarter. On-site you'll find the clubby **Grant Grill** (619-744-2077), as well as a popular lobby bar. Service is impeccable, as you would expect with these prices. Very expensive.

Westgate Hotel (619-238-1818; www.westgatehotel.com), 1055 Second Ave. Unless you were born into royalty, this palatial hotel is as close as you're likely to get to staying overnight in Versailles: the lobby is decked out to impress, with museum-quality 18th-century French antiques, fine oil paintings and tapestries, gorgeous silk fabrics, and enormous crystal chandeliers. The exceedingly polite staff offers among the best concierge service in the city. Guest rooms are spacious and decorated with European imported furniture, with ritzy marble- and brass-appointed bathrooms, many with convenient separate dressing rooms. Some rooms on higher floors have lovely views of the harbor and the burgeoning downtown skyline. Exceptional hospitality ensures that all this opulence doesn't feel stuffy. Expensive to very expensive.

Westgate Hotel

CORONADO

Lodging in Coronado offers the best of both worlds: easy access to the excitement and cultural wealth of downtown via a short drive over the Bay Bridge *and* a beach experience in a friendly community that feels like a small town. Although there are many fewer overnight options in Coronado than in downtown—and most of the available properties are much smaller than what you'll find in the city center—the hotel options reviewed here offer charm, history, and relative value. Coronado is an especially good home base for those traveling with young children, because the area is of manageable scale, easily walkable, and family friendly.

El Cordova Hotel (800-229-2032; www.elcordovahotel.com), 1351 Orange Ave. This friendly boutique hotel, which was originally built as a mansion in 1902 for Elisha Babcock, one of the masterminds behind the Hotel del Coronado, sits across the street from the Del, and although the views and the ambiance cannot compare with its grand neighbor, guests of the El Cordova can still avail themselves of the expansive Coronado Beach nearby. The Mediterranean décor carries throughout the property, and the lush open courtyard features tiled barbecues and pretty picnic seating. There are a wide variety of accommodations available, many of which feature kitchenettes and patios. Moderate.

Glorietta Bay Inn (619-435-3101; www.gloriettabayinn.com), 1630 Glorietta Blvd. A luxe option, this beautiful historic property was built in 1906 as the dream home for John Spreckels, a major booster of early San Diego. At one time Spreckels owned a good chunk of Coronado as well as downtown San Diego, including the Hotel del Coronado. The old mansion is on Glorietta Bay, which today has jaw-dropping views of the downtown San Diego skyline Spreckels helped build. There are 11 suites in the old mansion, as well as 89 contemporary rooms available next door. Expensive.

Hotel del Coronado, with Point Loma in the background  Courtesy of the Hotel del Coronado

Hotel del Coronado (619-435-6611; www.hoteldel.com), 1500 Orange Ave. Hands down, this is the most famous resort in San Diego, and it is considered one of the top destination hotels in the country. Built in 1888, the beautiful white-washed resort is sited on a wide, sugary white-sand beach. The public rooms are rich in carved mahogany, plush rugs, and extravagant Victorian furnishings. Romantic guest accommodations are sited in the original and historic Victorian Building, the Towers and Cabana, or the sumptuous Beach Village, featuring condo properties for rent. (If you have a choice, opt for the older period rooms to fully appreciate the history of this classic beauty.) This is a full-service resort, with a large sparkling pool and new state-of-the-art spa featuring hydrotherapy, steam rooms, and a full complement of treatments; numerous boutiques, including upscale clothing stores and fine jewelry stores; kids' and teens' activities in the summer; and several on-site bars and restaurants. Visit **Babcock and Story** for cocktails with a view of the ocean in a setting that is straight out of the 19th century. **1500 Ocean** offers contemporary California coastal cuisine with impeccable views. And the historic **Crown Room** has long been voted the best Sun. brunch in San Diego by local newspapers and magazines. Very expensive.

POINT LOMA

Point Loma is one of the oldest neighborhoods in the city. Although the point is a little far-flung from some of the downtown sights, proximity to the Cabrillo National Monument, the Old Point Loma Lighthouse, and its grand residential neighborhoods make this a good choice for history buffs. In addition, adjacent Shelter Island, a human-made peninsula just off Point Loma, is only 6 miles from downtown and right on the water. Staying here offers both proximity to the nightlife of the hot Gaslamp Quarter and the beauty of waterfront San Diego. The area is also very close to the airport, which makes sense if you're coming to town for a brief stay. The lodging options are limited, but the choices are nostalgic, a bit kitschy, and offer a real value.

Humphrey's Half Moon Inn (619-224-3411; www.halfmooninn.com), 2303 Shelter Island Dr. Surrounded by the adjacent San Diego Bay, perennially chock-full of sailboats and yachts, a stay here feels less like San Diego and more like the South Pacific. The grounds are thick with tropical palms, brightly colored flowers bloom year-round, and the lushly landscaped pool could be in Polynesia. Guest rooms are a mix of airy Hawaiian exotica and contemporary Mediterranean style. The inn hosts the **Humphrey's Outdoor Concerts by the Bay**, a series popular with locals that runs from May through Oct. and features jazz, comedy acts, blues, and international music. Moderate.

Kona Kai Hotel and Spa (619-221-8000; www.resortkonakai.com), 1551 Shelter Island Dr. The proprietors of this tropical hotel surrounded by magnificent water views of the marina and the bay like to boast that guests can experience Hawaii at the hotel without having to leave the mainland. Guest rooms are light, airy, and decorated with Polynesian-style fabrics and rattan, and each offers a balcony or patio to enjoy the many views. In the summer the hotel offers authentic luaus, complete with lei greeting, a Polynesian dance show, and an extensive buffet featuring Kahlúa pork. The hotel offers a fun water taxi service that runs from the property to Coronado and to the downtown harbor. Moderate.

The Pearl Hotel (619-226-6100; www.thepearlsd.com), 1410 Rosecrans St. The proprietors of this tiny midcentury modern property have taken what was a classic (and heretofore not so interesting) two-story motel and reinvented it into a retro-chic gem. Small rooms offer modern, clean-lined furniture and include platform beds, wall-mounted LCD televisions, and stylish bathrooms. The playful property sponsors special events like Dive-In Theater every Wed., in which a movie is projected on a large screen suspended over the classic oyster-shaped pool, as well as theme parties and food and wine events. The **Restaurant at the Pearl** offers full bar service, happy hour nibbles that attract locals, and poolside cabana service. This is a fun and lively place for young couples, straight or gay, and the atmosphere is friendly and whimsical. Inexpensive.

Local Flavors

Taste of the town . . . local restaurants, cafés, bars, bistros, etc.

There is a higher density of restaurants in this area than any other in San Diego County, and you're sure to find something to please just about every palate and pocketbook. Look for upscale dining in trendy, chic restaurants in the historic Gaslamp Quarter downtown; Mexican restaurants that offer hearty portions and plenty of libation choices in tourist-centric Old Town; quirky ethnic eateries and comfort-food cafés throughout the Uptown area; fabulous (and pricey) foodie favorites in Coronado; and plenty of seafood in Point Loma.

Best Picks for Dining

Best Bet All Around: Jsix
Best Family Friendly: Corvette Diner
Best Romantic: Osetra: The Fish House
Best Splurge: 1500 Ocean
Best Waterside View: Bali Hai
Best Hidden Gem: El Indio
Best Longtime Favorite: Filippi's Pizza Grotto
Best Value: Café 222

FINE DINING

Downtown San Diego

Bandar (619-238-0101; www.bandarrestaurant.com), 825 Fourth Ave. Open daily for lunch and dinner. The elegant Bandar in the Gaslamp Quarter will remind visitors of restaurants in Paris and Brussels, but the food is pure Middle Eastern—for the past several years the place has been voted by local publications as the best Persian restaurant in the city. The dishes are prepared traditionally, but with an occasional nod to the Southern California influence—offering treats like hummus made with pureed avocado and accented with cilantro, olive oil, and lemon. You can't go wrong with the juicy and flavorful shish kebob of filet mignon, tomato, onion, and bell pepper served over saffron rice. Persian food is low in fat, so guests can keep their guilt level in check. Moderate to expensive.

Café Chloe (619-232-3242; www.cafechloe.com), 721 Ninth St. Open daily for breakfast, lunch, and dinner. No details were overlooked in this adorable European-style bistro and wine bar, from the black-stained wooden floors, gleaming white demilune bar, tiny tables tucked next to floor-to-ceiling foldaway windows, and a small sidewalk café. Weekday breakfasts offer a fines herbes omelet stuffed with Brie and served with duck sausage, or

Café Chloe

a decadent and creamy breakfast bread pudding served with seasonal fruits. For lunch consider the mussels with saffron broth and incredible crispy *pommes frites* or the steak tartine with Gorgonzola mousse and cipollini onions. For dinner, lamb chops with couscous and roasted veggies or a roast half chicken with *pommes lyonnaise* are indulgent, Francophile comfort food. Whatever meal you choose, don't miss the *affogato*—a scoop of Chloe's buttery homemade vanilla ice cream topped with a shot of hot espresso. Moderate.

Café 222 (619-236-9902; www .cafe222.com), 222 Island St. Open daily for breakfast and lunch. This quirky tiny diner within walking distance of the convention center is wildly popular for breakfast—for good reason: the food is astonishing, and the prices are rock-bottom. The café is famous for its pumpkin waffles, which are light and delicately flavored, as well as the incredible Mexican Scramble with chiles, Mexican gravy, and cheese. My favorite menu item is the oversized

peanut butter and banana stuffed French toast, which is the perfect mix of sweet and salty. Be forewarned: portions are huge. Because of its diminutive interior, Café 222 is usually packed on weekend mornings, but weekdays are slightly less hectic. Inexpensive.

Café Zucchero (619-531-1731; www.cafezucchero.com), 1731 India St. Open daily for breakfast, lunch, and dinner. Famed for its desserts and breakfast pastries, including plump cannoli, flourless chocolate cake, and authentic fruit gelato, all created on-site by a Sicilian-trained pastry chef, this Italian bistro in Little Italy is also a fine place to dine on more substantial fare. Don't miss the fresh *pollo alla Limone*, moist chicken breast sautéed with lemons, white wine, and capers and served over a bed of spinach. Pizzas are also a good bet; Zucchero makes their own sausages, so meat toppings are especially good. Moderate.

Cowboy Star (619-450-5880; www.thecowboystar.com), 640 10th Ave. Open Mon.–Sat. for lunch and dinner, Sun. for dinner only. The brick-

and-timber exterior of this restaurant promises a more rustic experience than actually awaits guests inside: this cowboy has gone urban and upscale. The sophisticated dining room has a loft aesthetic, with clean-lined furniture, romantic lighting, and a gleaming stainless-steel open kitchen. The chic approach to the Wild West is reflected in many of the menu offerings, in dishes like fried sweetbreads in bourbon sauce, crispy pork cheeks, and duck with a lavender and honey glaze. Despite the fancified backdrop and fine-dining ambiance, the real draw at this swaggering chophouse are the exquisite steaks, which include a flavorful 10-ounce skirt steak, a 22-ounce cattleman's cut rib chop, and a gut-busting 40-ounce porterhouse (which is intended for two). Although the vibe feels far from Fort Worth, it also feels far from San Diego—there really is no other restaurant in town quite like it. Expensive.

Currant American Brasserie (619-702-6309; www.currantrestaurant .com), 140 W. Broadway. Open daily for lunch and dinner. Step into this oasis on bustling Broadway and escape to a European café, with black-and-white tile floors and stone bistro tables. Floor-to-ceiling windows slide open to a sidewalk café. Restaurant offerings are built around seasonal veggies, fresh fish, and choice cuts of meat served California style, with a nod to Continental cooking traditions. The large bar is also quite popular—and noisy during happy hour. Try the Cool Cucumber, with champagne, cucumber-infused vodka, and elderflower syrup, or the slightly oddball Bubblegum Martini, with vodka, crème de banana, and bubble gum soda. Moderate.

Flemings (619-237-1155; www .flemingssteakhouse.com), 380 K St. Open daily for dinner. Across from the convention center and in the heart of the hottest tourist section of the city, Flemings *feels* like a neighborhood steakhouse, with exceptional personal service, true quality, and a huge wine list (there are more than one hundred options available by the glass). Meats are prepared simply—seared off with only a light dusting of salt and pepper—and everything comes à la carte. The filet mignon is exceptional, and the special steak Oscar—served with béarnaise sauce and chunks of crab—is a crowd-pleaser. Don't miss the side of mashed potatoes with Gorgonzola, served family style and easily enough for two or three to share. Expensive.

Jsix (619-531-8744; www.jsixsan diego.com), 616 J St. Open daily for breakfast, lunch, and dinner. The Jsix restaurant belongs to the hip **Hotel Solamar,** but it draws the bulk of its crowds from locals flocking to try Chef Christian Graves's coastal California cuisine. Graves uses local all-organic produce, free-range meat and chicken, and Pacific Coast fish caught by harvesters practicing sustainability. All breads, desserts, and dips are made on the premises. Look for "small bites" like lobster risotto served with a watercress and orange salad, or the rich chowder that is studded with fresh clams in the shell. Leave room for the signature grilled ahi tuna, served rare with Tuscan white beans and a Meyer lemon and almond chutney, or the enormous portion of wine-braised short ribs with a black truffle aioli served over a bed of rosemary-flavored potatoes and Swiss chard. Expensive.

Lou and Mickey's (619-237-4900; www.louandmickeys.com), 224 Fifth Ave. Open daily for dinner (lunch when major conventions are in town). Conveniently located across the train tracks from the convention center, Lou and Mickey's is an evocative, romantic homage to East Coast steak and martini houses from the midcentury. The clubby atmosphere offers plenty of dark woods, black leather chairs, moody lighting, and World War II–era tunes. Carnivorous delights include top sirloin, lamb chops, rib eyes, and extra thick porterhouse steaks. You can pair the turf options with lobster or crab legs as well. Desserts are traditional favorites like root beer floats, apple cobbler, and hot fudge sundaes. Don't miss the Coronado Cosmo, a blend of Absolut Citron and white cranberry juice. Expensive.

Monsoon (619-234-5555; www.monsoonrestaurant.com), 729 Fourth Ave. Open daily for lunch and dinner. A vertical wall of rain (a clever allegory) runs through the middle of this northern Indian restaurant and drowns out the considerable noise of bustling Fourth Ave. outside. The menu is extensive, with starters like vegetable fritters served with yogurt and mint dipping sauces, and entrées like curries in lamb, chicken, fish, and tofu; juicy, flavorful tandoori-grilled meats; and plentiful vegetarian choices—all of which can be prepared as spicy (or not) as you want. Finish with a steaming cup of chai with milk. For lunchtime you'll find an exceptionally diverse, well-priced buffet. Moderate.

Nobu (866-751-7625; www.hardrockhotelsd.com/dining-&-nightlife/nobu), 207 Fifth Ave. Open daily for dinner. The signature restaurant at the **Hard Rock Hotel**, this gleaming hot spot is part of the empire created by world-famous chef Nobu Matsuhisu and offers classical sushi and modern Japanese cuisine. Expect creative dishes you won't see anywhere else in the city, like octopus carpaccio served with a jalapeño dressing, sashimi tacos with yellowfin tuna and crab, and live local uni in the shell. Desserts are whimsical and luxurious, like the Bento Box, a warm Valrhona chocolate cake with

Nobu sushi bar   Courtesy of the Hard Rock Hotel

shiso syrup and green tea ice cream, and the Gingered Kabocha, a pumpkin cream layered with gingersnaps and served with mandarin granita. The bar offers an extensive selection of wine and saki. Beware: this is a *popular* restaurant, and advance reservations are an absolute must. Very expensive.

The Oceanaire (619-858-2277; www.theoceanaire.com), 400 J St. Open daily for dinner. Dim lights, subtle background jazz, and lush red-leather booths create an East Coast ambiance, but the fresh fish and high-quality produce speak to this elegant restaurant's prime location in Southern California. The menu changes daily to reflect the catch of the day, although there are a couple of menu standards: Start with the incredible oysters Rockefeller, succulent, vaguely smoky, and served piping hot. Swordfish and sea bass are especially delicious entrées. Side dishes are served à la carte, and the portions are ridiculously large: the hash browns Oceanaire (studded with bacon and caramelized onions) is easily large enough to feed six people. If you save room for dessert, you'll find equally generous servings of creamy cheesecake and Key lime pie, or the fantastically theatrical baked Alaska, which is flamed tableside. Expensive.

Osetra: The Fish House (619-239-1800; www.osetrafishhouse.com), 904 Fifth Ave. Open daily for dinner. This sexy, two-tiered dining room is dominated by a glowing multistory glass tower housing an extensive wine collection, tended to by "wine angels" who will float (via cables) to retrieve bottles. The bar packs in a crowd, especially on weekend nights, but first and foremost, this is a dining destination. Don't miss the lobster three-way, a heavenly ménage à trois of creamy lobster bisque, subtle lobster salad with avocado, and lobster dynamite,

a spicy and tangy custard that is bursting with lobster meat. The show-stopping bouillabaisse is an orgy of shellfish: a half lobster, crab legs, clams, mussels, and whitefish piled into a dish and dressed with a delicate and fragrant broth flavored heavily with sherry. Very expensive.

The Prado (619-557-9441; www .cohnrestaurants.com/restaurants/the prado/), 1549 El Prado, Ste. 12. Open daily for lunch, Tues.–Sun. for dinner. You can't find a closer restaurant to Balboa Park, because The Prado is *in* the park—the only evening dining option here. The large space is decorated in hacienda style, and the candlelit outdoor patio is an especially nice option on warm evenings, when you are likely to hear the calls of the peacocks from the nearby San Diego Zoo. The menu changes frequently; look for the grilled grand shrimp simmered in a coconut-lime mole sauce and served with mashed sweet plantains and an avocado salad dressed with ancho chile and orange vinaigrette. The Prado is especially good at accommodating pretheater diners (the **Old Globe** is a stone's throw away), but be sure to make reservations well in advance for this busy eatery. Expensive.

Rama (619-501-8424; www.rama restaurant.com), 327 Fourth Ave. Open daily for lunch and dinner. This one-time firehouse has been transformed into an exotic, tranquil venue with low lights and candles, an evocative weeping wall, and floating orchids on every table, and, in my opinion, offers the best Thai food in the city. A favorite starter is the golden shrimp, served juicy and wrapped in noodles that are flash fried and with a slightly spicy plum dipping sauce. Also delicious is the meaty chicken satay, served with a creamy peanut sauce. If you are in the mood for comfort food, don't miss the

Tom Kha, a coconut lemongrass soup prepared with tofu, chicken, or shrimp and brought to the table steaming hot in a big family-style tureen. Desserts, if you can fit them in, include fresh mangos in season and exotic sorbets. Moderate to expensive.

Red Pearl Kitchen (619-231-1100; www.redpearlkitchen.com), 440 J St. Open daily for dinner. Walk through the pulsing music, past the bar lounge full of low-slung tables and backless ottomans, and into a moody, high-style dining room that is one of the favorite dining spots in the city. Take note: this is not your mother's Chinese restaurant. Red Pearl specializes in dim sum offerings, including delectable crispy chicken-ginger pot stickers; sticky five-spice chicken wings; aromatic Korean barbecue short ribs; hot Thai chile-glazed calamari; and subtle steamed barbecue pork buns. Or try wok-fried specialties like Meyer lemon–honey chicken, Kobe beef stir fry with tender papaya, and black pepper caramel shrimp. Desserts have the barest of Asian influences and include lavender lemongrass panna cotta, refreshing passion fruit sorbet, and a caramelized banana served with coconut ice cream. Moderate.

Roy's (619-239-7697; www.roys restaurant.com), 333 W. Harbor Dr. Open daily for lunch and dinner. Roy Yamaguchi opened his first restaurant in Honolulu to great acclaim; now this master chef has several dozen Roy's around the world, and this one on the harbor (affiliated with the adjacent **San Diego Marriott**) is my all-time favorite. Cocktails are inventive (try the refreshing minty Hawaiian colada), and the appetizers are stunning—I'd be happy to graze my way through several and call it a meal. Surefire winners include lobster pot stickers, lemongrass clam chowder served with a Dunge-

ness crabcake, and succulent sticky pork ribs. Signature entrées include the rich macadamia-encrusted mahimahi smothered in brown butter sauce; the blackened island ahi, served rare with a spicy mustard sauce; and the scallops, cooked with smoked ham hock and served with braised Swiss chard and truffle-scented corn. For dessert indulge in the melting hot chocolate soufflé: dip your spoon in, and hot fudge oozes out like magma from a tropical volcano. Expensive.

Uptown San Diego

Bleu Boheme (619-255-4167; www .bleuboheme.com), 4090 Adams Ave. Open daily for lunch and dinner, weekends for brunch. This tiny bistro in Kensington has a distinct European flair, evocative both of the Bohemian Paris of the 1950s and of the Provençal countryside. The quaint, friendly eatery offers traditional French cuisine that includes luscious cheese and meat boards, favorites like garlicky escargots in the shell, onion tarts, a large selection of mussels and *frites,* coq au vin, *boeuf* bourguignon, and roast rack of lamb with ratatouille. Don't miss desserts like fresh crêpes filled with chocolate and hazelnut spread, apple tarts with crème fraîche, and white chocolate bread pudding. The restaurant offers a bargain three-course fixed-price menu (currently for $22) every evening before 6 PM, which includes their fabulous chocolate mousse to end the evening. Moderate.

Ortega's Mexican Bistro (619-692-4200; www.ortegasbistro.com), 141 University Ave., Ste. 5. Open daily for lunch and dinner. Puerto Nuevo lobster is a treat that used to be available only south of the border: whole Pacific lobster is boiled in oil and then sliced down the middle. The result is a tender, juicy lobster tail that is flavorful and meaty. Ortega's in Hillcrest offers the delicious shellfish with melted butter, rice, refried beans, and delicate handmade tortillas—and all without the wait to cross the border. At about $30 for a pound and a quarter of the delicacy, it's a real bargain as well. Before the show-stopping crustaceans arrive, try the guacamole prepared tableside. This neighborhood favorite is a little out of the way in a tiny strip mall—and parking can be a headache—but it's well worth the effort. Moderate.

Saigon on Fifth (619-220-8828), 3900 Fifth Ave. Open daily for lunch and dinner. This serene restaurant in Hillcrest, just north of downtown, is regarded as one of the best Vietnamese dining options in the city. The signature crunchy pan-fried dumplings are a delicious first choice and come stuffed with marinated chicken and vegetables. When soft-shell crabs are in season,

don't miss them. Saigon on Fifth also serves traditional pho, a classic rice noodle dish, and Vietnamese-style fried rice flavored with crab, chicken, or shrimp, or pineapple fried rice with cashews, shrimp, roasted garlic, and egg. You can even prepare your own food, Vietnamese-fondue style: try vinegar fondue beef, thin slices of filet simmered in a vinegar broth and then wrapped with veggies in rice paper, or Saigon fondue, with beef balls, tofu, or shrimp simmered in a lightly seasoned broth. Moderate.

Coronado

Coronado Boathouse (619-435-0155; www.coronado-boathouse.com), 1701 Strand Way. Open daily for dinner. This eye-catching restaurant built on a pier overhanging the water in Glorietta Bay, just across the street from the **Hotel del Coronado**, specializes in steak and seafood, and premier views

Beachside at the Hotel del Coronado

of nearby downtown San Diego. The stuffed prawns with Dungeness crab and smoked bacon served with a cream sauce is a perennial favorite, as is the authentic Key lime pie for dessert. Moderate to expensive.

Crown Room (619-522-8490; www.hoteldel.com/dining), 1500 Orange Ave. Open for Sun. brunch only. If you are looking for the Sun. brunch of a lifetime, look no further. The glowing wood interior of this barrel-vaulted, high-ceiling beauty within the historic **Hotel del Coronado** speaks to an earlier era, when dining at a fine resort like this one was gracious, unrushed, and eminently civilized. A bottomless glass of champagne is paired with a staggering selection of buffet items, which include glorious eggs Benedict, smoked salmon and bagels, shrimp, crab legs, sushi, a waffle station, an omelet station, exotic fruits, and a mouthwatering collection of pastries and chocolate-covered morsels. There is also a kids-only section that offers cereals, pancakes, and finger sausages. Do not miss the chocolate buffet, which overflows with luscious truffles and hand-dipped strawberries. Be sure to make reservations at least two weeks in advance. Very expensive.

1500 Ocean (619-522-8490; www.dine1500ocean.com), 1500 Orange Ave. Open daily for dinner. Don't dismiss this as just another hotel restaurant (it is the anchor eatery at the **Hotel del Coronado**). The premium views of the ocean would be worth the visit alone, but the cuisine is sublime as well—much better than it has to be to get repeat customers at this prime location. Seafood is a specialty, but steak is done equally well. Don't miss the delicate northern halibut served with baby artichokes and a saffron emulsion, along with sides like French green beans with walnuts and the oh-so-creamy baked macaroni and cheese. Moderate to expensive.

Peohe's (619-437-4474; www.peohes.com), 1201 First St. Open daily for lunch and dinner. Located in the **Ferry Landing Marketplace** in Coronado and offering amazing views of the San Diego Harbor, Peohe's is a longtime local favorite. To be sure, this island-inspired restaurant—decorated with a lava "cave" and indoor waterfall—comes with a hefty price tag, but the experience is worth the occasional splurge. Start with the huge Pacific fire shrimp, a spicy appetizer prepared with garlic, butter, and island spices; or the oversized crispy Maui-style onion rings, served with Peohe's homemade chipotle ketchup. For the main course, consider the crab-stuffed tilapia, a delicate whitefish coated with bread crumbs, stuffed with lump crabmeat, and finished with a light caper and butter sauce; or the seared Maine scallops, prepared with fresh ginger and lemongrass, and topped with a sesame oil vinaigrette. You'll also find a full-service sushi bar on-site. Expensive.

Point Loma

Bali Hai (619-222-1181; www.balihairestaurant.com), 2230 Shelter Island Dr. Open daily for dinner, Sun. for brunch. The Bali Hai has been an institution in San Diego since 1955, and for generations, the "tiki temple" décor inside, the red-eyed tiki god on the roof, and the awesome views of the downtown skyline across the bay have attracted locals and tourists. The restaurant recently underwent a complete renovation, and the exterior and interior got a good sprucing up. The cuisine is predominately Polynesian and Pacific Rim, and the presentation of dishes is nothing short of artistic. Don't miss the coconut shrimp to start, served with a very spicy dipping sauce; the snow-white halibut served with tempura squash blossoms and a dollop of caviar; and to top off the meal, the divine banana egg rolls, dipped in white chocolate, rolled in crushed pretzels, and drizzled with caramel. Hawaiian cocktails are a kick, too, like the potent mai tais and the peachy Gilligan's Island. And surprise—the price point is a *lot* less than you'd expect for a place with killer views in a neighborhood populated by hotels and yacht clubs. Moderate.

View from Island Prime

Courtesy of the Cohn Restaurant Group

Island Prime (619-298-6802; www .cohnrestaurants.com/restaurants/island prime), 880 Harbor Island Dr. Open daily for lunch and dinner. With views of downtown and Coronado across the bay, this waterfront restaurant offers plenty of ambiance; it's especially romantic at dusk, when the lights of the city begin to twinkle. It is easy to become addicted to whimsical sides like the nut-crusted Brie served warm with jalapeño jelly, and the lobster, bacon, and cheddar twice-baked potato—but save room for the meaty entrées, like center-cut filet mignon, prime porterhouse, and bone-in rib eye. Executive Chef Deborah Scott is a local legend and has been racking up accolades for this trendy eatery since it opened a few years back. Expensive.

Kaiserhof Restaurant and Biergarten (619-224-0606; www.kaiserhof restaurant.com), 2253 Sunset Cliffs Blvd. Open Tues.–Sun. for dinner. At the Kaiserhof, the city's only true German restaurant, there's no need to wait for Oktoberfest: the restaurant hosts a heated outdoor beer garden year-round, with 14 brews on draft and a lively atmosphere guaranteed every weekend. In addition, the restaurant serves authentic German specialties like Wiener schnitzel, sauerbraten, and house-made bratwurst. Do not miss the fabulous apple strudel. Moderate.

CASUAL DINING

Downtown San Diego
BASIC (619-531-8869; www.barbasic .com), 410 10th Ave. Open daily for dinner (until 2 AM) and sporadically for lunch. In the East Village of downtown, near Petco Park, this favorite with the before- and after-Padres baseball crowd serves thin-crust Connecticut-style pizzas and top-shelf cocktails. The chic space is industrial—it was converted

from a 1912 warehouse—with exposed brick, high ceilings, and garage doors. Locals have voted this the best pizza in the city for several years, thanks to simple, high-quality ingredients. BASIC takes on a second life as an über-cool hangout when the cocktail crowd moves in after midnight. Moderate.

Dick's Last Resort (619-231-9100; www.dickslastresort.com/domains/san diego), 345 Fourth Ave. Open daily for lunch and dinner. Although some downtown restaurants take themselves and their customers too seriously, Dick's provides a fun, irreverent atmosphere where you are sure to be insulted by the waitstaff and assaulted by the loud music. The huge street-side outdoor patio reminds me of cafés on the beach, but Dick's is just blocks from the convention center, smack in the heart of the Gaslamp downtown. Food here is messy and hearty: strap on your plastic bib and dive into a bucket of sticky ribs or a pile of chicken-fried steak smothered in jalapeño gravy. Moderate.

Filippi's Pizza Grotto (619-232-5094; www.realcheesepizza.com), 1747 India St. Open daily for lunch and dinner. One of the original restaurants in Little Italy (and now with several locations throughout the city), Filippi's has been a San Diego institution since 1950. In addition to extra cheesy meatball and pepperoni pizzas, Filippi's serves an exceptionally loaded vegetarian special, with black olives, mushrooms, bell pepper, and onions. The red-and-white vinyl tablecloths and inexpensive bottles of Chianti remind you that this restaurant was a mainstay even before the neighborhood underwent a dramatic revitalization in the past decade. Inexpensive.

Fred's Mexican Café (619-232-8226; www.fredsmexicancafe.com), 527 Fifth Ave. Open daily for lunch and dinner. Eat under palapas on the sidewalk at this energetic, loud Gaslamp Quarter Mexican joint. Celebrate "Cinco de Fred" the fifth of every month, and don't miss "Kiss My Taco" Tuesdays, when the crunchy treats sell for $2. Fred's also has locations in Old Town (619-858-8226) and Pacific Beach (858-483-8226). Inexpensive.

Greek Islands Café (619-239-5216), 879 W. Harbor Dr. Open daily for lunch and dinner. This little takeout Greek restaurant is the best dining value in Seaport Village—and is the only eatery facing the harbor that doesn't tack on a premium for the water view. You'll find classic Greek appetizers like hummus and *tzatziki* (yogurt with cucumber); especially good spinach pie and dolmades (marinated grape leaves wrapped around seasoned rice); gyros and souvlaki; and Greek salads loaded with feta, onions, and kalamata olives. The service is generally fast. Inexpensive.

Kansas City Barbeque (619-231-9680; www.kcbbq.net), 600 W. Market St. Open daily for lunch and dinner. Made famous by the 1986 Tom Cruise movie *Top Gun*, in which it was featured, Kansas City Barbeque is the real deal—and true fans will appreciate that the downtown gentrification hasn't affected the place one bit: it's just as rough around the edges as it was when Maverick bellied up to the bar. Try the meaty baby back ribs (ask for extra sauce) or the pulled beef sandwiches served with heavily breaded onion rings. Moderate.

Maryjane's Coffee Shop (619-702-3000; www.hardrockhotelsd.com), 207 Fifth Ave. Open daily for breakfast, lunch, dinner, and late-night dining. This neo-midcentury modern coffee shop on the ground floor of the **Hard Rock Hotel** offers typical diner fare

Maryjane's Coffee Shop

Courtesy of the Hard Rock Hotel

like hamburgers, sandwiches, and salads—but with a twist. Try the Hot Elvis, a grilled peanut butter and banana sandwich. There's also a full bar, and happy hour drink prices are rock-bottom. Grab a booth and enjoy the individual televisions showing an endless stream of old rock videos and sitcom clips. Moderate.

O'Brothers Burgers (619-615-0909; http://obrothersburgers.com), 188 Horton Plaza. Open daily for lunch and dinner. In the Horton Plaza shopping mall, this hip burger joint offers organic, locally raised grass-fed beef burgers, a huge selection of beers, and house-made condiments—a high-end experience in an inexpensive, fast-food environment. Check out the Western Burger, piled with onion rings and slathered with barbecue sauce. Inexpensive.

Richard Walker's Pancake House (619-231-7777; www.richardwalkers .com), 520 Front St. Open daily for breakfast and lunch. In the Harbor District, Richard Walker's has a line out the door most mornings of folks eagerly waiting for German pancakes, lobster omelets, and fluffy crêpes. The fabulous apple pancakes are roughly the size of a pizza. Moderate.

Uptown San Diego

Big Kitchen (619-234-5789; www.big kitchencafe.com), 3003 Grape St. Open daily for breakfast and lunch. The neighborhood has been gentrified a bit since Whoopi Goldberg bussed tables and worked as a dishwasher more than 25 years ago in this Golden Hills establishment, but were she to return, she would still recognize the homey menu—and probably some of the friendly longtime servers. This funky place attracts an eclectic clientele who come from all around the county for the generous portions of homestyle breakfasts served up by owner "Judy the Beauty." Expect long waits on weekends. Inexpensive.

Hash House A Go-Go (619-298-4646; www.hashhouseagogo.com), 3628 Fifth Ave. Open Tues.–Sun. for breakfast and lunch. This extremely popular uptown café in Hillcrest (an artsy neighborhood just north of downtown) merits the standing-room-only crowd that lines up every weekend. Portions are massive and reasonably priced. Although the hash for which the place is named is extraordinary (especially the unusual meat loaf hash with spinach and mozzarella), I'm a big fan of the oversized flapjacks. Moderate.

Jimmy Carter's Mexican Café (619-295-2070; www.jimmycarters mexicancafe.com), 3172 Fifth Ave. Open daily for lunch and dinner. No, it's not *that* Jimmy Carter, but this Mexican café in Mission Hills serves up food good enough for a president. Try the *carnitas*, and prepare to wait for a table on weekends. Moderate.

Lefty's Chicago Pizzeria (619-295-1720; www.leftyspizza.com), 3448 30th St. Open daily for lunch and dinner. Authentic Chicago-style deep-dish creations are piled high with toppings, including fresh herbs and high-quality cheeses. You can also find a stuffed crust variety, which features more than 3 pounds of cheese. Inexpensive.

The Linkery (619-255-8778; www .thelinkery.com), 3794 30th St. Open daily for lunch and dinner. You won't find nitrates or fillers in the sausages at this North Park restaurant, because everything is made from scratch on the premises. Come here for exceptional wursts, as well as the unusual sausage tacos served with cabbage and jalapeño sauce in a corn tortilla. Moderate.

Urban Mo's Bar and Grill (619-491-0400; www.urbanmos.com), 308 University Ave. Open daily for breakfast, lunch, and dinner. This is a revamped version of the beloved (and now defunct) Hamburger Mary's in Hillcrest; the management is the same, but the décor is upscale, to match the increasingly gentrified neighborhood. Try the stuffed burgers for a gourmet treat, or build your own burger with their long list of fixings. Inexpensive.

Old Town San Diego

El Indio (619-299-0333), 3695 India St. Open daily for lunch and dinner. To call this fast food is a disservice to the consistently high quality of El Indio, a San Diego favorite since 1940. Soft grilled chicken tacos and *carnitas* are among the best in town. In Dec., you can find sweet tamales, something normally available only in home kitchens. Inexpensive.

Old Town Mexican Café (619-297-4330; www.oldtownmexcafe.com), 2489 San Diego Ave. Open daily for breakfast, lunch, and dinner. Old Town Mexican Café is a longtime favorite with locals and tourists. Start with the ever-popular guacamole and chips or, for the more adventurous, try the shrimp and octopus cocktail served with cucumber and sliced avocados. Combinations featuring typical Mexi-

can fare (tacos, enchiladas, burritos, fajitas) are all good choices, but for a real treat, check out the chicken mole, smothered in a sauce flavored with dark chocolate. The famous "tortilla ladies" of Old Town Mexican Café crank out more than seven thousand corn and flour tortillas a day for patrons—and it's worth visiting just to watch their quick hands. Moderate.

Coronado

Beach-n Diner (619-437-6087; www .nadolife.com), 1015 Orange Ave. Open daily for breakfast, lunch, and dinner. This homey art deco diner in the heart of Coronado serves comfort food in colorful surroundings. Breakfasts are especially popular, and portions are large: check out the pile of homemade waffles or any entrée that comes with the delicious crispy hash browns. The soda fountain selections are worth a try, too, especially the purple cows. Moderate.

Clayton's Coffee Shop (619-435-5425), 979 Orange Ave. Open daily for breakfast and lunch. This longtime neighborhood coffee shop in Coronado is frequently crowded, thanks both to the diminutive interior—an authentic midcentury diner with a horseshoe-shaped counter—and to the homestyle cooking and generous portions. For breakfast, don't miss the corned beef hash and the banana pancakes. Inexpensive.

Lil' Piggy's Bar-B-Q (619-522-0217; www.nadolife.com/lilpiggys/index.html), 1201 First St. Open daily for lunch and dinner. In the Coronado Ferry Landing shopping center, Lil' Piggy's packs them in for authentic Southern barbecue that includes pulled pork, beef brisket, and sticky baby back ribs. The restaurant also offers a huge selection of beers. Dine inside or out, and don't miss the fried pickles. Moderate.

Miguel's Cocina (619-437-4237; www.brigantine.com/locations_miguels .html), 1351 Orange Ave. Open daily for breakfast, lunch, and dinner. This is one of the best places for Mexican food in the city—and in San Diego, that's high praise. Across the street from the Hotel del Coronado, Miguel's is a sit-down restaurant on the ground floor of the **El Cordova Hotel** that offers authentic carne asada burritos and tacos, along with interesting entrées like calamari rellenos and jalapeño shrimp. The fish tacos are also especially good. Snag a table on the outside patio for a festive atmosphere. Moderate.

Stretch's Café (619-435-8886), 943 Orange Ave. Open daily for breakfast and lunch. This casual eatery offers wholesome, tasty dishes, with many vegetarian options. Check out the Spinach Fandango, a casserole of spinach, mushrooms, brown rice, and cheese; homemade soups served with corn bread or banana bread; and the healthy smoothies. Inexpensive.

Point Loma
Corvette Diner (619-542-1476; www.cohnrestaurants.com/restaurants /corvettediner), 2965 Historic Decatur Rd. Open daily for lunch and dinner. Formerly located in Hillcrest, the Corvette Diner recently moved to the revamped Liberty Square shopping mall in Point Loma. Despite the change in latitude, there's very little change in attitude: you'll still find a mint-condition vintage Corvette parked inside, loud 1950s music, and lively waitstaff dressed in poodle skirts and fishnet stockings. As the surroundings suggest, the cuisine is midcentury comfort food, and portions are large. Start with the fried pickles and finish with a mile-high banana split or an authentic New York egg cream. Moderate.

Miguel's Cocina

Little Italy

Point Loma Seafoods (619-223-1109), 2805 Emerson St. Open daily for lunch and dinner (closes at 6:30 PM). In addition to being a quality seafood mart, the wildly popular Point Loma Seafoods is also a no-frills café that sells take-out prepared foods. There's generally a chaotic line of locals waiting to order, but push yourself to the front, take a number, place your order, and then grab a picnic table outside to enjoy the view of the boats at the marina next door while you wait. The seared ahi salad and the simple fish combo plate are outstanding. Moderate.

Venetian (619-223-8197; http://venetian1965.com), 3663 Voltaire St. Open daily for dinner. Vince Giacalone started this restaurant in 1965, and now his sons Joey and Frank (and their children) continue to turn out exceptional, traditional pizzas; they still use the same recipes and even the same pizza ovens, and still top their pies with

sausages they make on the premises. Moderate.

SNACKS

Downtown San Diego
Extraordinary Desserts (619-294-7001; www.extraordinarydesserts.com), 1430 Union St. Open Mon.–Fri. 8:30 AM–11:30 PM, Sat.–Sun. 10 AM–11 PM. This sleek bistro serves up desserts that deserve the name *extraordinary*. Try the rich *gianduia*, heady chocolate cake soaked in Myers's Rum and slathered with hazelnut butter cream, chocolate mousse, and berry jam; or the lighter blood orange ricotta torte with orange whipped cream and fresh berries. Moderate.

Ghirardelli Soda Fountain and Chocolate Shop (619-234-2449), 643 Fifth Ave. Open Sun.–Thurs. 10 AM–midnight, Fri.–Sat. 10 AM–1 AM. Although Ghirardelli is generally associated with San Francisco rather than

Southern California, chocoholics welcome this old-fashioned soda fountain to the downtown Gaslamp district anyhow. Don't miss the hot fudge sundaes—a large is easily big enough to split. Moderate.

Heavenly Cupcakes (619-235-9235; www.heavenlycupcake.com), 518 Sixth Ave. Open Tues.–Thurs. 10–9:30, Fri.–Sat. 10 AM–11:30 PM. Billing itself as a "cupcake lounge," this outlet of decadence serves a variety of gourmet cupcakes, including the signature orange chip and a divine version of s'mores. Call ahead for curbside pickup. Inexpensive.

Panificio e Ristorante Solunto's (619-233-0595), 1643 India St. Open Mon. 11–9:30, Wed.–Fri. 10–9:30, Sat.–Sun. 8 AM–9:30 PM. An unassuming bakery and restaurant in Little Italy, Solunto's sells fresh-baked cookies by the pound, including pignole, amaretti, and pecan-studded Mexican wedding cakes, as well as delightful fresh breads. This is also a great bargain for breakfast; enjoy a large pancake for about $2 outside on the small sidewalk patio. Inexpensive.

Coronado

Coronado Cupcakery (619-437-0166; http://coronadocupcakery.com), 1201 First St. Open Mon.–Thurs. 9:30–8:30, Fri.–Sat. 9:30 AM–10 PM, Sun. 9:30–7:30. In the Coronado Ferry Landing mall, this tiny bakery offers a variety of yummy, homestyle cupcakes, with specialties featured daily. Inexpensive.

Dolce Vita Candy (619-552-0713), 1330 Orange Ave., Ste. 140. Hours vary by season. You don't have to be a kid to appreciate being in this candy store: in addition to favorites like jelly beans, lollipops, and gum drops, this colorful emporium offers sinful fudge and handmade truffles. Inexpensive.

MooTime Creamery (619-435-2422; www.nadolife.com/mootime /loc-coronado.html), 1025 Orange Ave. Open Sun.–Thurs. 11–9, Fri.–Sat. 11–10. This longtime local favorite ice cream shop sells traditional flavors as well as fun varieties like creamy toasted coconut, brownie batter, and cinnamon. Inexpensive.

Point Loma

Chi Chocolat (619-546-0650), 2690 Historic Decatur Rd. Open Tues.–Fri. 8–3, Sat. 10–6. Serious chocoholics will not want to miss this bistro in the Liberty Square shopping mall in Point Loma. The shop features some seriously good artisan-crafted candy. Indulge in fudge fondue and chocolate-dipped ginger, or for something a little different, try a dark-chocolate raspberry peppercorn truffle or a heart-shaped bon bon filled with rosewater ganache. Moderate.

Cupcakes Squared (619-226-3485; www.cupcakessquared.com), 3772 Voltaire St. Open Mon.–Fri. 10–6:30, Sat. 11–6, and Sun. 11–5. This Point Loma outlet serves traditional cupcakes made with all natural ingredients in a nontraditional package: square. You can't go wrong with the red velvet. Inexpensive.

Living Room Coffeehouse (619-222-6852; www.livingroomcafe.com/ point-loma.php), 1018 Rosecrans St. Open daily 6 AM–midnight. This local coffeehouse chain (which includes other venues scattered around the city) is meant to be as comfortable as your own living room. This outlet is housed in the historic Jennings House, a two-story home with an expansive front porch. Look for the delicious walnut cinnamon cookies. Moderate.

Marvelous Muffins (619-223-0403), 2907 Shelter Island Dr. Open daily for breakfast. This longtime neighborhood muffin outlet is a bargain (most muffins are $2) and a great place to grab an inexpensive breakfast to go. Their Cuban coffee is a real eye-opener, and the apple-spice muffins are addictive. Inexpensive.

Don't Miss

Must-see attractions, in San Diego and nearby . . .

San Diego has long been a top destination for live theater, with the Tony-award-winning Old Globe Theatre in Balboa Park setting the standard. Balboa Park is the cultural center of downtown, boasting more than a dozen museums and several world-class gardens. The city also has its fair share of architectural history, on display in the lovingly restored Gaslamp Quarter. And thanks to new clubs that seem to spring up overnight, downtown is *the* place to enjoy live music, sip hundreds of varieties of martinis, and dance until the wee hours.

Best Picks for Local Attractions

Best Cultural Attraction: Balboa Park

Best Historical Place: Mission San Diego de Alcalá

Best Beach: Coronado Beach

Best Garden: Botanical Building and Lily Pond

Best Outdoor Activity: Deep-sea fishing in Point Loma

Best Family Fun: San Diego Zoo

Best Shopping: Seaport Village

Best Nightlife: Altitude Sky Lounge

BEST CULTURAL ATTRACTIONS

Balboa Park (619-239-0512), off Park Blvd., San Diego Balboa Park was built to commemorate the 1915–16 Panama–California Exposition, and today the El Prado pedestrian thoroughfare running through the center of the park appears much as it did then, with elaborate Spanish Renaissance architecture, expansive subtropical gardens, and several major theatrical venues, including the award-winning **Old Globe**. The park is home to more than a dozen museums; several cultural venues, including the **Centro Cultural de la Raza** (619-235-6135; open Tues.–Sun. noon–4), which is dedicated to educating the public about Chicano, Mexican, and Native American art and culture; the **House of Pacific Relations** (619-234-0739; open Sun. noon–4), a group of 20 cottages representing the culture and history of 31 different nations; and plenty of park grounds on which to picnic or just enjoy the eucalyptus and jacaranda trees spread out over 1,200 acres. You'll even find a Frisbee golf course at the **Balboa Park Disc Golf Course** (619-692-3607). In addition, the world-famous **San Diego Zoo** anchors the north end of the park. The one-hundred-bell carillon housed in the **Balboa Tower** chimes every 15 minutes. Children will not want to miss the 1922 carousel near the zoo—grab the brass ring and get a free ride. The Balboa Park Visitors Center offers one-hour audio tours, which highlight the park's history, botanical features, and architecture.

Mingei International Museum (619-239-0003; www.mingei.org), 1439 El Prado, San Diego. Open Tues.–Sun. 10–4. Rotating exhibits at this tiny museum feature international art and cultural artifacts. There's an especially interesting gift shop (which can be accessed without a ticket) selling handmade pottery, jewelry, and imported textiles. Adults $7, children $3.

Museum of Contemporary Art San Diego—Downtown (858-454-3541; www.mcasd.org), 1100 Kettner Blvd., San Diego. Open Thurs.–Tues. 11–5, every third Thurs. 11–7; closed Wed. This center-city venue of MCASD (its sister museum is in La Jolla) recently expanded into a second downtown exhibition space, located across the street in the old baggage building of the historic Santa Fe Depot, and together the two downtown locations explore national and regional trends in contemporary art, with an emphasis on works by artists from San Diego and Tijuana. On the first Thurs. of every month, the museum hosts a fun cocktail party called TNT. Adults $10, seniors and active military $5, 25 years and younger free.

Old Globe Theatre (619-234-5623; www.theoldglobe.org), 1363 Old Globe Way, San Diego. The Tony-award-winning Old Globe is the oldest professional theater in California, located at the center of Balboa Park; it is home to more than five hundred

Balboa Tower in Balboa Park

Jay Goede in *How the Grinch Stole Christmas* at the Old Globe

Photo by Craig Schwartz. Used with permission of Craig Schwartz and the Old Globe.

generally affordable, and it is usually not difficult to get seats at the last minute.

San Diego Museum of Art (619-232-7931; www.sdmart.org), 1450 El Prado, San Diego. Open Tues.–Sun. 10–6. As the largest art museum in the county, the SDMA in Balboa Park gets world-class touring exhibits. The small permanent collection includes a few memorable pieces by William Bouguereau, Renoir, and El Greco. Adults $12, seniors and active military $9, children $4.50.

San Diego Opera (619-232-7636; www.sdopera.com/Home), 1200 Third Ave., San Diego. The longest established opera company in Southern California, with productions staged at the downtown Civic Theater, the San Diego company has been ranked by Opera America as one of the top 10 opera houses in the country. Award-winning director Ian Campbell oversees lavish productions that have featured international stars like Joan Sutherland, Luciano Pavarotti, and Beverly Sills. Tickets for performances usually sell out several months in advance, and season ticket holders often nab the best seats, but it is possible to score last-minute cancellations.

San Diego Repertory Theatre (619-544-1000; www.sdrep.org), 79 Horton Plaza, San Diego. The nationally acclaimed San Diego Repertory Theatre started out in 1976 as a street theater company in which one-time San Diegan Whoopi Goldberg was involved. A decade later, the Rep. partnered with the City of San Diego when it moved into the downtown Lyceum Theater at Horton Plaza and became steward to the Lyceum complex. Today the Rep. and other community organizations coproduce two thirds of the more than four hundred performances per year.

performances a year on its three stages, and an astonishing number of original shows have gone on to Broadway. The intimate outdoor Lowell Davies Festival Stage features the Summer Shakespeare Festival from mid-June through the end of Sept. Throughout late Nov. and into Dec., the Old Globe main stage presents *How the Grinch Stole Christmas*, a screenplay adaptation of Dr. Seuss's famous tale.

Old Town Theater (619-337-1525; http://cygnettheatre.com/shows.php ?show_id=48), 4040 Twiggs St., San Diego. In the **Old Town State Historic Park**, this small theater is operated by the acclaimed Cygnet Theatre Company, which offers productions throughout the year. Note that tickets are

San Diego Symphony Orchestra (619-235-0804; www.sandiego symphony.com), 750 B St., San Diego. The San Diego Symphony performs world-class classical and contemporary orchestral works year-round in Copley Symphony Hall downtown, in addition to the well-attended outdoor Summer Pops concert series on Fri. and Sat. nights at Embarcadero Marina Park South. The symphony also sponsors family festivals and community concerts throughout the city, and in the past has played host to eclectic musicians like Aaron Neville (conducted by Marvin Hamlisch) and Woody Allen's jazz band.

Spreckels Organ Pavilion (619-702-8138), south of El Prado in Balboa Park, San Diego. The pavilion in Balboa Park, which seats 2,400, houses the Spreckels Organ, the largest outdoor musical instrument in the world. The concert organ comprises 73 ranks of more than four thousand pipes, ranging in size from 32 feet long down to little more than an inch. There are free year-round concerts every Sun. from 2 to 3.

Starlight Theatre (619-232-7827; www.starlighttheatre.org), 2005 Pan American Plaza, San Diego. The Starlight Bowl in Balboa Park hosts outdoor musical productions in a venue that is smack-dab in the middle of the flight path of the jets landing at Lindbergh Field. An intricate warning light system cues the actors and the orchestra to freeze during performances (often in the middle of a song!) to let especially loud aircraft pass, which is often as entertaining to watch as the revival musical productions themselves.

Timken Museum of Art (619-239-5548; www.timkenmuseum.org), 1500 El Prado, San Diego. Open Tues.–Sun. 10–4. This tiny museum next to the Lily Pond in Balboa Park displays a

Insider Tip: For half-price theater tickets on the day of the performance, head to Horton Plaza's downtown ArtTix booth (858-381-5595; www.sdartstix.com; 28 Horton Plaza). You can purchase half-price day-of tickets for dance and music events here as well. Or save yourself the wait time and go online at www.sandiegoperforms.com to see daily listings of available performances and purchase your tickets directly from the Web site.

Rembrandt and a very lovely Albert Bierstadt painting of Yosemite Falls—and is well worth stopping in. Admission is free.

BEST HISTORICAL PLACES

Cabrillo National Monument and Old Point Loma Lighthouse (619-557-5450; www.nps.gov/cabr), 1800 Cabrillo Memorial Dr., Point Loma. Open daily 9–5. Juan Rodriguez Cabrillo, said to be the first European to set foot on the west coast of what is now the United States, sailed into the San Diego harbor on Sept. 28, 1542, on his way to search for a shortcut from Central America to Asia. He never found this route, but he did claim San Diego (he named it San Miguel) for Spain. The Cabrillo National Monument, at the very tip of the Point Loma peninsula, memorializes his accomplishments with a sculpture of the famous conquistador, which looks out onto one of the greatest views in the city. From this vantage point you can view the San Diego skyline, the graceful Coronado bridge, and beyond to the mountains of Mexico. On-site is a small museum that displays Cabrillo artifacts and a scale model of Cabrillo's flagship, the *San Salvadore.*

There's also a bookstore that sells prints and posters.

Also on-site is the picturesque **Old Point Loma Lighthouse**, which dates to 1854. Visitors can peek into re-created living space of the light keeper and his family. Farther up, a ladder leads to the lighthouse lens (although guests are permitted to the very top only two days a year).

Because Point Loma juts out into the sea, this is an excellent place to watch gray whales, which migrate from the Arctic Sea down to Baja Mexico, starting in late Dec. and through March. Hike past the lighthouse, and you'll find a short trail that loops to the **Whale Overlook**, a glass-enclosed structure that has educational displays on the whales. The adjacent coastline is a protected park as well and includes a small, rocky beach and some of the best tide pools in the city. Hike down native scrub landscape via the steep Bayside Trail or drive down to access the tide pools (look for the sign on the west side of the road going into the park, and you'll see the turnoff). $8 per vehicle.

Mission San Diego de Alcalá (619-281-8449; www.missionsandiego .com), 10818 San Diego Mission Rd., Mission Valley. Open daily 9–4:45. Padre Junípero Serra, along with explorer Gaspar de Portolá, arrived in San Diego in 1769 to establish this first of 21 Spanish missions in California. The San Diego mission was originally located on Presidio Hill, site of the current **Serra Museum** in Presidio Park, but the fathers moved it 6 miles inland in 1774 for better farmland and a more reliable source of water. The mission was built and rebuilt many times after it was destroyed by fires, and what is displayed today dates to 1931, when the mission was remodeled to look like the church in 1813. The picturesque *campanario*, or bell tower, is nearly 50

Old Point Loma Lighthouse

feet tall. On-site is the Padre Luis Jayme Mission Museum, which displays artifacts from the mission era, including religious vestments and statuary. Adults $3, seniors and students $2, children $1.

Whaley House (619-297-7511; www.whaleyhouse.org), 2476 San Diego Ave., Old Town. Days and hours are seasonal. Built in 1885 as the home of wealthy businessman Thomas Whaley and his family, and also used as the site of the county courthouse, the Greek Revival Whaley House is carefully decorated with period furniture and accessories. But its real claim to fame comes from its longtime occupants. It is famously acknowledged by experts in such things as one of the most haunted structures in America. The Whaley House was the site of many tragedies

Mission San Diego de Alcalá

throughout the years, and no doubt this adds to its ghostly reputation. For example, in 1885, after a scandalous divorce from her first cousin and a prolonged battle with depression, Whaley's daughter Violet committed suicide in the home by shooting herself through the heart. There have been reports from visitors and museum employees of seeing the spirits of Mr. and Mrs. Whaley and their tragic daughter; a parapsychologist even reported seeing the ghost of a spotted fox terrier, resembling the dog the Whaleys owned while living in the home. Adults $10, seniors $5, children $4.

BEST GREEN SPACES

Beaches

Coronado Beach, off Coronado bridge in Coronado; follow the signs from Orange Ave. With the Hotel del Coronado as a backdrop, at this lovely beach you'll have a chance to get in touch with your inner Marilyn Monroe (parts of the 1950s film *Some Like It Hot,* starring Monroe, were filmed on this stretch of sand). The beach is exceptionally wide by Southern California standards, and the water gets deep gradually, which makes it a fine family beach. (An interesting tidbit: kite flying is prohibited north of the rock jetty, because kites interfere with the nearby North Island's military radar.)

Silver Strand State Beach, off Coronado bridge in Coronado; follow the signs from Orange Ave. This is the best beach in the area to find seashells; head out at dawn with a pail and be prepared to keep your eyes peeled on the powdery sand to find the morning's treasures. It's also a gentle swimming beach for children, because the water gets deep very gradually here, too.

Sunset Cliffs, west on Sunset Cliffs Blvd. in Point Loma; staircases lead to beach access. This is a remote beach that is popular with locals and surfers, and you'll find more seclusion on the sands here than just about any other beach in town. Go toward the south near Cabrillo Point (also accessible from the Cabrillo National Monument) and find great tidepooling; in the north you'll find bigger waves and more surfers. Note that there are no facilities here, and riptides can be strong.

Gardens and Parks

Unless otherwise indicated, gardens and parks are free and open daily during daylight hours.

Botanical Building and Lily Pond, off El Prado, Balboa Park, San Diego. Open Fri.–Wed. 10–4. The ornate wooden lath Botanical Building in the center of Balboa Park houses more than two thousand orchids and exotic palms, as well as a wide variety of herbs and rotating seasonal flowers. It makes the perfect backdrop for the much-photographed reflecting Lily Pond, which blooms in summer and is home to koi year-round.

Embarcadero Park (North and South), off Harbor Dr., downtown San Diego. These parks surround Seaport Village and the San Diego Convention Center, and feature walking paths with spectacular views of the water and the pricey sailboats and yachts that call it

Sunset Cliffs in Point Loma

Courtesy of Jon Preimesberger

Botanical Building in Balboa Park

home, picnic areas, and large expanses of grassy lawn.

Inez Grant Parker Memorial Rose Garden, over the footbridge that crosses Park Blvd. at the east end of El Prado, Balboa Park, San Diego. More than two hundred varieties of roses bloom in this often-overlooked garden, which is at its most spectacular Mar.–Dec.

Japanese Friendship Garden (619-232-2721; www.niwa.org), next to Spreckels Organ Pavilion, Balboa Park, San Diego. Open Tues.–Sun. 10–4. An entertaining bamboo water fountain greets visitors to this small, serene garden, which features a bonsai exhibit and a well-stocked koi pond. Adults $4, seniors $3.

Presidio Park (www.sandiego.gov /park-and-recreation/parks/presidio /index.shtml), 2727 Presidio Dr., Mission Valley. This hilltop park is anchored by the **Junípero Serra Museum**, which features archaeological treasures from early San Diego and boasts a far-off view of the harbor (and the tangle of freeways that fall between here and there). But most local kids prefer the steep grassy hills, which they can roll down to their hearts' content.

Japanese Friendship Garden

BEST OUTDOOR ACTIVITIES

Even in this urban region of San Diego, the moderate temperatures and nearly constant sunshine afford abundant outdoor recreational activities, especially on and along the waterfront. In addition, downtown San Diego has the expansive Balboa Park, with venues for Frisbee golf, bocce ball, circuit training, and nice, long walks.

Boating

Proximity to the "Big Bay" of San Diego makes this area a favorite with sailors. But even if you don't know your jib from your boom, there are still plenty of opportunities to get out on the water and enjoy the downtown skyline, the pretty inlets of Coronado, and the stunning views off Point Loma.

Dennis Connor's America's Cup Experience (800-644-3454; www.stars -stripes.com), next to the USS *Midway*, San Diego. Dennis Connor's offers two-hour harbor cruises, charters, and sailing lessons aboard 80-foot International America's Cup Class yachts, the fastest mono-hull sailing vessels in the world. Book in advance, because excursions are limited, and this company is popular.

Gondola Company (619-429-6317; www.gondolacompany.com), 4000 Coronado Bay Rd., Coronado. Imagine a gondolier in a straw hat plying the waters of a canal, traditional Italian music playing softly in the background, as you sit back and sip a beverage of your choice. A romantic outing in Venice, you say? No! Coronado has its very own Gondola Company, with vessels imported from Italy (as well as replicas made in the United States). For about $100 an hour, two guests enjoy a scenic cruise through the canals of the Coronado Cays; included in the price is a dessert or appetizer plate, and ice buckets and glasses are provided to chill whatever libation you choose to bring along. For a little more cash they'll throw in a three-course dinner at a restaurant on the water and live mandolin or violin music.

Hornblower Cruises (888-467-6256; www.hornblower.com/hce/home /sd), 1066 N. Harbor Dr., downtown San Diego. One of the best ways to see

Sailboats in the "Big Bay"

the skyline in San Diego is by boat. Hornblower offers nightly dinner cruises through the harbor, leaving just in time to catch the sunset and the city lights. They also have champagne brunches on weekends and private charters, as well as daily one- and two-hour tours throughout the bay.

San Diego Harbor Excursions (619-234-4111; www.sdhe.com), 1050 N. Harbor Dr., downtown San Diego. San Diego Harbor Excursions offers a wide variety of services, including day cruises on the harbor, nightly dinner dance cruises, guided whale watching tours, and holiday excursions.

Seaforth Coronado Boat Rental (619-437-1514; www.seaforthboat rental.com), 1715 Strand Way, Coronado. Skiff rentals are available for a half day or a full day. This organization also offers sailing classes and rents speedboats, water skis, and kayaks.

Diving and Snorkeling

The Point Loma kelp beds are a popular diving destination and can be accessed from a number of companies, including **Aqua Tech Dive Center** (619-237-1800; 1800 Logan Avenue, San Diego) and a number of dive shops in Mission Bay, Mission Beach, and La Jolla (see chapter 2). Although the water quality is sometimes poor (as a result of occasional sewage spills from nearby Mexico), Imperial Beach, south of Coronado, has one of the best diving attractions in Southern California: a sunken submarine known as S-37. The wreck's bow is buried in the sand, at a depth of about 30 feet. The World War II–era sub saw action in Japan but was decommissioned in 1945 and was to be used as a target for aerial bombing. However, as she was being towed out for positioning, the line broke, the sub sank, and the navy left her to rest on the ocean floor, originally positioned much farther from the beach. A private salvage company tried to rescue the submarine in the late 1970s; it was floated toward the beach, but it buried its nose in the sand and remains in this stuck position, with the conning tower sometimes visible from the shore at low tide. Only experienced divers should enter the vessel, and all divers should use caution. The 219-foot hull is only 20 feet wide, lists to the port side, and is extremely cramped.

Fishing

San Diego County is known as one of the best fishing destinations in the world, and south bay is the hub for deep-sea fishing. Note that nearly 650 acres off Point Loma are protected as the Point Loma Ecological Reserve.

Deep-Sea Fishing

The San Diego and Baja coastlines are a dream for those who love deep-sea fishing. You'll find yellowtail, albacore, skipjack, and several species of tuna, and the deeper out you go, the bigger the fish you're likely to land. In December 2010 a 405-pound, 7-foot yellowfin tuna was caught off the coast of Baja by a sportfishing vessel based in San Diego. It was a record-setting weight—the average tuna caught weighs closer to 15 or 20 pounds.

Popular six-hour day trips are available from a number of sportfishing tour operators, which will take you out to the Point Loma kelp beds and along the coastline of Imperial Beach. Nine- and 10-hour trips go out deeper, as well as south along the Baja coast. Overnight trips are available during winter months to fish the 60 Mile Bank or 43 Fathom, where you'll fish for more than 50 varieties of rock cod and bottom fish. If you're hankering for an old-man-and-the-sea experience, check out the multiple-day options (3 to 28 days in length) aboard San Diego's famous long-range fleet, huge platform ships with accommodations akin to cruise ships. In summer and fall you can board five-day trips to the offshore Baja islands to fish for dorado, tuna, and yellowtail. Longer trips will travel up to 1,000 miles south of San Diego to places like Alijos Rocks and Thetis Bank, where you'll fish for bluefin tuna and wahoo, and to the more distant islands of Revilla Gigedos-Clarian and Socorro, where it's possible to catch 300-pound yellowtail and wahoo up to 100 pounds.

Prices vary, but figure an average of $300–350 per day on multiday trips (meals and accommodations onboard included). Day trips range from $200 to $300. Most trips of any length include rods and other equipment in the price, and when fishing in Mexican waters, sportfishing trips generally include the price of the required Mexican fishing license. If you want to bring your own gear, make sure you have a minimum 20-pound tackle—or you won't be reeling in the really big ones. Sportfishing boats leaving from Point Loma in San Diego Bay include **Fisherman's Landing** (619-224-1421; 2838 Garrison Street), **H&M Landing** (619-222-1144; 2803 Emerson Street), and **Point Loma Sportfishing** (619-223-1627; 1403 Scott Street).

Pier and Surf Fishing

Smaller fish live in the shallows, and there are plenty of small fish to be had along San Diego's piers and beaches. If you're casting in waters up to 6 feet deep, expect to catch croaker, corbina, and perch; from 6 to 20 feet, expect to haul in halibut, mackerel, and even bonito. Fishing licenses are not required at any of the San Diego piers, but anyone 12 or older will need a license to surf fish. Catch limits apply. The

Imperial Beach Pier (at Seacoast Drive, south of Coronado) is picturesque and extends out into water at least 20 feet deep—but don't even think about eating the fish here, because the waters are apt to be too polluted. Another good spot for the small ones is **Coronado Pier** (at the foot of Orange Avenue). Try the **Silver Strand Beach** in Coronado for surf fishing.

Golfing

Plenty of folks come to San Diego just for golfing. There are a number of courses in the North County (see chapter 3), but there are also a handful of championship courses southeast of downtown, in the established suburb of Chula Vista, as well as connected to outlying Indian gaming casinos. (Note that many of these courses are well inland from downtown San Diego and the neighborhoods that are highlighted in this chapter. Be sure to consult a map—or talk to your concierge—before heading out for the day, to make sure you have a sense of how far these locations are from your lodging.)

Barona Creek Golf Club (619-387-7018; www.barona.com/golf), 1000 Wildcat Canyon Rd., Lakeside. Thirty miles east of downtown San Diego and part of the Barona Casino complex, Barona Creek Golf Club was rated the fifth-best modern golf course in California by *Golfweek* magazine. The rugged terrain and scenic beauty of Barona are different from other courses in the county, and it's well worth the drive east. Green fee: $120–160.

Carlton Oaks Lodge and Country Club (619-448-4242; www.carltonoaks golf.com), 9200 Inwood Dr., Santee. Pete Dye designed this challenging 18-hole course in Santee, about 20 miles east of downtown, which features beautiful landscaping and extensive water hazards. Green fee: $55–80.

Barona Golf Course

Courtesy of Barona Casino

Coronado Municipal Golf Course (619-435-3122; www.golfcoronado .com), 2000 Visalia Row, Coronado. A relatively hidden gem with some of the best views of San Diego Bay and the Coronado bridge you'll find in the city, this course is well maintained and challenging; the $35 green fee makes it one of the best golf values in California. Local golfers rate this as among their favorite courses in the city. Green fee: $35.

Eastlake Country Club (619-482-5757; www.golfsd.com/eastlake.html), 2375 Clubhouse Dr., Chula Vista. Good for all levels, this par 72 course in Chula Vista has 18 holes and a driving range, with a few challenging water hazards and a beautiful open-air pavil-

ion—and is another great golfing value. Green fee: $69–89.

Riverwalk Golf Club (619-296-4653; www.riverwalkgc.com), 1150 Fashion Valley Rd., San Diego. Centrally located in Mission Valley, just a few miles north of downtown, the Riverwalk Golf Club was the site of the San Diego Golf Open back in the 1950s; more recently, the course has been redesigned by Ted Robinson Sr. and his son Ted Jr. You'll find 27 holes with lots of water features and well-maintained greens. Green fee: $89–99.

Salt Creek Golf Course (619-482-4666; www.saltcreekgc.com), 525 Hunte Pkwy., Chula Vista. This Scottish-links style course is bordered on the north by a state park and in all other directions by protected habitats, so the natural serenity of the area is ensured. Generous fairways and flat bunkering promise an approachable course for golfers of most levels. Green fee: $59–79.

Sycuan Resort Golf Club (800-457-5568; www.sycuanresort.com/golf), 3007 Dehesa Rd., El Cajon. These two 18-hole championship courses in El Cajon, east of downtown San Diego, wind through old-growth trees and offer challenges for seasoned golfers.

This club is part of the Sycuan Indian gaming resort. Green fee: $57–79.

Hiking
Urban hiking is an enjoyable pastime in San Diego, where the weather is almost always pleasant and the terrain is relatively flat. There are wide sidewalks along the harbor, as well as many meandering pathways throughout the oasis-like Balboa Park.

If you'd like to get a bit of history with your exercise, consider taking a

Petco Park

Courtesy of Petco Park

Petco Park: Home of Padres Baseball

Since President Jimmy Carter threw out the first pitch in 2004, **Petco Park** (619-795-5011; www.padres.com; 100 Park Boulevard, San Diego)—the dazzling $453.4 million home of the San Diego Padres baseball team—has drawn hundreds of thousands of fans to enjoy the parklike surroundings of the new game field, as well as to attend the 80 baseball games a year, played from early April through October. Naysayers complain that ticket prices are steep at the new ballpark, but there are plenty of fun and affordable alternatives. For only $5, visitors can gain admission to the extremely popular "Park in the Park" behind center field; this is a pretty grassy area elevated enough to see into the ballpark or to watch the game on a giant video screen. Kids love to run the bases at the small baseball diamond. Or for $10, you can sit at "the Beach," a sandy area with bleachers. Note that the Park in the Park is open for free on nongame days, and for a small fee, baseball fans can arrange for a behind-the-scenes tour of Petco any time of the year.

guided walking tour through the city. For $10 for adults, you can take a two-hour tour to learn about the city's somewhat sordid past and to hear the stories behind the beautiful facades of downtown buildings with **Gaslamp Quarter Walking Tours** (619-233-4692). You don't need to make advance reservations for these tours, sponsored by the Gaslamp Historic Society; just come to the William Heath Davis House (at the corner of Fourth Avenue and Island) on any Saturday at 11 AM and purchase tickets 10 minutes prior.

Bayside Trail, follow signs off Cabrillo Memorial Dr., Point Loma. This 3-mile out-and-back gravel trail near the Cabrillo Lighthouse in Point Loma offers stunning views of San Diego Bay and beyond to Tijuana. The U-shaped trail, which used to be a military patrol road, winds down a 300-foot descent along the cliffs through native wildflowers and scrub bushes; in the winter, you might even see migrating gray whales from this vantage point. $5 fee for parking.

Tijuana River National Estuarian Research Reserve, 301 Caspian Way, Imperial Beach. Open daily. Access the north and south McCoy Trails from the visitors center at the Tijuana Estuary Reserve; both trails pass through prime bird-watching habitat at the mouth of the Tijuana River. Included in this reserve is the Tijuana Slough National Wildlife Refuge, more than 1,000 acres of wetlands where the Tijuana River runs into the Pacific. More than 370 species have been recorded here, including the Belding's Savannah sparrow, the American peregrine falcon, and the northern harrier, as well as the endangered California least tern. The western snowy plover, which is a threatened species, nests on the beaches of the refuge and makes its home here year-round.

BEST FAMILY FUN

Knott's Soak City (619-661-7373; www.knotts.com), 2052 Entertainment Circle, Chula Vista. Open daily Memorial Day weekend through early fall; hours

Knott's Soak City

Courtesy of Knott's Soak City

Insider Tip: Save money on admission prices to Knott's Soak City by purchasing tickets online, which will save $5 per adult admission. Look for special package deals online as well, which often discount tickets an additional 20 percent when purchased in multiples.

vary. Set amid the otherwise dry hills of southern Chula Vista, southeast of downtown, the 32 colorful acres of water park at Knott's Soak City San Diego remind visitors of the San Diego long-board surfing scene in the 1950s. Attractions include the Pacific Spin, a 132-foot spiral ride that terminates in a six-story funnel; the La Jolla Falls, which offers up a quartet of high-speed, fast-action tube slides; and the Palisades Plunge, which features a triplet of wild and steep inner tube slides. For somewhat tamer fun, try the Coronado Express, a family raft ride that plunges down milder dips, or the Sunset River, lazy river rapids where you can sit back, float, and catch some rays. Kids will also love Balboa Bay, an 800,000-gallon wave pool that generates swells suitable for body surfing. The Gremmie Lagoon, a themed section designed for toddlers and young children, has its own paddling pool and kinder, gentler water slides. There are locker rentals on-site, as well as plenty of casual dining options. Come early to secure a beach chair—or if you're willing to plunk down some extra cash, rent a private cabana. Adults $31, children and seniors $20.

Marie Hitchcock Puppet Theater (619-544-9203; www.balboaparkpuppets.com), 2130 Pan American Plaza, San Diego. Open Wed.–Sun.; hours vary. Marie Hitchcock was a beloved fixture in the San Diego school district as far back as 50 years ago, traveling from classroom to classroom, introducing schoolchildren to puppetry. Today this quaint puppet theater in Balboa Park, named in her honor, continues to enchant children with marionettes and hand puppets in short-format plays. Adults $5, seniors $4, children $3.

New Children's Museum (619-233-8792; www.thinkplaycreate.org), 200 West Island Ave., San Diego. Open daily 10–4; closed Wed. Opened in May 2008, the New Children's Museum is a light-filled, three-story glass and concrete space with soaring ceilings, open steel beams, and floating staircases. The museum is filled with interactive experiences, giving kids the opportunity to play with, create, and experience art. Throughout are murals kids can color in, blackboards they can draw on, and graffitied walls they can climb. This is appropriate for the ankle-biter set—toddlers and kids up to seven will find endless opportunities for exploration. Aside from the Teen Studio, which allows teenagers to engage in a more in-depth art project, there is very little for older kids to do. Admission $10.

Old Town San Diego State Historic Park (619-220-5422; www.oldtownsandiegoguide.com), 4002 Wallace St., San Diego. Open daily 10–5. Located on the site of one of the first European settlements on the West Coast, the restored and reconstructed buildings in Old Town make up a Westernized version of Colonial Williamsburg. With docents and shopkeepers in period costumes, historic reenactments and period demonstrations, and nearly 40 themed buildings—some museums and some shops—that highlight the early pueblo era of 1821–72, Old Town gives visitors a chance to step into history. Museum exhibits highlight the commercial and personal lives of the missionaries, Spanish colonists, wealthy Mexican families, and the native Kumeyaay Indians who lived in early San Diego. Visitors can tour the Blackhawk Livery Stables and view historic carriages; wander through the original newspaper office of the *San Diego Union;* visit the old courthouse museum, and then check out the jail next door; and stroll through the Robinson Rose Building, the one-time house and law offices of prominent attorney James W. Robinson, which currently serves as the park's visitors center. La Casa de Estudillo, built for a former commander of the presidio, has been preserved with period furniture and decorations. The adjacent entertainment zone

A quiet courtyard within Old Town San Diego

known as **Fiesta de Reyes** (2754 Calhoun St.) is chock-full of historically themed restaurants and shops. Admission is free.

Reuben H. Fleet Science Center (619-238-1233; www.rhfleet.org), 1875 El Prado, San Diego. Open daily at 10; closing times vary. A favorite field trip destination for local schoolchildren for decades, the Reuben H. Fleet in Balboa Park offers more than one hundred fun and interactive experiments demonstrating the principles of science. The museum also hosts a beautiful **IMAX Dome Theater**, which plays several regular features throughout the week (the offerings change every few months) as well as a wide variety of special after-hours shows on Fri. nights. Adults $10, seniors and children $8.75.

San Diego Air and Space Museum (619-234-8291; www.sandiegoairand space.org), 2001 Pan American Plaza, San Diego. Open daily 10–4:30; Thurs. until 11 PM. Peer into an *Apollo* service module mockup, stroll alongside 1920s-era barnstormers, and see original fighter planes from World War II. Adults $16.50, seniors and students $13.50, children $6, active military free.

San Diego Aircraft Carrier Museum (619-544-9600; www.midway .org), 910 N. Harbor Dr., San Diego. Open daily 10–5. The decommissioned USS *Midway*, the longest-serving aircraft carrier in U.S. Navy history and, since 2004, permanently docked at the Navy Pier, provides a unique experience for civilian visitors. It is 1,001 feet long, 258 feet wide, and has more than 4 acres of flight deck up top, so you can lose yourself wandering what remain surprisingly authentic surroundings. Visit the cavernous hangar, sit in the cockpit of a Phantom fighter jet, and engage in a virtual dogfight with networked video simulators. Let children climb aboard a Seasprite or try out an ejector seat—disconnected, of course. On the flight deck, wander among Hornets, a Sea King helicopter, and an F-14 Tomcat. My favorite is the Second Deck, where visitors can stroll the narrow (and low) corridors among the officers' staterooms and get a taste of what it must be like to live on one of these floating cities; here you can also see the laundry room, with dozens of industrial-sized washers and dryers that in the carrier's commissioned days ran 24–7; the mess and serving line (complete with rubber re-creations of navy favorites like chipped beef and bacon and eggs); and the galley, which used to process 10 tons of food daily for the sailors onboard in a shockingly cramped space. Adults $18, seniors $15, active military and children over five $10.

San Diego Maritime Museum (619-234-9153; www.sdmaritime.org), 1492 N. Harbor Dr., San Diego. Open daily 9–8. This longtime local favorite on the harbor front features seven sailing vessels that have been converted into museums, including the magnificent sailing ship the *Star of India*, built in 1863 and currently the oldest active ship in the world; the *Berkeley*, an 1898 steam ferry; the HMS *Surprise*, a replica of an 18th-century Royal Navy frigate; the *Medea*, a 1914 steam yacht; and a B-39 Russian attack submarine (avoid the latter exhibit if you are claustrophobic). An unusual summertime activity hosted by the Maritime Museum is Movies before the Mast (in July and Aug.), at which nautical-themed movies are projected onto the sails of the *Star of India;* the tall ship also has family sleepovers held onboard a few nights in June and July. Adults $14, seniors and active military $11, children $8.

San Diego Model Railroad Museum (619-696-0199; www.sd modelrailroadm.com), 1649 El Prado, San Diego. Open Tues.–Fri. 11–4, Sat.–Sun. 11–5. Located downstairs from the Museum of San Diego History in Balboa Park, this museum has more than 28,000 square feet of scale model railroad layouts, which boast amazing detail. Young children will go crazy for this place. Adults $7, children under 15 free with a paying adult.

San Diego Zoo (619-234-3153; www.sandiegozoo.org), 2920 Zoo Dr., San Diego. Open daily; hours vary by season. Although the San Diego travel industry's mantra for the past two decades has been "more than just a great zoo," the fact is that the San Diego Zoo helped put this city on the tourist-destination map. The zoo

The HMS *Surprise,* San Diego Maritime Museum

remains one of the largest and most innovative in the world, and it's a favorite stop for visitors and locals alike. With more than 100 acres set aside just minutes from downtown in Balboa Park, the zoo houses more than 3,500 rare and endangered animals representing more than four hundred species. In addition, the extensive botanical gardens contain more than 700,000 exotic plants, many of these endangered species as well. The zoo was one of the first in the world to create animal habitats that do not resemble traditional animal enclosures. Animals that would normally cohabitate in the wild are housed together in "biomes" that simulate the animals' natural habitat, in the least restrictive environment possible to ensure the safety of the animals and visitors. Some of the most popular exhibits include the Polar Bear Plunge, where you can watch the arctic creatures frolic in a 12-foot-deep, 130,000-gallon water tank; Gorilla Tropics, which is considered by conservationists as one of the best gorilla exhibits in the world; and the Koala Exhibit, which allows visitors to get close to several of the nocturnal cuties. Another perennial favorite is the oftentimes crowded Giant Panda Research Station. You'll find live entertainment scheduled throughout the day, including bird shows, puppet theater, and special presentations for children. Animal enrichment encounters are also available and include feeding giraffes. For an additional charge, you can hop aboard a double-decker bus for a 35-minute guided tour of the zoo, which will take you past Asian and African elephants, rare deer and antelope, meerkats, and spectacled bears, among others. The bus is a good way to save a little shoe leather—and because the zoo is a big place, with uneven and hilly terrain in spots, this is

Insider Tip: If you plan to visit both the San Diego Zoo and the San Diego Zoo Safari Park in Escondido, you can save considerably on admission costs by purchasing a two-park ticket.

sometimes a welcome alternative to hoofing it. The ever-popular Skyfari Aerial Tram is another must-see: a gondola car will carry you from the east side of the zoo to the west side and back again. You'll cross directly over the gorilla enclosure, for premier viewing access. Note that in the summer

Panda bear at the San Diego Zoo

the park stays open late for Nighttime Zoo, with additional shows, live music, and animal encounters. During the entire month of Oct., the zoo is free to children, which is a nice benefit if you're traveling with little ones, but the congestion increases as a result. Adults $37, children 3–11 $27.

BEST SHOPPING

There are a number of eclectic, entertaining shopping areas in downtown and Old Town, including **Westfield Horton Plaza** (324 Horton Plaza, downtown), a mainstream outdoor mall with dazzling multilevel architecture. Just to the north on the waterfront, you'll find charming **Seaport Village** (619-235-4014; the end of Pacific Highway, downtown)—a 14-acre waterfront shopping district that is designed to look like a well-manicured fishing village at the turn of the 20th century. Be sure to let little ones ride the relocated 1895 carousel, with Coney Island–style wooden animals carved by the famous artisan Charles I. D. Looff. In Old Town, look for **Bazaar del Mundo** (619-296-3161; 4133 Taylor Street, Old Town), just a few blocks from the Old Town State Historic Park. This colorful, intriguing place with eclectic stores sells imported items you're not likely to find elsewhere. Adjacent to the historic area is **Fiesta de Reyes** (2754 Calhoun Street, Old Town), which features period restaurants, live music and entertainment on the weekends on an open-air stage, and small shops scattered throughout that sell mission-era souvenirs, toys, crafts, and books. Across the bay in Coronado, be sure to browse through **Coronado Ferry Landing Marketplace** (1201 First Street, Coronado), which offers a lively collection of restaurants, shops, and galleries; the

Bazaar del Mundo

pretty outdoor space also offers premier views of the downtown skyline and boasts live entertainment most weekends.

Following is a list of unusual stores scattered throughout the area, where you'll find good bargains, unusual wares, and impressive displays:

Architectural Salvage San Diego (619-696-1313; www.architectural salvagesd.com), 2401 Kettner Blvd., San Diego. Relocated in the past few years a few blocks north of its former Little Italy home, this jam-packed store specializes in antique stained-glass windows, salvaged doors, fireplace surrounds, and ironwork. You'll also find an amazing collection of doorknobs and other vintage hardware, and racks of old tin ceiling tiles.

Bay Books (619-435-0070; www .baybookscoronado.com), 1029 Orange Ave., Coronado. An outdoor coffee bar, a good children's section, and an extensive collection of international magazines and newspapers make this large, open store a relaxing stop for the afternoon.

Blick Art Materials (619-687-0050; www.dickblick.com/stores/california /sandiego), 1844 India St., San Diego. Artists and crafters will flip over this two-story warehouse in Little Italy filled with high-end art supplies, oversized canvases, professional portfolios, and a nice collection of art books.

Kite Flite (877-234-8229; www .kiteflitesd.com), 849 W. Harbor Dr., San Diego. Friendly salespeople will help children of all ages explore the huge collection of kites at this little shop in Seaport Village; you'll find beautiful hand-painted kites in the shape of butterflies and surfboards, windsocks, and Frisbees that come equipped with built-in headlights.

Le Travel Store (619-544-0005; www.letravelstore.com), 745 Fourth Ave., San Diego. Travel buffs will not want to miss this downtown store, which, in addition to an extensive collection of durable and versatile luggage, wrinkle-resistant clothing, and miniaturized personal care essentials, boasts one of the best travel book collections in the city.

Seaside Papery (619-435-5565; www.seasidepapery.com), 1162 Orange Ave., Coronado. In addition to exquisite stationery, invitations, and unique gift cards, you'll also find interesting trinkets like seashell nightlights and blown-glass paperweights.

So Good (619-238-3599), 450 Fifth Ave., San Diego. This brightly lighted store glitters with hundreds of thousands of faux jewels in the largest collection of costume jewelry I've ever seen. Look for sparkling necklaces, bracelets, dangling earrings, and hair adornments, most for under $20.

Upstart Crow (619-232-4855; www.upstartcrowtrading.com), 835 W. Harbor Dr., Ste. C, San Diego. The

Seaport Village

original San Diego coffee shop/book-store, the Upstart Crow in Seaport Village nestles tables among the stacks. You'll find a good children's book collection, as well as games and puzzles. They also make a pretty good cup of joe.

BEST NIGHTLIFE

Nightlife in this part of San Diego ranges from trendy Hollywood-style clubs with velvet rope lines, to premier live-music venues that play to increasingly discerning local crowds, to plentiful Irish pubs and sports bars, to intimate wine bars. Especially for folks staying in the Gaslamp Quarter and East Village neighborhoods of downtown, there are nearly endless opportunities for nightlife and late-night entertainment. On weekend nights, especially, the popular downtown corridor is crawling with revelers out for a good time. If you have a hard time deciding on the right venue, the compact locale of the downtown area makes it easy to barhop.

Downtown San Diego
Altitude Sky Lounge (619-446-8086; www.altitudeskylounge.com), 660 K St. This rooftop beauty, 22 stories up on the top of the San Diego Marriott in the Gaslamp, overlooks the Coronado bridge and the sparkling San Diego skyline, as well as into **Petco Park**; on game days you can even watch the action from here. The vibe is comfortable, hip, and quintessentially San Diego. Try the Del La Sol martini, a tequila, pineapple, and white cranberry juice cocktail.

Anthology (619-595-0300; www.anthologysd.com), 1337 India St. This beautiful three-story venue in Little Italy boasts superior acoustics, a sophisticated setting, and exceptional eclectic live music that includes jazz, blues, and Latin. Enthusiasts will appreciate the large collection of single-malt scotch available from the bar.

Croce's Restaurant and Jazz Bar (619-233-4355; www.croces.com), 802 Fifth Ave. Owner Ingrid Croce (widow of singer/songwriter Jim Croce) invested in the Gaslamp Quarter well before it was cool, and now Croce's is firmly established as a destination for sophisticated nightly live entertainment, as well as fine dining. The comfortable space is decorated with Croce family photographs, gold albums, and other memorabilia. Croce's has an extensive wine list and full bar.

East Village Tavern and Bowl (619-677-2695; www.bowlevt.com), 930 Market St. This downtown newcomer in East Village is part sports bar, part bowling alley, part pool hall, part gastropub—and 100 percent fun. Food selections are typical (burgers, tacos, some salads) but tasty, and the bar is extensive.

The Fleetwood (619-702-7700; www.thefleetwood.com), 639 J St. This Gaslamp restaurant and bar is casual and hip, and for these reasons is the very essence of San Diego nightlife. In addition to a $4 cocktail "Power Hour" and a well-loved Sun. champagne brunch, The Fleetwood offers karaoke every Sun. at 9 PM, dancing and DJs every Thurs.–Sat., and 50 percent off all wine bottles every Wed. The signature cocktail is the La Parma, fashioned from vodka, pear puree, and Parmesan cheese. (Trust me: it's better than it sounds.)

4th and B (619-231-4343; www.4thandb.com), 345 B St. One of the premier live-music venues in town, this 20,000-square-foot, one-thousand-seat Gaslamp Quarter facility features music from just about every genre, including hip-hop, jazz, alternative rock, and country. In addition to world-class sound and lighting systems, you'll find luxurious sky boxes and private mezzanine booths.

House of Blues (619-299-2583; www.houseofblues.com), 1055 Fifth Ave. Near the Gaslamp Quarter, this outlet of the House of Blues restaurant and nightclub chain is an extremely popular nightspot and draws name acts as well as local bands. (On Sun. mornings, look for the Gospel Brunch, a hearty buffet with live entertainment.)

Jimmy Love's (619-595-0123; www.jimmyloves.com), 672 Fifth Ave. Housed in the beautiful old City Hall building (and one-time city library), dating to 1887, this large Gaslamp restaurant and bar features contemporary American cuisine and live music nightly, including jazz, blues, and 1980s dance music.

Joltin' Joes (619-230-1968; www.joltnjoes.com), 379 Fourth Ave. Another popular offering in the Gaslamp Quarter, this 15,000-square-foot sports bar and grill features flat-screen televisions scattered throughout the vampy red-carpeted main dining room, as well as an upstairs outdoor "beach" patio, championship billiard tables, and a video arcade. All this fun, and they also serve up decent pasta and burgers.

Noble Experiment (619-888-4713; http://nobleexperimentsd.com), 777 G St. In East Village, this establishment has won rave reviews for primo cocktails. The head bartender insists on perfection and chisels ice from hand-cut blocks to avoid overquick melting and watered-down drinks. The décor is a little over the top (check out the wall of golden skulls), but the concoctions are the real deal. Order up one of the best old-fashioneds you'll ever have.

Red Velvet (619-501-4561; www.redvelvetwinebar.com), 750 W. Fir St.,

Ste. 101. A newcomer to Little Italy, this welcoming and intimate wine bar offers dozens of rare wines by the glass, along with a menu of small plates that pair well with wines.

Starlite Lounge (619-358-9766; www.starlitesandiego.com), 3175 India St. In midtown, this hip new restaurant and bar is hugely popular with locals and always draws a crowd. Try the Starlight Mule, a ginger beer and vodka concoction served in a copper mug, and don't miss the house-made pickles.

Stingaree (619-554-9500; www.stingsandiego.com), 454 Sixth Ave. This stylish and ultrapopular bar is known to attract LA celebs, but whether you spot a member of the Hollywood glitterati or not, this is one of the hottest places to see and be seen.

The Tipsy Crow (619-338-9300; http://thetipsycrow.com), 770 Fifth Ave. This trendy lounge attracts a young, upwardly mobile crowd every night of the week (3 PM–2 AM), with long lines forming on the weekends. There are three distinct levels—The Nest, The Main, and The Underground, each with its own vibe. Expect live music and enormous crowds on the weekends.

Vin de Syrah (619-234-4166; www.syrahwineparlor.com), 901 Fifth Ave. This trendy bar features an underground entrance and a whimsical down-the-rabbit-hole ambiance, with cozy high-backed booths, eclectic artwork, and greenery on the walls. Look for the drink special: bourbon infused with duck liver and raspberry.

Whiskey Girl (619-236-1616; http://whiskeygirl.com), 600 Fifth Ave. This rowdy bar and grill features live bands most nights of the week, four giant screens to catch sporting events, as well as high-octane cocktails like whiskey and Red Bull. Enjoy decent pub food as

Las Vegas–Style Casinos

San Diego County has the largest concentration of Native American tribes (18) in the United States. Approximately five thousand tribe members in the county live on tribal land, which accounts for nearly 130,000 acres. Of these, several local tribes run gaming casinos that feature Las Vegas–style gambling, entertainment, world-class restaurants and accommodations, spas, and golf, and host big-name live entertainment. Most of these are within 30 to 45 minutes from downtown. Among the largest are **Barona Casino** (619-443-2300; 1932 Wildcat Canyon Road, Lakeside), **Harrah's Rincon Casino and Resort** (760-751-3100; 3375 Valley Center Road, Valley Center), **Sycuan Resort and Casino** (619-445-6002; 5469 Dehesa Road, El Cajon), and **Viejas** (619-445-5400; 5000 Willows Road, Alpine).

well, like a six-pack of sliders, a meatball sub, and build-your-own pizzas.

Coronado

Babcock and Story Bar (619-435-6611; www.hoteldel.com/babcock-and-story.aspx), 1500 Orange Ave. Inside the historic **Hotel del Coronado,** Babcock and Story is a gracious throwback to the turn of the 20th century. The charming establishment was named after the founders of the famous resort and boasts a 46-foot hand-carved mahogany bar that dates to 1888, as well as billion-dollar views of the ocean and expansive sandy beach just beyond the resort. Don't miss the strawberry basil martini.

Coronado Brewing Company (619-437-4452; www.coronadobrewing company.com), 170 Orange Ave. Coronado Brewing makes small batches of handcrafted beers on-site that range from the pale, crisp Golden Ale to the black, malty Outlet Stout. You'll also find seasonal favorites like cranberry wheat for Thanksgiving and Independence Day Ale in July. Enjoy a pint inside by the fireplace or outside on the large heated patio. You can also buy wood-fired pizzas, steaks, and other grill staples for lunch and dinner; on Tues. nights children under 12 eat for free.

Eno (800-468-3533; www.hoteldel .com/eno-wine.aspx), 1500 Orange Ave. This delightful hidden gem inside the Hotel del Coronado offers guests a gourmet trifecta: wine, cheese, and chocolate.

McP's Pub (619-435-5280; www .mcpspub.com), 1107 Orange Ave. This friendly Irish pub and restaurant on the main drag in Coronado serves lunch and dinner daily, as well as a late-night menu; nightly live music draws a loyal local crowd. There are 10 brews on tap, including Wyder's Pear Cider and Guinness stout, as well as fine wines, frozen drinks, and a collection of premium whiskeys.

McP's Pub

48 Hours

ITINERARY FOR COUPLES

Friday Night
- Arrive in town in time for dinner at the dark and moody **Lou and Mickey's**, in the heart of the Gaslamp Quarter; to ensure a romantic evening, start with the juicy oysters Rockefeller (and for the sake of your partner, skip the otherwise divine garlic mashed potatoes).
- Enjoy a nightcap and live music at the sophisticated **Croce's Restaurant and Jazz Bar**; if money is no object, order up a bottle of Dom Pérignon from the extensive wine list. Or if you're looking for more action, head to **The Tipsy Crow** next door and party the night away.
- Overnight at **The Keating Hotel**—within walking distance of both nightspots suggested above; if you want to get some sleep, skip the in-room espresso and turn up the soothing white-noise machine to drown out the world outside.

Saturday
- Breakfast on a stack of whole-wheat pancakes with cherry syrup and applewood bacon at the intimate **Café Chloe**, in the East Village of downtown; leave the driving to public transportation and order a sublime lavender-lemon mimosa.
- Stroll hand in hand through the **Japanese Friendship Garden** in

Keating Building, downtown

Balboa Park, then take time to smell the roses at the nearby **Inez Grant Parker Memorial Rose Garden,** just over the footbridge east of El Prado.

- Split a portobello quesadilla and a huge order of guacamole made fresh at your table at **Ortega's Mexican Bistro** in Hillcrest, just north of the park; wash it down with their famous pomegranate margaritas.
- Head over the bridge to Coronado to enjoy an afternoon plying the canals with the **Gondola Company;** spring for the live violin music.
- Dine on kung-pao-style calamari and blackened ahi at the lovely harbor-side **Roy's;** don't miss the chocolate marquis custard dusted with cocoa powder to share.
- Stroll next door to the **Top of the Hyatt** to enjoy the sparkling lights of Coronado across the bay and to sip a wicked dirty martini nightcap.

Sunday

- Partake of the *divine* champagne brunch at the **Crown Room** at the Hotel del Coronado; do not miss the crab legs and the chocolate fountain (not necessarily at the same time).
- Walk off some of the calories from brunch by window shopping along Orange Ave. in Coronado; stop in at **Bay Books** to browse the stacks.
- Although it's unlikely you'll have much of an appetite by lunchtime, drop by **Miguel's Cocina** across from the Hotel del Coronado for the appetizer sampler of calamari strips, beef taquitos, quesadillas, ceviche, and pollo asada with guacamole or a small bowl of Mexican meatball soup.
- Drive out to the **Cabrillo National Monument** on Point Loma to catch the sights; head to the lookout point

to watch for migrating whales or frolicking dolphins.

ITINERARY FOR FAMILIES

Friday Night

- Rustle up the kids for dinner at the entertaining **Cowboy Star** for a hunk of prime beef, a side of potatoes, and nary a green vegetable in sight. Save room for dessert (see below).
- Take a pedicab tour through the Gaslamp Quarter; ask the driver to stick to Fifth Ave. so the views remain family friendly. Stop by for a late-night fudgy indulgence at the **Ghiradelli Soda Fountain.**
- Overnight at the **San Diego Marriott Hotel and Marina,** which boasts the best pool in downtown— sure to be a hit with young children and teenagers. Snag a room in the North Tower, and parents can sip a beverage on the balcony and enjoy jaw-dropping views after the kids go to bed.

Saturday

- Start the day right with a rib-sticking breakfast at **Café 222,** where kids will be encouraged to play with their food (and then will happily eat it): be sure to check out the green eggs and Spam (and come early to avoid a long wait for a table).
- Head to the **Old Town State Historic Park;** stroll by the restored Cosmopolitan Hotel, then head to the Colorado House, a historic hotel that now houses the Wells Fargo Museum.
- Meander down the street to the **Old Town Mexican Café** for lunch; cheese enchiladas or the ever-popular chicken tacos are kid-pleasers. Encourage the children to watch the tortilla ladies while

waiting for their meal to arrive—they might even get a free sample.

- Walk down to the "haunted" **Whaley House** for a tour; tell your children to ask a docent about the ghost of Yankee Jim.
- Head back to the 21st century in downtown and grab organic burgers from **O'Brothers Burgers** in Horton Plaza; don't miss the crispy onion rings.
- Return to the Marriott for an evening swim in the tropical heated pool; the water is pleasant even if the air is nippy. Order up hot chocolate from room service afterward.

Sunday

- Breakfast at **Richard Walker's Pancake House**; check out the delicious (and enormous) German pancake dusted with powdered sugar (or for tiny diners, consider the Dutch pancake, which is a smaller version of the same dish).
- Walk down the harbor to the **USS Midway** at the **San Diego Aircraft Carrier Museum** to check out the impressive collection of fighter jets; or if you're traveling with very young children, go instead to the **New Children's Museum**.
- Lunch at **Maryjane's Coffee Shop**, downstairs from the Hard Rock Hotel in the Gaslamp Quarter; parents, be prepared to explain the cast of characters from the 1970s music videos and sitcoms that play on the TV sets at each booth. Don't miss the ice cream shakes. Head inside the **Hard Rock Hotel** to check out the awesome collection of music memorabilia in the lobby; stop in at the Rock Shop to purchase an unusual souvenir. Or for families with younger children, head to the **San Diego Model Railroad Museum** instead.

ITINERARY FOR OUTDOORS ENTHUSIASTS

Friday Night

- When visiting in season, park the car, drop off the bags, and go directly to **Petco Park** in the East Village of downtown for a Padres game; pick up a free scorecard at the entrance. (If you miss the boys of summer, check out the action at the **East Village Tavern and Bowl**.)
- Afterward, enjoy a late dinner at the atmospheric **Oceanaire** restaurant; don't miss the horseradish-crusted halibut with a side order of steamed asparagus with hollandaise.
- Overnight at the trendy **Hotel Solamar**; request a room with an extra-deep soaking tub, in case lots of outdoor activities result in sore muscles.

Saturday

- Start the day with a protein-packed breakfast omelet with Italian sausage and tiny cup of authentic espresso at **Café Zucchero** in Little Italy.
- Head across the Bay Bridge for a round of golf at the **Coronado Municipal Golf Club**; bring a camera, because views from the links are impressive.
- Enjoy a restful lunch at **Peohe's** in Coronado; grab a table outside to enjoy the view of downtown across the San Diego Bay—and don't miss the lobster bisque.
- Join the crew at **Dennis Connor's America's Cup Experience** on the harbor for an exhilarating high-speed sail through San Diego Bay. Don't worry about seasickness: this organization promises that if you lose your lunch while sailing with them, they will reimburse the cost of the cruise or buy you a new lunch.

- Unwind at the evocative **Rama** downtown; check out the Yum Talay, a spicy seafood salad that is light and exotic.
- Finish out the night shooting pool at **Joltin' Joes**; head upstairs to the beach bar (complete with sand and tin-roofed shack) for a nightcap.

Sunday
- Recoup your strength with the Popeye Omelet, made with spinach and Egg Beaters, at **Stretch's Café** in Coronado; order fresh fruit or (better yet) grits on the side.
- Suit up for surf fishing off the Silver Strand in Coronado; if the fish aren't biting, go swimming or boogie boarding instead.
- Dry off and head back to downtown. Pull up a waterfront picnic table overlooking the harbor to enjoy a healthy Greek salad from **Greek Islands Café** in Seaport Village.
- Take a brisk run or bike ride through **Embarcadero Park** and along the harbor, where the cool breezes keep the temperatures pleasant for vigorous exercise. Or head to **Kite Flite**, purchase a flying treasure, and then test it out at the harbor-side park.

ITINERARY FOR CULTURE ENTHUSIASTS

Friday Night
- Start off the weekend with an exotic dinner at **Monsoon**, considered among the best Indian restaurants in the city. For a particularly authentic treat, try the Goan fish in a fragrant ginger curry sauce.
- Walk to the **Lyceum Theater** in Horton Plaza to see a live performance by the **San Diego Repertory** company.

- Overnight at the palatial **Westgate Hotel** downtown, just up the street from the theater. Request a top floor for the best views across the harbor.

Saturday
- Don't stray from the hotel for breakfast: go directly to the **Westgate Room** downstairs and look for the house-smoked salmon hash.
- Make the half-hour walk to Balboa Park and head to the **Mingei International Museum** near the central fountain; be sure to save time to shop at the eclectic museum store that features imports from around the world.
- Stroll across the parking lot to lunch at **The Prado** in the park; look for the pan-seared duck breast served with spaghetti squash or the delightful ahi tacos.
- Roll out of the restaurant and head across the street to see the touring exhibit at the **San Diego Museum of Art**; if there's time, drop by the small **Timken Museum of Art**, too, just across from the reflecting pond behind the SDMA.
- Take a minivacation to Iran via the **Bandar** restaurant in downtown, and dine on authentic Persian cuisine like *Ada Polo,* marinated charbroiled chicken served with rice studded with currants and dates.
- Enjoy a stunning **San Diego Opera** performance at the San Diego Civic Theater downtown; for added interest, attend a preopera lecture to learn about the composer, artists, and history of the performance. (Be sure to purchase tickets well in advance.)

Sunday
- Enjoy European ambiance at **Currant American Brasserie**; check out

Ornate architecture in Balboa Park

the almond French toast with lemon-sugared blueberries, and access your inner Hemingway with a refreshing morning Bellini.

- Peruse the stacks at the **Upstart Crow** bookstore and coffee shop in Seaport Village.
- Fortify yourself with a lemon-coconut cupcake at **Heavenly Cupcakes** downtown.
- Walk off the sugar with an educational **Gaslamp Quarter Walking Tour** through historical downtown; be sure to ask your tour guide about Wyatt Earp's influence on what was once called the "Stingaree" district.

ITINERARY FOR TIGHT BUDGETS

Friday Night

- Start the night at perhaps the only dive restaurant left in the gentrified harbor district of downtown: **Kansas City Barbeque.** Ask for extra sauce to accompany whatever tasty meat you order, and save room for the chewy walnut pie for dessert.
- Drive over the Bay Bridge to enjoy a pint of the latest microbrew from **Coronado Brewing Company;** don't miss the Islander Pale Ale—and if you really like it, purchase a six-pack to go.
- Overnight at the quaint **El Cordova Hotel** in Coronado; book a room with a kitchenette, and you'll be able to store drinks and snacks in the fridge.

Saturday

- Elbow your way past clamoring locals to order coffee and dangerously crispy hash browns at the iconic **Clayton's Coffee Shop** in Coronado.

- Rent a four-wheel bike on the Coronado boardwalk and ride along the thoroughfare fronting the beach—or save cash and hoof it; stop by long enough to check out the live piano music in the **Hotel del Coronado** lobby.
- Purchase picnic supplies at the **Babcock and Story Bakery** at the Hotel Del, and enjoy the spread on the wide sands of **Coronado Beach**.
- Move on to nearby Point Loma to hike the Bayside Trail from the **Old Point Loma Lighthouse**. Be sure to check out the tide pools and the views of the towering cliffs.
- Make an early dinner of it at **Point Loma Seafoods** (arrive any later than 6:30, and the place will shut down on you). Enjoy a crab sandwich at a picnic table on the water, and watch out for foraging seagulls.
- Grab a Guinness stout at **McP's Pub** in Coronado, and the designated driver in your party can enjoy a free cup of coffee.

- Spend the early morning in the quaint Little Italy section of downtown; feast on inexpensive pastries at a sidewalk table at **Panificio e Ristorante Solunto's**—or go for broke and wash down Solunto's decadent cannoli with a cup of $1 coffee.
- Visit the exquisite **Botanical Building and Lily Pond** in Balboa Park before the crowds arrive; walk along El Prado to the nearby Alcazar Garden near the iconic Balboa Tower. Listen for the carillon chime at noon.
- Grab a premade salad or sandwich at the outdoor **San Diego Museum of Art Cafe**; choose a table overlooking the sculpture garden to enjoy the view gratis.
- From 2 to 3, check out the free organ concert at the **Spreckels Organ Pavilion** in Balboa Park.

2

La Jolla and the Beaches

COASTAL JEWELS

Few places have the cachet of La Jolla. In addition to miles of lovely (costly) shoreline, arguably the most important contemporary art museum in California, and multimillion-dollar homes, La Jolla offers hot new restaurants and bars, cutting-edge boutique hotels and elegant historic properties, and shopping along Prospect Street that rivals Rodeo Drive in Beverly Hills. La Jolla has been home to the likes of Gregory Peck, Raquel Welch, and Dr. Seuss (aka Theodor Geisel), and hosts world-class scientific research centers like the Scripps Institute of Oceanography, the Salk Institute, and the University of California, San Diego. The art scene is vibrant, thanks to the famed La Jolla Playhouse, which has sent dozens of plays to Broadway, and to a plethora of galleries featuring internationally recognized artists. La Jolla is the Riviera of California and attracts a cosmopolitan, upscale crowd that keeps the manicured streets humming every night of the week.

Inland La Jolla encompasses the Golden Triangle, an area bordered by I-5 on the west, I-805 on the east, and CA 52 in the south. This area centers on the Westfield University Towne Center shopping mall (known as UTC by locals) and includes a number of financial and scientific research institutions, as well as several large-scale chain hotels and a wide selection of fine dining opportunities. Northern La Jolla includes the neighborhood that revolves around the Torrey Pines State Reserve and includes the adjacent beach, the Torrey Pines Glider Port, and the internationally recognized Torrey Pines Golf Course.

Just to the south, Pacific Beach is a densely packed blend of hip new design and beach-cottage chic; increasingly you'll find sleek restaurants and bars in "PB," but this is still surfer central, and bare feet on the boardwalk are as common as little black dresses. This vaguely retro neighborhood is the place to find live music, Bohemian boutiques, and bikini shops. Merging nearly seamlessly into PB from the south is youth-centric, party-hearty Mission Beach, a community that revels in sun, surf, and suds. You'll find board shops and funky bars here, along with a vintage roller coaster just off the most populated shoreline in the city. To the east is Mission Bay, which is vacation central for families visiting San Diego: here you'll find miles of walkways for strolling hand in hand or for a leisurely bike ride, all the

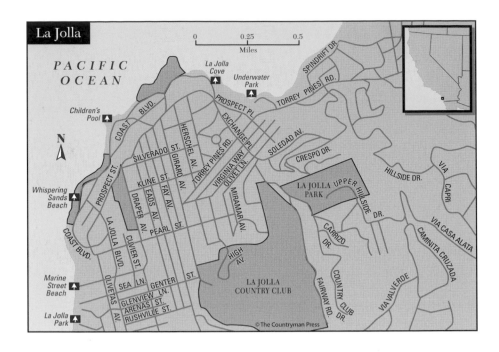

while surrounded by tall palm trees, calm waters, and a relaxed atmosphere. You can rent all manner of water toys or just pull up a hammock and soak up the sun.

Just south of Mission Bay, Ocean Beach (affectionately known to locals as "OB") is an insular neighborhood that is home to iconoclasts of all sorts and popular with vegans and surfers; OB is the epitome of laid-back, with a strong community spirit and a welcoming vibe. This is very much a locals neighborhood, so you won't find a lot of lodging options or tourist attractions, but the area is scenic and the natives are friendly.

Pick Your Spot

Best places to stay in La Jolla, and what you'll find nearby . . .

La Jolla and the coastline neighborhoods just to the south comprise the most popular beaches in San Diego County, and there are plentiful hotel options on the water. You'll find that in general the prices edge up as you move northward along the coast, with La Jolla being significantly more expensive than Mission Beach and Mission Bay.

LA JOLLA

Bed and Breakfast Inn at La Jolla (858-456-2066; www.innlajolla.com), 7753 Draper St. Famed local architect Irving Gill, who worked with Frank Lloyd Wright, built this charming bed and breakfast as a private residence in 1913. The lush gardens were planned by Kate Sessions, who landscaped much of Balboa

Park, and the house was once home to John Philip Sousa, the legendary conductor. The charming residential location, with 15 guest rooms, offers ocean and garden views, and is elegantly decorated with fine antiques and art in a restrained Victorian style. Many rooms feature fireplaces and claw-foot tubs, and the enormous beds are piled high with fine linens. Guests enjoy a complimentary full breakfast in the mornings and a wine and cheese reception in the afternoons. Expensive.

Best Picks for Lodging

Best Family Friendly: Hyatt Regency Mission Bay Spa and Marina

Best Romantic: The Grande Colonial

Best Historical: La Valencia

Best Luxurious: La Jolla Beach and Tennis Club

Best Views: Crystal Pier Hotel

Best Trendy: Tower 23 Hotel

Best Service: Paradise Point Resort and Spa

Best Value: La Jolla Cove Suites

Estancia La Jolla Hotel and Spa (858-550-1000; www.estancialajolla .com), 9700 N. Torrey Pines Rd. The Estancia is in inland La Jolla, across the street from the University of California, San Diego, so no true ocean views here—but this hotel does offer lovely vistas of its natively landscaped property and mission-style architecture. The luxurious 210-room property offers a full-service spa and fitness facility; on-site dining at **Adobe El Restaurante, The Library Dining Room,** and the casual **Mustangs and Burros;** a relaxing small pool; business and conference space; and myriad private enclaves hidden among the gardens. The hotel has gotten a lot of attention after being listed on *Condé Nast Traveler*'s hot list, and likely because of this remains well booked throughout the year. For these prices, hospitality and efficiency should be top-notch, but to be honest, I have found the service to be somewhat lacking. Very expensive.

The Grande Colonial (858-454-2181; www.thegrandecolonial.com), 910 Prospect St. Dating to 1913, the immaculately restored Grande Colonial is the oldest hotel in La Jolla. The comfortable lobby invites guests to relax over a drink or just warm up by the cozy fireplace, but I would be happy to sequester myself in an idyllic guest room. Large windows—and lots of them—actually open to let in fresh ocean breezes (and highlight the magnificent ocean views). The Grande Colonial is located to allow nearly instant access to La Jolla Cove, upscale shopping, and fine dining, but guests needn't stray off property to experience exquisite California cuisine: **Nine-Ten** on-site is one of the most highly regarded restaurants in the city.

In addition to the main hotel, the property also owns and manages the eight-room **Little Hotel by the Sea** next door and the adjacent 10-room **Garden Terraces,** each of which offer small kitchens and more room to spread out. Both accommodations are quite pricey but offer the chance to feel like a resident, thanks to homey touches like wooden floors, deep whirlpool tubs, and extra seating areas. Expensive to very expensive.

Hotel Parisi (858-454-1511; www.hotelparisi.com), 1111 Prospect St. Imagine a European castle designed according to Chinese feng shui principles: this is the Hotel Parisi, which aims to present guests with peace and well-being, wrapped in a contemporary Zen-inspired package. Clean-lined, contemporary guest rooms are decorated with dark woods, snow-white linens, organic prints, and flat-screen TVs. Amenities include an on-site yoga instructor, an acupuncturist, and a massage therapist. A beautifully presented continental breakfast, with fresh fruit and French pastries, is included. The hotel also has eight apartments for short-term rent, located across the street on Herschel. Very expensive.

La Jolla Beach and Tennis Club (858-454-7126; www.ljbtc.com), 2000 Spindrift Dr. An elite gathering place for locals who come for the 12 championship tennis courts and the landmark **Marine Room** restaurant, the distinctly upscale La Jolla Beach and Tennis Club on the sands of La Jolla Shores is an exclusive enclave for the well-heeled. The property offers 90 guest rooms and suites, including recently remodeled one- to three-bedroom beachfront accommodations that are big enough for families. Public spaces show off gleaming wood and clubby accents, and private interiors are decorated with soft fabrics in beach-inspired colors. If you aren't up for sand between your toes, pull up a comfortably padded chaise lounge by the uncrowded pool, or try your luck at the par 3 nine-hole golf course on-site. In the evening, indulge in a sophisticated barbecue on the beach, where you'll dine on fine china at tables set with fresh linens. Very expensive.

Tide pools near La Jolla Cove

La Jolla Cove Suites (888-525-6552; www.lajollacove.com), 1155 Coast Blvd. I recommend this hotel to budget-minded out-of-town friends who want to stay on the water—although I caution them that the La Jolla Cove Suites isn't luxurious or trendy. However, it *is* just across the street from a storybook beach (the Cove for which the property is named), with a grassy park nearby and a mile of ocean-view sidewalk to stroll. The spacious suites feature seating areas, full kitchens, and expansive balconies—and those that face the ocean have incomparable views over La Jolla Cove (better views, in my opinion, than many pricier hotels in the same area). The place isn't in the best repair, and décor is a little tired, but despite steady rate increases over the years, this is still a bargain for otherwise ultraexpensive La Jolla. The property has a small pool and spa in the back, and the views from the rooftop deck where daily breakfast is served will take your breath away. Moderate.

La Jolla Shores Hotel (858-459-8271; www.ljshoreshotel.com), 8110 Camino del Oro. Formerly known as the Sea Lodge, the La Jolla Shores Hotel is directly on the sands of La Jolla Shores, among the most swimmable and family-friendly beaches in San Diego, extremely popular with divers and kayakers. The lodge offers a small heated pool and a tiny spa, as well as a spacious courtyard that reminds me more of Hawaii than San Diego, thanks to extensive palms and ferns. Oceanside accommodations have balconies or patios looking toward the sea, just a few dozen yards from the water's edge. The architectural design screams 1970s, but the overall vibe is understated elegance. Many of the 128 rooms have kitchenettes, and the pricey La Jolla Suite has a full kitchen, dining room, and large living area—perfect for long stays. Expensive.

La Valencia (858-454-0771; www.lavalencia.com), 1132 Prospect St. Since 1926, the much-lauded Spanish Colonial "pink lady" has lured the rich and famous, like old-time Hollywood luminaries Groucho Marx, Mary Pickford, and Greta Garbo, who were frequent guests. La Valencia offers impeccable service and boasts one of the most spectacular lobbies in the world, decorated like a grand hacienda that just happens to have a drop-dead gorgeous view of the Pacific. You can plant yourself in one of the intimate seating arrangements, listen to live piano music nightly, and sip cocktails until the wee hours, all without leaving the rarified air of this regal hotel. On-site is the well-regarded **Mediterranean Room** restaurant, which serves California cuisine in a beautiful setting. Or step into the clubby on-site **Whaling Bar** and rub elbows with gentrified locals. Thanks to an impressive reputation, La Valencia commands blisteringly expensive rates, but note that the standard guest rooms (which can be priced at close to $400 in season *without* an ocean view) are tiny, as are the bathrooms. Very expensive.

The Lodge at Torrey Pines (858-453-4420; www.lodgetorreypines.com), 11480 N. Torrey Pines Rd. This immaculate Craftsman-style property sits on the 18th green of the famous **Torrey Pines Golf Course** and is considered one of the finest resort desti-

Insider Tip: The Torrey Pines Golf Course is wildly popular, and without advanced reservations, it can be tough to get a tee time. Guests at The Lodge at Torrey Pines enjoy the inside edge: on all but the busiest weekends, the concierge will find tee times for hotel guests.

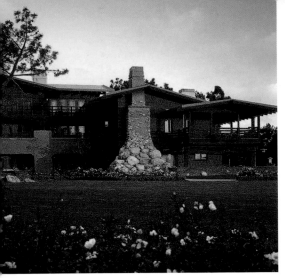

nations in the state. Although the lodge isn't directly on the beach, many rooms offer views of the water, as well as some equally spectacular views of the golf course. Due to the premier on-site **Spa at Torrey Pines**, casual dining at the **Grill and Bar**, and world-class dining at **A.R. Valentien**, many guests find it hard to leave the property. The posh lodging is surprisingly family friendly, too, with organized activities for kids like water-balloon fights, scavenger hunts, and Lincoln Log–building contests. Expensive.

The Lodge at Torrey Pines
Courtesy of The Lodge at Torrey Pines

MISSION BEACH AND MISSION BAY

Bahia Resort (800-576-4229; www.bahiahotel.com), 998 W. Mission Bay Dr. A Mission Bay fixture for 50 years, the Bahia is surrounded by water—which means good views are a sure bet. The landscaping is tropical, with meandering water features and palm trees. Although the exterior shows its age, the public rooms have been rejuvenated with thematic Moroccan style. There are two lighted tennis courts, and professional lessons and clinics are available by appointment. The resort is family friendly, with an active kids' club throughout the year and a Mad Science camp for the 5- to 12-year-old set in the summer. Moderate.

Insider Tip: Guests of the Bahia Resort can cruise aboard the *Bahia Belle*, a Mississippi stern-wheeler that departs from the hotel's dock and cruises the calm waters of the bay every evening.

The Dana (619-222-6440; www.thedana.net), 1710 W. Mission Bay Dr. The Dana is a hidden treasure tucked into a southwest peninsula of Mission Bay. The self-contained resort has its own marina and is surrounded by water. Guest rooms are decorated with clean lines and Asian-inspired textiles; many offer private balconies. Secure a pool-view room in the Marina Cove section of the hotel during the summer, and you'll enjoy outstanding views of nearby SeaWorld's seasonal fireworks. The hotel offers its guests two pools: one a lush, tropical oasis with Mexican-style palapas and the other an infinity pool that seems to melt into Mission Bay. There is almost nothing within easy walking distance, although excellent beaches, downtown dining, and La Jolla shopping are all easy car rides away. Moderate.

Hyatt Regency Mission Bay Spa and Marina (619-224-1234; http://mission bay.hyatt.com), 1441 Quivira Rd. This expansive property sits on a peninsula of its own within scenic Mission Bay (very close to SeaWorld—you can catch a water taxi from the resort to the park—and just across the bay from **Belmont Park**, a small seaside amusement park), with lovely water views in every direction. The hotel has been voted as having one of the top-10 hotel pools in the country: guests will find three free-form lagoon-style pools, which include kid-pleasing corkscrew slides that wind amid the lush landscaping. Recently refurbished guest rooms are bright, airy, and spacious, with tropical accents and clean lines. The resort offers the top-notch, ecofriendly **Blue Marble Spa**; several waterside lounges; the critically acclaimed **Red Marlin Bar and Terrace**; as well as the casual and convenient **Einstein Brothers Bagels**. Guests can also rent Jet Skis and kayaks on the property. Expensive.

Paradise Point Resort and Spa (858-274-4630; www.paradisepoint.com), 1404 Vacation Rd. This self-contained 44-acre island in Mission Bay has more than a mile of sandy beaches; expansive, lush gardens; an 18-hole putting course; five pools, one of them with a spectacular tropical waterfall; championship tennis courts; a full-service marina that rents a wide variety of boats and water toys; two on-site restaurants; and an exotic spa. On-site is the delightful **Baleen** restaurant, which specializes in local seafood. The recently rejuvenated rooms offer a "Bali modern" interior design, and each has a private lanai with comfy furniture and tropical views. Very expensive.

PACIFIC BEACH

Crystal Pier Hotel (800-748-5894; www.crystalpier.com), 4500 Ocean Blvd. This unique lodging option offers the opportunity to sleep *over* the water, in 29 individual Cape Cod–style cottages built directly on the historic Crystal Pier in Pacific Beach. Inside you'll find hardwood floors, simple furniture, and kitchenettes. The cottages have been around since the late 1920s—although they've been remodeled

Water slides at Hyatt Regency Mission Bay

Cottages on the Crystal Pier in Pacific Beach

several times over. Thanks to the relentless sun and saltwater exposure, they're a little rough around the edges, but the management keeps them clean and in good working condition. If you're looking for privacy and peace, this might not be the place for you: the pier is open to the public during daytime hours, when locals head to the far end to fish or people-watch—and hardly a person passes without trying to steal a peek inside. At night the waves below will drown out the worst noise from the PB revelers. Demand is high, and the manager suggests booking at least six months in advance for summer and holiday stays. Expensive.

Tower 23 Hotel (858-270-2323; www.t23hotel.com), 4551 Ocean Blvd. Tower 23 is a high-style, elegant lodging option in a neighborhood otherwise ruled by surfer bars and Hawaiian-themed eateries. Named after the nearby lifeguard tower of the same number, this ultrahip hotel sports minimalist design created in glass, concrete, and steel. Guest rooms have flat-screen TVs, equally minimalist interior design, and feature walk-in rain showers and aromatherapy baths. The upscale hotel is within easy walking distance to the Crystal Pier, numerous restaurants, and the rowdy nightlife that makes Pacific Beach a perennial favorite with 20-somethings. But you don't have to go off-site for a great cocktail lounge. The chic on-site restaurant, Jrdn, boasts a sleek interior and a large outdoor patio just off the boardwalk, with a sushi bar, a fireside patio, and a casual fire pit. Expensive.

Local Flavors

Taste of the town . . . local
restaurants, cafés, bars,
bistros, etc.

Best Picks for Dining

Best Bet All Around: Nine-Ten
Best Family Friendly: World
Famous
Best Romantic: Marine Room
Best Splurge: George's at the
Cove
Best Waterside View: Trattoria
Acqua
Best Hidden Gem: Kono's Café
Best Longtime Favorite: Cody's
Best Value: Rubio's

Proximity to the ocean, cool breezes
that come onshore during even the
hottest summer days, and a prevailing
vacation spirit make these coastal communities a popular choice for a romantic meal or a quick and casual bite.
Plentiful outdoor dining makes every
day feel like a holiday.

FINE DINING

La Jolla

A.R. Valentien (858-453-4420; www
.arvalentien.com), 11480 N. Torrey
Pines Rd. Open daily for lunch and
dinner. At the **Lodge at Torrey Pines**,
A.R. Valentien was voted by *Condé
Nast Traveler* as one of the top-10
farm-to-table restaurants in the country. Chef Jeff Jackson's food is clean,
bright, and surprising. The seasonal
menu can include braised pork belly
with blue-cheese-stuffed dates, roasted
chicken with fennel, and divine *tres
leches* cake with roasted apple cream.
Every Thurs. the restaurant features a
communal Artisan Table, with a four-
course menu served family style and
paired with wines selected by the chef
($75). Between courses guests have the
opportunity to meet the chefs and dis-
cuss the evening's menu. Very expensive.

Cody's (858-459-0040; www.codys
lajolla.com), 8030 Girard Ave. Open
daily for breakfast, lunch, and dinner.
Housed in a charming yellow cottage
surrounded by a white picket fence,
Cody's is a comfortable place to enjoy a
casual meal on the patio while looking
out over the beaches near La Jolla
Cove. For breakfast, the classic eggs
Benedict are served over crispy oniony
home fries or grits. Or for an intimate
dinner, dine inside in the bistro-style
dining room on duck confit quesadilla
with jalapeños and red onions, or the
crostini with Brie, pear-jalapeño jam,
and fig compote. For an unusual entrée,
try the pumpkin seed and coriander
crusted tuna served rare with white
bean and garlic puree. Desserts are
homey and include apple pie à la mode,
Southern red velvet cake, and a decadent flourless chocolate cake. Moderate.

George's at the Cove (858-454-
4244; www.georgesatthecove.com),
1250 Prospect St. Open daily for dinner. For decades, George's in La Jolla
(perched just above the La Jolla Cove)
has been *the* place to celebrate a special occasion, thanks to impeccable cuisine and spectacular oceanfront views.
The recently renovated George's is
actually a collection of three venues:
George's Modern, a fine-dining option
with an ever-changing seasonal menu
of California dishes, featuring Nieman
Ranch beef and sustainable seafood;
the **Ocean Terrace**, which offers a
more casual atmosphere and rooftop
dining; and **George's Bar**, a gastropub
that offers entrées like steak *frites* and

spaghetti with clams. Moderate to very expensive (depending on venue).

Jai (858-638-7778; www.wolfgang puck.com/restaurants/fine-dining /3896), 2910 La Jolla Village Dr. Open Tues.–Sun. for dinner, selected days. Adjacent to the **La Jolla Playhouse** and located on the campus of the University of California, San Diego, Jai is the brainchild of über-celebrity Wolfgang Puck, who serves as its executive chef. Cuisine is a mixture of Asian and contemporary California style, with eclectic menu items like Kobe beef burgers with wasabi mayonnaise, Shanghai lobster with green curry sauce, and miso-glazed butterfish with orange noodles. The atmosphere is relaxed and elegant, and perfectly suited for a pretheater dinner. In fact, note that the restaurant is open *only* on those nights when the La Jolla Playhouse has a performance. Expensive.

Marine Room (866-644-2351; www.marineroom.com), 2000 Spindrift Dr. Open daily for dinner. This La Jolla landmark is considered by many locals to be the most romantic place to dine in San Diego. The restaurant juts out over the sand, and during high tide the waves sometimes crash against the expansive windows. The white, nondescript dining room is a clean canvas to allow the mesmerizing views of La Jolla Shores to come into full focus, and waiters are so reverential of these vistas that they will pause their service to let diners watch the sunset. This venerable institution hardly needs more to recommend it, but in addition to being a feast for the eyes, come here for a *true* feast: exotic ingredients, inventive French recipes, and classically prepared dishes are brought to the table with formality and panache. Menus change constantly, but look for the signature appetizer, a delicately flavored blue-crab cake served with duck confit hash and butternut squash, and the sweet corn and mascarpone brûlée

View of La Jolla Shores from the Marine Room

with lightly dressed organic greens and fig jam. This is a splurge, for sure, but dining at the Marine Room is an experience you will not soon forget. Very expensive.

Nine-Ten (858-964-5400; www .nine-ten.com), 910 Prospect St. Open daily for breakfast, lunch, and dinner. This intimate restaurant in The Grande Colonial serves "evolving California cuisine," and menus change regularly to reflect what's in season. Look for first courses like the baby beet salad served with roasted carrots, toasted walnuts, baby fennel, and arugula, and the marinated black mission figs with white truffle oil. Second courses can include spicy marinated shrimp with feta cheese and melon salad, or the spoon-tender, port-wine-braised short ribs drizzled with potato froth. Final courses might include Hudson Valley duck breast with black rice, Valencia oranges, red currants, and candied juniper; perfectly *sous vide* halibut; and slightly spicy flat iron steak and onions. Desserts also change with the seasons, but count on the half-baked chocolate cake served with caramel sauce, which is like a hot brownie soup. Or for $120, you can put yourself at the "Mercy of the Chef" for an unforgettable five-course menu dreamed up by Chef Jason Knibb and paired with wines (or $80 without wines). Expensive.

Roppongi (858-551-5252; www .roppongiusa.com), 875 Prospect St. Open daily for lunch and dinner. This popular weekday happy-hour destination has a lively sidewalk patio, as well as a large indoor dining room, a full bar, and a small sushi bar. Roppongi is known for its high-quality sushi, and in addition to traditional offerings like California rolls and a variety of sashimi, the restaurant has a few unusual selections, like the beautiful spicy scallop sushi rolls with cucumber and Tobiko

caviar, and the spicy albacore jalapeño roll with sesame seeds. The signature starter is the Polynesian crab stack, a gorgeously engineered tower of crab-meat, avocado, mango, red onions, and pea shoots served with an oil-free ginger sauce, which servers are inexplicably hell-bent on smashing up the minute it arrives. Expensive.

Tapenade (858-551-7500; www .tapenaderestaurant.com), 7612 Fay Ave. Open daily for lunch and dinner. A few blocks off pricey Prospect St., Tapenade's charming facade opens up to an expansive, elegant dining room and bar, with intimate lighting and comfortable black leather booths. There is also sidewalk dining available. Lobster medallions served on top of a chopped mango relish and floated with a frothy coconut milk emulsion are particularly fine. Another favorite is the classic steak au poivre, fork tender and served with crispy *pommes frites*. The imaginative pastry chef always presents an assortment of inventive final choices, including a traditional cheese plate accented with dried fruits and walnut bread, and a luscious trio of tiny crème brûlées. There is an extensive wine list and live jazz on Thurs. nights. Expensive.

Trattoria Acqua (858-454-0709; www.trattoriaacqua.com), 1298 Prospect St. Open Sat. for breakfast, lunch, and dinner; Sun. for brunch and dinner; Mon.–Fri. for lunch and dinner. Outdoor terraces, cozy patios, and a gazebo room provide several choices for intimate dining at Trattoria Acqua, located just above La Jolla Cove, with breathtaking views of the calm waters. The yummy lobster bisque is served in a generous tureen and topped with a pillow of puffed pastry, and the soup is loaded with large chunks of lobster. Also fabulous is the succulent lobster potpie, made with a half pound of

Maine lobster tail and accompanied by herbed French fries. The dessert menu presents you with an impossible choice: Will it be the Meyer lemon tart with fresh berries, the warm blueberry bread pudding served with blueberry gelato, or the fried bananas with chocolate and caramel dipping sauce? If you can't decide, split the *il piatto di dolci acqua,* a sampler plate with a little taste of everything. Expensive.

Whisknladle (858-551-7575; http://whisknladle.com), 1044 Wall St. Open daily for lunch and dinner. Tucked into a quiet section off the main drag of La Jolla, this pretty patio bistro has created a buzz in the culinary world. In 2008, Condé Nast picked this locavore eatery as among the top 125 tables in the world. Chef Ryan Johnston controls *everything* he serves by making it all in-house: Whisknladle bakes its own breads, smokes its own meats, pickles its own

Stuffed squash blossoms from Whisknladle
Courtesy of Whisknladle

pickles, and churns its own ice creams and sorbets. The management is committed to securing everything else locally, from the best organic farms in Southern California. The result is a menu that changes constantly with the seasons. Moderate.

Pacific Beach

Green Flash (858-270-7715; www .greenflashrestaurant.com), 701 Thomas Ave. Open daily for breakfast, lunch, and dinner. Relax on the large outdoor patio and watch the parade of characters stroll down the Pacific Beach boardwalk, or dine inside and take advantage of the large windows looking toward the water. This is a favorite place to watch the sun go down (the place is named after the green flash of light that can sometimes be seen the moment the sun sets into the ocean), but the view of the sea and beach are quintessentially San Diego no matter what time of day you visit. For dinner, start with seafood favorites like oyster shooters, shrimp cocktail, and calamari strips. Entrée choices include fresh seafood—the seafood kabobs with shrimp and scallops are especially good—and beef filets. Don't miss the signature cocktail, the Green Flash: lemon-lime Bacardi, pineapple and orange juices, and melon liqueur. After a few of these, you'll be seeing green flashes long after the sun sets. Moderate.

Jrdn (858-270-5736; www.jrdn .com), 723 Felspar St. Open daily for breakfast, lunch, and dinner. Part of the hip **Tower 23 Hotel,** the very trendy Jrdn restaurant overlooks the sands of Pacific Beach and offers a large outdoor dining space to make the most of the views. The interior dining room is no less impressive, with sleek design and theatrical lighting. The sophisticated cuisine focuses on local

Insider Tip: Jrdn draws a large happy-hour crowd and is famous for its well-crafted cocktails as much as its food: try the prickly pear margarita or the watermelon mojito.

ingredients and specializes in upscale surf and turf. Look for grilled ahi tuna served with Baja octopus, skirt steak from a nearby farm, and free-range chicken with chimichurri sauce. Expensive.

World Famous (858-272-3100), 711 Pacific Beach Dr. Open daily for breakfast, lunch, and dinner. World Famous serves fresh seafood and California coastal cuisine in a relaxed atmosphere. Eat in or soak up the sun on the outdoor sidewalk patio. Breakfast options are creative and reflect San Diego's eclectic ethnic heritage. Try the Kahlúa pork hash, eggs scrambled with Hawaiian-style, slow-cooked shredded pork; the banana macadamia nut pancakes; or the inventive carne asada eggs Benedict, served with avocado and traditional hollandaise sauce. The staff likes children, who are exceedingly well tolerated here. Moderate.

CASUAL DINING

La Jolla
Bubba's Smokehouse BBQ (858-551-4227; www.bubbassmokehousebbq.com), 888 Prospect St. Open daily for lunch and dinner. This messy, friendly restaurant is in the heart of upscale La Jolla Village—and not exactly the kind of place you expect to see on tony Prospect St. Look for inexpensive comfort food like fried chicken, chili, grilled tri-tip, and their famous sticky-sweet ribs. Moderate.

Burger Lounge (858-456-0196; www.burgerlounge.com), 1101 Wall St. Open daily for lunch and dinner. Looking for a quality, guilt-free carnivorous experience? This is the place. The restaurant uses energy- and water-efficient technology; recycles extensively; and uses only sustainable food products, including free-range meat raised humanely without hormones. Bonus: the burgers are awesome. Moderate.

Forever Fondue (858-551-4509; http://foreverfonduesd.com), 909 Prospect St. Open Mon.–Sat. for dinner. Enjoy made-at-your-table cheese fondue served with fruits and vegetables, or indulge in chocolate fondue concoctions served with strawberries, pineapple, peanut-covered marshmallows, and chunks of cheesecake. Moderate.

Goldfish Point Café (858-459-7407), 1255 Coast Blvd. Open daily for breakfast, lunch, and dinner. This tiny café, just across from the Sunny Jim Cave in La Jolla, has the best views of any coffeehouse I know. Grab a sidewalk table overlooking the Cove and enjoy a buttery croissant or a blueberry muffin as you watch the waves roll in. Inexpensive.

Harry's Coffee Shop (858-454-7381), 7545 Girard Ave. A local hangout and breakfast favorite since 1960, this friendly coffee shop is open daily 6–3. Don't miss the corned beef hash and eggs, and the incredible raisin walnut French toast. Inexpensive.

Porkyland (858-459-1708; www.goporkyland.com), 1030 Torrey Pines Rd. Open daily for lunch and dinner. Quality Mexican take-out reaches its zenith at Porkyland in La Jolla (and their second location at 2196 Logan Ave. in San Diego). Try the succulent pork loin tacos or, my favorite, the carne asada tacos made with marinated flank steak. Moderate.

Smashburger (858-750-2532; www.smashburger.com), 1000 Prospect St. Open daily for lunch and dinner. This trendy build-your-own-burger joint in the heart of upscale La Jolla offers third-pound burgers served on butter-toasted buns, with a plethora of add-ons you can choose yourself. (The guacamole is exceptional.) Inexpensive.

The Spot (858-459-0800; www .thespotonline.com), 1005 Prospect St. Open daily for lunch and dinner. This place hasn't changed much over the past few decades: the wood paneling creates a moody atmosphere, the servers are friendly (though a little slow), and the food is reasonably priced. Specials include pizza and specialty burgers, but the restaurant also often offers a three-course lobster meal for under $25. Moderate.

Mission Beach and Mission Bay

Rubio's (858-272-2801; www.rubios .com), 4504 E. Mission Bay Dr. Open daily for lunch and dinner. This walk-up taco stand, brainchild of a San Diegan who fell in love with the food in the surfing town of Ensenada, Mexico, during his college years, is the original location of a beloved local chain of Mexican grills that can now be found throughout Southern California. Ralph Rubio started this first small taco shop in the early 1980s to bring Baja cuisine home, and it was here that locals were first introduced to the Baja-style fish taco, now unofficially recognized as *the* signature dish of San Diego. You'll find Rubio's throughout the county, but this loca-

> **Insider Tip:** On Tuesdays Rubio's features $1.25 fish (or sometimes shrimp) tacos—one of the best bargains in the city.

tion is my favorite because you never forget your first love. Inexpensive.

Sandbar Sports Grill (858-488-1274; www.sandbarsportsgrill.com), 718 Ventura Pl. Open daily 9 AM–2 AM. Close to the ocean and in the heart of the action in Mission Beach, the Sandbar is a favorite local hangout, especially for happy hour (4–7), when you can get bottle and draft beer for $3 and half-off appetizers. Check out the breakfast burger, with an Angus patty, a fried egg, Tater Tots, and cheddar cheese. Moderate.

Taco Surf Taco Shop (858-272-3877), 4657 Mission Blvd. Open daily for lunch and dinner. At this popular surfer hangout a few blocks from the shores, the fast service and modest surroundings complement the huge portions at modest prices. Try the monster burrito to get the biggest bang for your buck. Inexpensive.

Pacific Beach

Australian Pub (858-273-9921; www .australianpub.com), 1014 Grand Ave. Open daily for lunch and dinner. Expect to be greeted with a friendly "G'day" at this Aussie pub in Pacific Beach, which offers delights like sausage rolls and meat pies. Knock back a pint on the sunny outdoor patio, or play darts or shoot pool in the dim interior. Although the connection to the land down under isn't clear, this is fan central for the Green Bay Packers; you'll find memorabilia everywhere, and on game days, don't even think about watching anything else on the pub's TVs. Inexpensive.

The Eggery (858-274-3122; www .theeggery.com), 4150 Mission Blvd. Open daily 7 AM–2 PM. As the name implies, this quaint breakfast and lunch restaurant specializes in anything made with eggs—scrambles heady with sausage and veggies; Benedicts with crab, turkey, or avocado; crêpes stuffed with crab or fresh fruit; and gloriously overstuffed omelets that come with just about anything. Come early on weekends, or expect a long wait. Moderate.

Kono's Café (858-483-1669), 704 Garnet Ave. Open daily for breakfast and lunch. Just inland from the famous Crystal Pier, this Hawaiian-themed diner in Pacific Beach is a local favorite, serving up huge portions of good food at an exceptional value (the average cost of a meal is about $7). This place is *busy,* and on weekends there is sure to be a line around the corner, although it moves pretty quickly, and you'll have great views of the ocean while you wait. Once you squeeze in, order one of their famous hamburgers, or consider the breakfast items, which are served all day long. Inexpensive.

Rocky's Crown Pub (858-273-9140; www.rockyburgers.com/Rockys _Home.html), 3786 Ingraham St. Open daily for lunch and dinner. Large, juicy burgers; a side of greasy fries; and beer on tap at this unassuming joint in Pacific Beach—what more could you want? My friend Pat says that "this is what heaven must taste like." Inexpensive.

Zanzibar Café (858-272-4762; www.zanzibarcafe.com/home), 976 Garnet Ave. Open daily for breakfast, lunch, and dinner. This welcoming, artsy café and coffee bar in Pacific Beach has live music a couple of nights a week (call for a schedule). Enjoy the pretty sidewalk dining area, a great spot to people-watch. Inexpensive.

SNACKS

La Jolla
Cups (858-459-2877; http://cupslj.com), 7857 Girard Ave. Open daily 9–9. Cupcakes are all the rage these days, and Cups in La Jolla is one of the most styl-

ish places to find them. They offer more than 50 organic choices on a rotating basis (look for the fig cake with goat cheese frosting), and there is always one gluten-free and one vegan item. Inexpensive.

Gelateria Frizzanie (858-454-5798), 1025 Prospect St. Open daily 10–10. A tiny shop decorated with photographs of Italy, this gelateria serves up intensely flavored treats like passion fruit sorbet, tiramisu gelato, and chocolate and hazelnut frozen yogurt. You can also pick up a panini for lunch. Inexpensive.

Girard Gourmet (858-454-3325; www.girardgourmet.com), 7837 Girard Ave. Open daily for breakfast, lunch, and dinner. This gourmet deli and Belgian bakery specializes in flaky breakfast croissants, delectable cookies, and gourmet items sold by the pound. There are a handful of tables to eat onsite, but most folks take their food to go; this is a great place to gather supplies for a picnic at the nearby Ellen Browning Scripps Park. Moderate.

Michele Coulon Dessertier (858-456-5098; www.dessertier.com), 7556-D Fay Ave. Open Mon.–Sat. 9–4. This beloved pastry shop in downtown La Jolla specializes in fruit tortes (don't miss the strawberry, when in season), French breads, and even homemade jams. All ingredients are organic, and most are local. Moderate.

Pacific Beach
Charlie's Best Bread (858-272-3521), 1808 Garnet Ave. open daily. This bakery sells some of the best bread in the city, hands down. Try the banana chocolate chip loaf and the pumpkin walnut. Inexpensive.

French Gourmet (858-488-1725; www.thefrenchgourmet.com), 960 Turquoise St. Open daily for breakfast, lunch, and dinner. This French restaurant has one of the most authentic European-style bakeries in the city and has been a longtime favorite with locals, who come for the chocolate mousse cups; lemon buttercream cakes; and the strawberry bagatelle with marzipan, white chocolate, and Bavarian cream. Moderate.

Mr. Frostie's (858-274-9977; www.mrfrosties.com), 1470 Garnet Ave. Open daily 10–9. In Pacific Beach since 1949, Mr. Frostie's is famous for its banana splits and hand-dipped soft cones. Inexpensive.

Don't Miss

Must-see attractions, in La Jolla and nearby . . .

La Jolla is eminently civilized, and there is no better place to browse fine art galleries than Prospect Street; add to the mix the famed contemporary art museum and the La Jolla Playhouse, and La Jolla comes in second only to downtown as San Diego's premier spot for highbrow culture.

Best Picks for Local Attractions

Best Cultural Attraction: La Jolla Playhouse

Best Historical Place: Mount Soledad Veterans' Memorial

Best Beach: La Jolla Cove

Best Park: Mission Bay

Best Outdoor Activity: Kayaking in La Jolla

Best Family Fun: SeaWorld

Best Shopping: Anything along Prospect Street, La Jolla

Best Nightlife: Whaling Bar

BEST CULTURAL ATTRACTIONS

La Jolla Playhouse (858-550-1070; www.lajollaplayhouse.org), campus of UCSD, La Jolla. Considered one of the finest regional theaters in the country, the La Jolla Playhouse has premiered more than 30 productions that have gone on to Broadway, including the Tony-award-winning *Jersey Boys* in 2004, Matthew Broderick's *How to Succeed in Business Without Really Trying*, and Lee Blessings's *A Walk in the Woods*. The theater was founded in 1947 by La Jolla native Gregory Peck and his Hollywood pals. Today the theater performs in four venues, all located on the UCSD campus in La Jolla. The theater is open May–Nov.

Insider Tip: To avoid intermission crowds, place your drink order at the theater bar at the La Jolla Playhouse before the show; your drink will be waiting for you at intermission.

Museum of Contemporary Art San Diego (858-454-3541; www.mcasd .org), 700 Prospect St., La Jolla. Open Mon.–Tues. and Fri.–Sun. 11–5, Thurs. 11–7. This internationally known museum has a permanent collection of more than three thousand works representing myriad art genres from the past half century and includes paintings, sculpture, photography, video, and multimedia works. The expansive museum also attracts arguably the most important touring exhibits of contemporary art in Southern California. There's a nice café in the front and an eclectic bookstore that also sells high-style jewelry and decorating accessories. General admission $10, individuals 25 and younger free.

Off La Jolla Cove

Note that there is now also a downtown venue for exhibits (see chapter 1).

Stuart Collection UCSD (858-534-2117; http://stuartcollection.ucsd.edu), 9500 Gilman Dr., La Jolla. UCSD in La Jolla has a secret attraction that most locals don't even know about: arrayed on several miles of pathways that meander through the 1,200-acre campus is an impressive outdoor sculpture collection. Visitors can crisscross the expansive university to view 17 installations, including a group of "talking trees" and an oversized phoenix sculpture affectionately known as the Sun God, which is the unofficial mascot of the campus. Before beginning your tour, stop at the

Nancy Rubins's *Pleasure Point* (2006) is on permanent display at the Museum of Contemporary Art San Diego.

Photo by Pablo Mason. Used with permission.

Insider Tip: Visit the Stuart Collection at UCSD on a weekend day, when parking is plentiful and free, and the campus is much quieter.

information kiosk at the campus's south entrance on Gilman Dr., where you can pick up a brochure and map (or download a map at http://stuartcollection.ucsd.edu/StuartCollection/Map.htm). The full circuit takes approximately two and a half hours to walk. Free.

BEST HISTORICAL PLACES

Crystal Pier, 4500 Ocean Blvd., Pacific Beach. Opened in 1927, the Crystal Pier (a beautiful wooden construction) continues to be a draw for fishermen and people watchers. At the foot of the pier is a cluster of 29 cottages (**Crystal Pier Hotel**) built in the 1930s directly over the water.

Mount Soledad Veterans' Memorial, 6905 La Jolla Scenic Dr. S., La Jolla. Perched at the top of a mountain more than 800 feet high and overlooking the expanse of La Jolla, Mount Soledad offers a gorgeous panoramic view of the area. In addition, on-site is a veterans' memorial comprising six block-granite walls engraved with the names and photos of more than 2,700

Seals ashore at Children's Pool beach in La Jolla

war veterans, as well as a large cross. The memorial is the site of annual Memorial and Veterans Day ceremonies.

Ocean Beach Pier, at the end of Niagara St., Ocean Beach. This favorite with locals offers a fully stocked bait and tackle shop. The Ocean Beach Pier is nearly 2,000 feet long—the longest pier on the West Coast.

BEST GREEN SPACES

This strip of coastline offers some of the finest opportunities for outdoor activities in the state. Beaches range from pristine seaside oases to sand-lot party spots; visitors can bare it all and bask in the sun, grab a water toy and dive into the waves, or just kick back and enjoy the show.

Beaches

Black's Beach. From Torrey Pines Rd., follow the signs to the Glider Port; park in the dirt lot and hike down the cliff pathways. Or walk in past the Scripps Pier from La Jolla Shores, La Jolla. Between 1974 and 1977, Black's Beach, just north of La Jolla Shores, was officially designated as a swimsuit-optional beach. Because nudity was (and still is) banned at all other San Diego–area beaches, uninhibited people were attracted in droves to Black's. Although Black's lost its official designation as a nude beach decades ago, the tradition continues at the northern end.

Children's Pool, off Coast Blvd., south of La Jolla Cove. Don't let the name fool you; this crescent-shaped beach just south of La Jolla Cove is not overrun with children but rather with seals. The shallow cove is protected by a seawall (it's fun to walk to the end of the curving concrete walkway, with waves crashing all around), and it

La Jolla Cove

would have made for a protected, calm place for youngsters to swim—if the noisy seals hadn't claimed it decades ago. Although the city has made attempts to take back the beach, environmentalists have balked—and federally protected seals are likely to rule the shore for years to come. You are not allowed to approach the wildlife, and thus the beach itself usually isn't accessible, but you can watch the amusing creatures bask on the sand from the walkway above.

La Jolla Cove, off Coast Blvd., west of Prospect St., La Jolla. This is by far my favorite place to enjoy the sea in San Diego; unfortunately, there are many others who share my enthusiasm for this tiny beach, which is protected on three sides by the C-shaped cliffs. Finding parking here would test Job's patience. As always, come early and be prepared to hike in if you can't find

something close. The waters are calm enough for snorkeling (and thanks to the San Diego–La Jolla Underwater Ecological Reserve, you have a decent chance of spotting sea life). If you're not up for the sand between your toes, try the **Ellen Browning Scripps Park**, an expansive grassy park at the top of the Cove stairs, or stroll around the sidewalk that rings the Cove and heads south to **Children's Pool**. This is an excellent place for tidepooling and is especially family friendly.

La Jolla Shores, off Vallecitos St., La Jolla. Crystal blue waters, white-sand beaches, and countless oiled bodies baking in the sun define La Jolla Shores, which has some of the loveliest views, calmest waves, and widest strips of sand in the city. This is a great place to kayak, thanks to the gentle waves, and it's a popular place to take surf lessons as well. From the parking lot walk north past the Scripps Pier, and you'll get away from the crowds—although be careful not to get stranded during high tide (and too far north will take you into the clothing-optional zone of **Black's Beach**).

Mission Beach, south off Mission Blvd., Mission Beach. There are 2 miles of sand from the north entrance of Mission Beach to Pacific Beach, and these 2 miles are packed body to body on weekends and all through the summer, making this one of the favorite—and most crowded—beaches in the city. The wide boardwalk is immensely popular with inline skaters, runners, and bikers—although it is possible for pedestrians to stroll the boardwalk safely if you keep your wits about you! Families will feel more comfortable staying on the southern portion of the beach—you can catch a beach volleyball game at Cohasset Court on the south end as well; the northern end tends to attract a rougher crowd.

Pacific Beach, north off Mission Blvd., Pacific Beach. Pacific Beach officially runs from the north end of Mission Beach, where the boardwalk terminates and becomes a sidewalk, north to the Crystal Pier. This can be a raucous scene and not necessarily the best for families, but it *is* one of the best places to people-watch—and what a lot of beautiful people there are! This beach is popular with surfers as well. Restroom facilities, showers, and fire rings are plentiful, even if parking is not.

Torrey Pines State Beach and Reserve (858-755-2063), off Hwy. 101, north of La Jolla. This is a quiet, relatively uncrowded beach on all but the hottest summer weekends. Even when it does get crowded, just walk a few minutes north or south from the beach parking lot, and you're likely to find secluded spots along the cliffs. You can also access the shores via the many trails coming down off the cliffs

Torrey Pines State Beach

(although be careful, because these can be unstable). This is one of the best family beaches in the city and is very popular with longtime locals.

Tourmaline Surfing Park, at the west end of Tourmaline St., Pacific Beach. No swimming is allowed on this beach; it is open only for surfers and sailboarders. And note: the wave riders are territorial here, so unless you are extremely skilled, better leave your board at home and just enjoy watching the locals.

Windansea, off Nautilus St., La Jolla. An offshore reef makes for huge waves (when the conditions are right), making this south La Jolla beach a world-class surfing destination—made famous by Tom Wolfe in *The Pump House Gang*. This is a popular beach for sunbathing as well, even though the shoreline is rocky; the extra effort to hike in helps seclude the beach.

Gardens and Parks

Kate Sessions Memorial Park, in Pacific Beach; take Lamont St. north. Named after the legendary landscape designer of Balboa Park (see chapter 1), this hilltop green space has a sweeping view of the ocean and bay, and beautiful city lights after dark (that's probably why so many teenagers come here to park in the evenings), as well as a large expanse of lawn for picnicking or a game of Frisbee or football. You'll find 79 acres of mature trees and plants, crisscrossed with dirt hiking trails.

Mission Bay Park, off Mission Bay Dr., Mission Beach. This picturesque human-made park encompasses more than 4,000 acres. Created more than 60 years ago when the city dredged the natural tidelands area, Mission Bay offers numerous recreational activities and is extremely popular with families and fitness buffs. The paved and nearly flat bike path that runs from DeAnza Cove on the northeast side of the park (accessed off the Mission Bay Dr. exit from I-5) through a 2.5-mile arc passes several children's playgrounds, acres of lush grass lawn, and follows the waterline to the Mission Bay Pkwy. bridge. This route is extremely popular with joggers and inline skaters as well, and on summer weekends the pathway can get congested.

If you want to be even closer to the water, you can rent sailboats, Jet Skis, powerboats, and aquatic bicycles at several junctions, or you can bring your own watercraft and use one of several public boat launches. Although there are always a few children splashing in the calm waters of Mission Bay and some die-hard swimmers, the pollution levels thanks to the powerboats and the fact that the bay is the terminus point for local drains makes this a fairly bad idea. Better to use this park for picnics, sports, and kite flying. You'll find fire rings, picnic tables, and large covered pavilions (most of the latter require a permit if you want to reserve them).

Fiesta Island, little more than a dirt mound in the middle of the eastern portion of the bay, is the site of the raunchy, boozy **Over-the-Line Tournament** every summer; the rest of the year it reigns as party central. You can drive to the island via the Fiesta Island Dr. bridge and park your vehicle right on the beach. The waters surrounding the island allow powerboating, so it is a good place to launch Wave Runners and ski boats, and thus it tends to be noisy, especially on the weekends.

SeaWorld is sited along the southern perimeter, and just north is the tiny Vacation Isle, accessed via Ingraham St. (going north from Mission Bay Dr.), where you'll find a model yacht pond and many quiet picnic spots. Sail Bay dominates the northwest portion.

Mission Bay Park

Unlike many waterfront parks in San Diego, the parking is plentiful at Mission Bay, both in the many lots along the eastern portion and street-side along Mission Bay Dr. You'll find every facility you could hope for, including public restrooms, boat launches, RV pump-out stations, and boat pump-out stations.

Mount Soledad Park, north of Mount Soledad Rd., La Jolla. The 43-foot cross on the top of Mount Soledad that is part of a monument to war veterans has been a source of controversy over the years, but recent court rulings have determined that the religious symbol is a local institution and thus will stay put—at least for now. The park provides panoramic views of La Jolla and, on really clear days, south to Mexico and north to the Channel Islands.

Torrey Pines State Reserve (868-755-2063), off Hwy. 101, north of La Jolla. At Torrey Pines State Reserve you'll find 2,000 pristine acres of sandstone mesas and canyons, marshes, and 8 miles of trails. Visitors will see native animals and plants (including the rare Torrey pine tree, which grows only one other place in the world), spectacular red and white wind-carved cliffs, and miles of unobstructed sea views. A visitors center that dates to 1922 made

Insider Tip: To save the $12 parking fee at Torrey Pines State Reserve—and get a cardio workout—snag a street-side spot just off Torrey Pines State Beach, then walk up the *steep* hill to the trails.

from adobe bricks hosts free guided naturalist tours every weekend to a point overlooking Peñasquitos Lagoon and the ocean beyond. The center also has a small theater showing a short video on the park, as well as a bookstore and tiny museum. At the foot of the mountain is the Torrey Pines State Beach, which can be accessed for free if you are lucky enough to nab one of the unmetered parking spaces along Hwy. 101.

BEST OUTDOOR ACTIVITIES

Boating

Bahia Belle (858-488-0551; www.bahia hotel.com/dining3.html), 998 W. Mission Bay Dr., San Diego. For only $10 ($3 for children), you can board this Mississippi riverboat stern-wheeler and cruise Mission Bay, all the while dancing and enjoying cocktails (for an addi-

tional charge). Purchase boarding tickets at the Bahia Resort. Early cruises are family friendly. Note that there are no cruises offered in Dec.

La Jolla Kayak (858-459-1114; www.lajollakayak.com), 2199 Avenida de la Playa, La Jolla. This establishment rents kayaks to experienced paddlers, and for novices offers one-and-a-half-hour guided tours through the La Jolla caves, including a special sunset tour.

Mission Bay Aquatic Center (858-488-1000; www.mbaquaticcenter .com), 1001 Santa Clara Pt., San Diego. The Mission Bay Aquatic Center claims to be the largest waterfront instructional facility in the world, offering classes in sailing, kayaking, rowing, windsurfing, and wakeboarding; it also has myriad equipment rentals.

Seaforth Boat Rental (619-223-1681; www.seaforthboatrental.com), 1641 Quivira Rd., San Diego. Located

Kayaking off La Jolla Shores

on Mission Bay (as well as Coronado and the harbor downtown), this company rents out sailboats, Jet Skis, and speedboats. They also provide crewed sunset sail cruises and charter fishing expeditions.

Diving and Snorkeling

Two favorite dive spots in this area are the La Jolla kelp forests and Wreck Alley, an artificial reef made up of sunken vessels, including an old weather station that blew over during a storm 20 years ago; a retired kelp cutter; a 160-foot Coast Guard cutter; a 366-foot Canadian destroyer; a sportfishing boat; two submarines; and a World War II bomber. Dive shops and charter boats will take you out to the wrecks, which are thriving with marine life.

The **San Diego–La Jolla Underwater Park Ecological Preserve**, just off the coast of La Jolla Cove and running north to Torrey Pines State Reserve, is a 6,000-acre marine habitat—the first coastal underwater preserve on the West Coast. The visibility is generally good and the waters are relatively calm, which makes for some of the best diving and snorkeling on the southern coast. In addition to the state fish, the golden Garibaldi (bright orange, with fluorescent blue markings in young fish), you are likely to see giant lobsters, sculpin, and harmless leopard sharks.

The San Diego City Lifeguard Service provides updated recorded diving information (619-231-8824). Note that spearfishing requires a license (available at most dive stores), although it is illegal year-round to take any sea life from the San Diego–La Jolla Underwater Park Ecological Preserve. Local dive shops include **Diving Locker** (858-272-1120; 6167 Balboa Avenue, San Diego) and the well-respected

Sunny Jim Cave

Kayakers in La Jolla Cove can explore six different ocean caves, carved through the years by the relentless waves. The most interesting of these is probably the Sunny Jim Cave, named by Frank L. Baum (author of *The Wizard of Oz*) after a 1920s cartoon character the opening of the cave is said to resemble. The cavity of the cave displays colorful mineral deposits from iron oxide and iodine from kelp. The cave is also accessible via a human-made tunnel and network of 145 steps (which can be slippery) through the **Cave Store** (858-459-0746; 1325 Cave Street, La Jolla). Adults $4, children $3.

Scuba San Diego (619-260-1880; 1775 E. Mission Bay Drive, San Diego).

Fishing

All fishing is prohibited along the marine reserve that runs from La Jolla Cove north to Torrey Pines.

Deep-Sea Fishing

Mission Bay has several launch points for deep-sea fishing, including **Islandia Sportfishing** (619-222-1164; 1551 W. Mission Bay Drive, San Diego) and **Seaforth Landing** (619-224-3383; 1717 Quivira Road, San Diego), which offer day trips to the Point Loma kelp beds and multiple-day trips aboard the long-range fleet.

Pier and Surf Fishing

Crystal Pier (at the west end of Garnet Ave., Pacific Beach) is a remnant of San Diego past; you'll find a small crowd of anglers casting from this 80-year-old structure, along with nonfish-

Beneath Scripps Pier, La Jolla Shores

ermen enjoying the peaceful atmosphere and the people watching. You won't need a fishing license here or for any other pier in San Diego.

Lagoons and Bays

San Diego County has an embarrassment of riches when it comes to the calm bay waters and abundant lagoons, and fishing is allowed in all but a few places that are otherwise reserved for swimming. **Mission Bay** has more than 4,000 acres to fish; check out **Quivira Basin**, in the southwest end of the bay; a public bait barge is located nearby, and the ubiquitous spills of anchovies attract a huge number of fish. You'll want to practice catch-and-release here, because the waters are not as clean as we wish they were. Fishing licenses are required for anglers 12 and older.

Golfing

Mission Bay Golf Course (858-581-7880; www.golfsd.com/mission_bay .html), 2702 N. Mission Bay Dr., San Diego. The only night-lighted public golf course in San Diego; you'll find a par 58 executive course with 18 holes. Green fee: $28–32.

Torrey Pines Golf Course (800-985-4653; www.torreypinesgolfcourse .com), 11480 N. Torrey Pines Rd., La Jolla. One of the nation's premier municipal golf facilities, with 36 holes, a driving range, and equipment rentals, this PGA-sanctioned course is extremely popular with serious local golfers. Deep canyons and dense vegetation make the course feel farther away from civilization than it really is. Almost every hole has a view of the ocean. The more expensive South Course is extremely difficult and has

Grunion Hunting

If someone invites you to a midnight "grunion hunt" at the beach, you might suspect fishy business. Have no fear: grunion hunting is an actual Southern California phenomenon. From March until August, schools of grunions (cousins of smelts) swim as far inland as possible during high tide at night to lay and then fertilize eggs. The process takes only a few seconds, and afterward they aim to swim back out with a retreating wave. But the 6-inch silver fish often get stranded for several minutes. Opportunistic grunion hunters scoop them up as they swim up the beach or when they are flailing on the sand awaiting the next wave. The largest runs are on the second through fifth nights following a new or full moon, and the heaviest part of any given run is about an hour into the run (which can last up to three hours). The best beaches in San Diego to hunt grunion are the Strand on Coronado, Mission Beach near the jetty, Torrey Pines State Beach north of La Jolla, and Del Mar Beach. Flashlight and firelight disturb the fish and minimize the number of grunion spawning. Hunters 12 years and older must have a valid fishing license, and nets and digging holes to trap the grunions are prohibited. April and May are closed season, so that the fish may replenish themselves.

And what do you do with your catch after a nighttime foray? Scale and gut the fish, coat them in cornmeal or flour, and fry them up whole. They aren't bad to eat, but they are extremely bony. A better use is probably as bait. To check expected grunion runs for the season, visit the Web site of the California Department of Fish and Game at www.dfg.ca.gov/mrd/gruschd.

challenged the best players in the world during the Buick Invitational played here every Jan. (as well as the 2008 U.S. Open). The North Course is a little less challenging but is the more scenic of the two. Green fee: $110–229.

Insider Tip: Torrey Pines Golf Course is popular and books up quickly. Nonresidents and residents of San Diego (who receive significant discounts at the course) can book a tee time up to 90 days in advance by calling the advanced reservation service (877-581-7171). Also note that twilight tee times (after 2:30) offer discounts of as much as 50 percent.

Hiking

La Jolla Cove Walkway, starting just above La Jolla Cove. An extremely easy 0.5-mile sidewalk stroll packs in the ocean scenery: traveling north to south, you'll pass La Jolla Cove, Shell Beach, Seal Rock—look for the seals basking in the sun—and Children's Pool. Along this route you'll also see cormorants drying their feathers, pelicans dive-bombing for snacks, enough seagulls to populate an Alfred Hitchcock thriller, and plenty of overfed ground squirrels.

Torrey Pines State Reserve (858-755-2063), off Hwy. 101, north of La Jolla. A number of well-worn trails wind through the native scrub brush and indigenous (and rare) Torrey pines, and along cliffs that lead to pristine ocean vistas—and these trails are heavily trafficked, especially on weekends. Once you pass through the ranger station entrance, drive up to the top of the mountain to access the trails. Or if you're looking for a serious workout, park at the beach and walk up (but watch out for cars—there are no sidewalks). Parking $12.

Surfing

You'll find some of the best surfing in this region, including the shores at Mission Beach, especially near the jetty off Mission Boulevard; Pacific Beach; Tourmaline Surfing Park; La Jolla Shores; Scripps Pier; and Black's Beach. You'll also find some of the most territorial locals. If you're going to surf these waters, make sure you know what you're doing, and mind your surfing etiquette.

If you're a beginner, surf lessons will get you up on a board in no time, although it takes years of practice and innate athletic ability to excel at the sport. Reliable surf schools include **Menehune Surf** (858-663-7299; 8070 La Jolla Shores Drive, #478, La Jolla), **Mission Bay Aquatic Center** (858-488-1000; 1001 Santa Clara Point, San Diego), **Ocean Experience** (619-225-0674; 4976 Newport Avenue, San Diego), and **Surf Diva** (858-454-8273; 2160 Avenida de la Playa, La Jolla), the latter of which offers girls- and women-only classes.

If the waves are flat at the beach, check out the **Wave House Athletic Club** (858-228-9300; 3115 Ocean Front Walk, San Diego) in Mission Beach, where you can ride one of three wave-generating devices that promise the perfect swell every time.

BEST FAMILY FUN

Belmont Park (858-488-1549; www .belmontpark.com), 3190 Mission

Surfing at La Jolla Shores

Courtesy of Jon Preimesberger

Blvd., San Diego. Open daily at 11 AM. Drive into Mission Beach, and you can't miss the whitewashed wooden roller coaster called the Giant Dipper, which has been rattling riders for eight decades. You'll also find the newer Beach Blaster, a giant arm ride, and the FlowRider, a simulated wave maker. Guests can purchase individual rides from $2 to $6 or an unlimited-ride wristband for $23 for adults and $16 for children 50 inches or shorter. (Height seems like a strange way to calculate admission prices, but this reflects the restrictions on the Giant Dipper; anyone shorter than 50 inches cannot ride.) The coaster closes down for several weeks in the winter for routine repairs, and then reopens Thurs.–Sun. until late May. Call ahead for updated hours.

Birch Aquarium at Scripps (858-534-3474; www.aquarium.ucsd.edu), 2300 Expedition Way, La Jolla. Open daily 9–5. A compact aquarium that is part of the Scripps Institution of Oceanography at the University of California, San Diego, the Birch sits atop a cliff overlooking one of the most spectacular ocean views in the city. Enjoy these vistas at the extensive outdoor tide pool exhibit, where visitors can touch creatures like starfish and sea cucumbers, and watch local Garibaldi fish swim through human-made ponds. More exotic specimens are available inside the aquarium, including ethereal jellyfish, leafy sea dragons that look like something out of a Dr. Seuss book, and

Insider Tip: Look for the sculpture of a life-sized gray whale and her calf outside of the Birch Aquarium to get an idea of the size of these amazing animals.

various varieties of small sharks. On-site is the **Splash Café**, a casual outdoor patio eatery with amazing views. Adults $12, seniors $9, children $8.50.

SeaWorld (800-257-4268; www.seaworld.com), 500 Sea World Dr., San Diego. Open daily; hours vary by season. Second only to the San Diego Zoo in fame, this marine zoological park on south Mission Bay is a must-see attraction in San Diego. Part aquarium, part amusement park, and part botanical garden, SeaWorld is deservedly world famous, and its feature killer whale, Shamu, has been San Diego's unofficial mascot for decades. Animal shows are the heart of Sea-World, so be sure to get a map and show schedule at the front entrance when you arrive so you can plan your day accordingly. During off-peak season, there are only two Shamu shows a day. On busy days plan to arrive about 30 to 45 minutes before showtime to get a good seat. If you see nothing else, plan your visit around the multimedia Shamu extravaganza. There are also dolphin shows and a comedic sea lion show—always a big hit with young children. If you visited SeaWorld a decade or so ago and haven't been back, you'll be surprised to find several water-themed thrill rides on the property, including Journey to Atlantis, a fast-paced water roller coaster ride that plunges 60 feet while riders listen to a soundtrack of dolphin calls; Shipwreck Rapids, a white-water raft adventure through waterfalls and spouting water jets that is guaranteed to leave you drenched; and Wild Arctic, a convincing simulator ride that will take you onboard a helicopter to see polar bears and caribou as you ride out an avalanche. Two original, tamer rides require additional tickets: Skyride, a six-minute gondola ride across Mission

Shamu and friend   Courtesy of SeaWorld

Bay that affords lovely views of the water; and the emblematic Skytower, a 265-feet-tall tower with a gently revolving compartment that shows off views up to 100 miles away. The real fun of SeaWorld is getting personally involved with the attractions. Pet a California bat ray at Forbidden Reef; watch the antics of the tuxedoed darlings at the indoor Penguin Encounter; stroll through a 57-foot acrylic tube as sand tiger and bonnethead sharks swim over your head at the 280,000-gallon Shark Encounter; or visit the classic Tide Pool exhibit, where you can pick up a starfish or pet a sea cucumber. Adults and children $59.

Whale Watching

Gray whales pass by the San Diego coastline every year during their 10,000-mile round-trip migration from the frigid Arctic Sea to the warm and shallow lagoons of Baja Mexico to mate and to calve, starting in late December and through the end of March. About two hundred whales pass by San Diego in a day during the peak migration period (late January and through February). To get a closer look, check out the whale-watching tours sponsored jointly by the **Birch Aquarium at Scripps Institution of Oceanography** (see *Best Family Fun*) and **San Diego Harbor Excursion** (619-234-4111; 1050 N. Harbor Drive, San Diego). As ships embark on three-hour tours to deep waters off San Diego, onboard Birch naturalists highlight biological and historical facts about gray whales. You really can't go wrong with these tours, because the San Diego Harbor Excursion promises that if you don't spot a whale, you can come back for a second tour at no additional cost. There are also longer whale-watching trips leaving from San Diego heading to Baja, starting in mid-February. These extended tours last between three and five days, and guests will visit Ojo de Liebre (Scammon's Lagoon) and secluded Bahia de San Ignacio, where the whales have their offspring. If you and your stomach are not up for a boat tour, try watching for whales from atop the hills at the **Cabrillo National Monument** in Point Loma or inside its partially glassed-in observatory, which is just a short walk from the **Old Point Loma Lighthouse.** Look about a mile offshore for water spouts 8 to 15 feet tall, the byproduct of whales breathing through their blowholes. Generally the whales blow four or five spouts, then sound (dive down) for about five minutes. You're apt to see the head or the tail surfacing shortly after a spout, and if you're really lucky, you'll see a whale breach.

The **Ocean Beach Antique District** on the 4800 block of Newport Avenue has one of the most concentrated areas for antiques and collectibles dealers in the city. You can find estate furniture, vintage jewelry, midcentury modern décor, Depression glass, and toys from the 1920s. But the greatest shopping in the area is likely along **Prospect Street** in La Jolla (as well as its perpendicular offshoot, Girard), which features upscale clothing boutiques, dozens of fine art galleries, and fine home-furnishing stores. Check out these independent stores in the beach area:

Bob's Mission Surf Shop (858-483-8837; www.missionsurf.com), 4320 Mission Blvd., San Diego. In addition to board sales and rentals, you can also get repairs in this one-stop shop, which sells its own brand of surfboards alongside a wide variety of designer brands.

Cottage Antiques (619-222-1967), 4896 Newport Ave., San Diego. Located in the heart of the Ocean Beach Antique District, this store specializes in fine English china, French furniture, and vintage quilts.

D.G. Wills (858-456-1800; www.dgwillsbooks.com), 7461 Girard Ave., La Jolla. A stuffed-to-the-rafters old-fashioned bookstore that specializes in new and used scholarly books as well as rare collector's items, D.G. Wills hosts regular readings by an eclectic mix of authors, poets, and journalists. The owner and staff are knowledgeable and extremely helpful.

Gone Bananas Beachwear (858-488-4900; www.gonebananasbeachwear.com), 3785 Mission Blvd., San Diego. Find some of the hottest beachwear at the largest mix-and-match swimwear shop on the West Coast. The store carries more than one hundred brands, including Billabong, Guess, Juicy, Body Glove, and Betsey Johnson.

Great News! (858-270-1582; www.great-news.com), 1788 Garnet Ave., San Diego. Tucked into a strip mall in Pacific Beach, this discount cookware store sells name brands of cookware for bargain prices and also offers reasonably priced on-site cooking classes.

Muttropolis (858-459-9663; www.muttropolis.com), 7755 Girard Ave., La Jolla. Appropriately located in dog-friendly La Jolla, Muttropolis offers exquisite food and water bowls, couture dog wear, and pet beds to complement the nicest interior designs. Canine companions are welcome.

Ocean Beach Antique Center (619-223-6170), 4926 Newport Ave., San Diego. A huge antiques mall that draws crowds on the weekends; there's almost nothing you can't find here, from estate jewelry to vintage toys to fine furniture.

Pangaea Outpost (858-581-0555; www.pangaeaoutpost.com), 909 Garnet Ave., San Diego. This unusual warehouse space hosts more than 50 international vendors under the same Pacific Beach roof. Browse through Mexican folk art, including a large collection of Day of the Dead pieces; carved wooden tiki masks from Indonesia; beaded cocktail purses; handcrafted jewelry; and beach clothing and shoes.

Pilar's Beachwear (858-488-3056), 3745 Mission Blvd., San Diego. This Mission Beach standard showcases the swimwear designs of two locals who've made a career out of beachwear for more than 30 years.

Warwicks (858-454-0347; www.warwicks.com), 7812 Girard Ave., La Jolla. This beloved independent bookstore manages to survive a market flooded with discount bookstores by offering unwaveringly good service and regular book signings by big-name authors. They also carry high-end gift papers and stationery.

BEST NIGHTLIFE

La Jolla and Pacific Beach offer plentiful nightlife options—but you'll find it is a tale of two beach cities. Whereas La Jolla tends to attract the upper crust and those dressing to impress for pricier, more refined establishments, Pacific Beach draws in a huge college crowd in mostly casual, raucous beach bars—many of which offer good, inexpensive food as well. Despite the dual nature of these locales, both are parking challenged, so consider taking public transportation or a taxi—a good idea, anyhow, if you plan to imbibe.

Cass Street Bar and Grill (858-270-1320), 4612 Cass St., San Diego. This old favorite in Pacific Beach is known for a laid-back atmosphere, inexpensive beer, and good food. The shuffleboard table is a fun addition.

Comedy Store La Jolla (858-454-9176; www.thecomedystore.com), 916 Pearl St., La Jolla. Some of the best comedy acts in the country have made their way to the stage at the famous Comedy Store. In its heyday during the 1980s, Robin Williams used to show up unannounced and unbilled, and Whoopi Goldberg got her start here. Wed. is open mike night.

La Jolla Brewhouse (858-456-6279), 7536 Fay Ave., La Jolla. One of the most unassuming establishments in upscale La Jolla, this paneling-clad bar decorated with surfboards and fishing trophies attracts an eclectic clientele, from longtime neighborhood devotees to college students, and offers a rotating menu of beers brewed on-site.

Miller's Field (858-483-4143; www.millersfield.com), 4465 Mission Blvd., San Diego. This rowdy sports bar in Pacific Beach offers $2 well drinks for weekday happy hours (3–7), as well as good barbecue selections from the grill. (Try the loin back ribs.)

Moondoggies (858-483-6550; www.moondoggies.com), 832 Garnet Ave., San Diego. With a no-worries atmosphere and dozens of screens playing surfing videos (as well as major sporting events), this casual sports bar and beach grill in Pacific Beach would make Gidget feel right at home. Come on a Mon. evening and enjoy all-night happy hour specials with amusing names like The Grateful Dog and Surf Wax shots.

Pacific Beach Alehouse (858-581-2337; www.pbalehouse.com), 721 Grand Ave., San Diego. This brewery and pub in Pacific Beach is a half block from the ocean and offers a comfortable microbrewery atmosphere and good food. Look for Burger Bliss Mondays, when burgers can be had for $5.

RT's Longboard Grill (858-270-4030; http://longboardgrill.com), 1466 Garnet Ave., San Diego. Another surf bar in Pacific Beach, RT's is crowded, loud, and youthful, often featuring local bands. Don't miss Taco Tuesdays ($1.50 per taco).

The Tap Room (858-274-1010; www.sdtaproom.com),1269 Garnet Ave., San Diego. In Pacific Beach, this popular watering hole offers a good selection of beer and surprisingly good pizza as well. Happy hour starts at 3 PM.

Whaling Bar (858-454-0771; www.lavalencia.com/dining/whaling-bar-grill.php), 1132 Prospect St., La Jolla. Within the hallowed halls of the exclusive **La Valencia Hotel**, the Whaling Bar is a clubby, old-fashioned lounge with mahogany tables, retro décor, and scrimshaw collections. Come for a subdued evening of cocktails and quiet discussions. Try the namesake Whaler, made with vanilla ice cream, brandy, cocoa, Kahlúa, Grand Marnier, and Baileys Irish Cream.

48 Hours

ITINERARY FOR COUPLES

Friday Night

- Set the mood for romance by dining at an ocean-view table at the incomparable **Marine Room** on La Jolla Shores; shoot the works with a forest mushroom torte followed by lobster tail basted with hand-churned tarragon butter.
- After one of the best meals of your life, stroll outside the restaurant to enjoy **La Jolla Shores** by starlight; if you're feeling adventurous, walk north past the Scripps Pier to **Black's Beach** and go skinny-dipping.
- Overnight at the romantic, historic **Grande Colonial**; splurge on an ocean-view room, and leave the windows open so you can fall asleep to the sound of the nearby surf.

Saturday

- Enjoy a cozy breakfast on the patio of **Cody's**; don't miss the "millionaire" buttermilk pancakes with blueberries.
- Head to **Torrey Pines State Beach**, where you have your choice of activities: lazing on the white sands below or hiking the stunning cliffs above.
- Meander south to Pacific Beach to pick up picnic supplies at **Charlie's Best Bread**; the *divine* Gorgonzola walnut loaf is a meal unto itself, and perfect enjoyed on a grassy patch overlooking **Mission Bay**.
- While at the bay, visit **Seaforth Boat Rental** to rent a sailboat or small powerboat for the afternoon.
- Return to La Jolla for Meyer lemon ravioli and local yellowtail at George's Modern at **George's at the Cove**; if you're celebrating a special

occasion, mention it when you make reservations, and it might just help you secure a table by a window.
- Wrap up the evening with a show at the legendary **Comedy Store** in La Jolla; consider the potent Long Island iced tea to fulfill the club's two-drink minimum—but then leave the driving to someone else.

Sunday

- Wake up with a breakfast panini and a chocolate espresso at the intimate **Goldfish Point Café**, across from La Jolla Cove.
- Hook up with **La Jolla Kayak** for a morning paddling tour through the caves off La Jolla; if you're an experienced paddler—and feel *really* comfortable in the ocean—the two of you can rent a double kayak and head out on your own.
- Refuel for lunch with a shrimp quesadilla from **Porkyland** in La Jolla.
- Take a luxurious swim in the perfectly round hotel pool at **The Grande Colonial**, which is kept at an idyllic 82 degrees, and then spend an hour or two lounging in the sun.

ITINERARY FOR FAMILIES

Friday Night

- Let the kids play with their food at **Forever Fondue** in La Jolla; top off the meal with strawberries dipped into a chocolate and caramel concoction.
- Walk off some of the sugar energy from dinner and head to **Children's Pool** in La Jolla to watch the sunset and to view the resident seals; you won't have to remind the kids to stay back, because the smell is appalling!
- Travel south along the waterfront via the scenic I-5 and overnight at the **Hyatt Regency Mission Bay**.

North end of La Jolla Shores

Saturday

- It's going to be tough to pry the kids away from the vacation atmosphere at this festive Hyatt outlet, so grab a bagel and egg sandwich from **Einstein Brothers Bagels** on-site and enjoy a casual breakfast poolside.
- Parents: soak up some sun at the hotel pool—maybe rent a cabana?—sip a beverage, and *relax*. Children: swim in all three free-form lagoon pools and see how many times you can make it down the corkscrew water slides.
- Grab a bowl of chowder or an ahi tuna sandwich at the waterfront **Red Marlin Bar and Terrace** on the hotel property.
- Spend the afternoon exploring the wonders of the sea at the entertaining **Birch Aquarium at Scripps**; be sure to look for the baby sharks, and don't miss the outdoor tide pool, where you can examine sea creatures up close.
- Most kids can't get enough burgers, so satisfy their cravings at the boutique-ish **Burger Lounge** in La Jolla, which also serves chicken tenders, grilled chicken salads, and wicked red velvet cupcakes.
- If you're visiting in the summer, check out the evening entertainment at **SeaWorld**, which includes a nightly fireworks spectacular visible

Colorful sea life   *Courtesy of the Birch Aquarium*

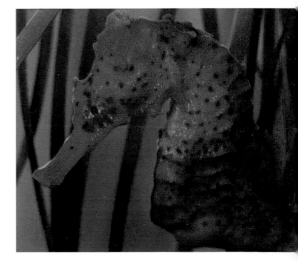

from the Hyatt; or head to nearby **Belmont Park** to ride the most exciting roller coaster in San Diego—a vintage wooden coaster that has primo views of Mission Beach.

Sunday

- Wakey, wakey, eggs and bakey at the local favorite, **Harry's Coffee Shop** in La Jolla.
- Hike to **Sunny Jim Cave** off La Jolla Cove; see if the kids can make out the face of the cartoon character after which this cave was named.
- Let the children play on the beach nearby while a parent waits in line for a lunch table at **Kono's Café** in Pacific Beach—believe me, the effort is worth it, and your wallet will be none the worse for your visit.
- If you can move after the massive portions at Kono's, try bicycling or in-line skating along the boardwalk in Pacific Beach—the flat pathway is ideal for beginners, and the ocean-side scenery can't be beat.

ITINERARY FOR OUTDOORS ENTHUSIASTS

Friday Night

- Pull up an oceanfront view on the patio at the sleek **Jrdn** restaurant in Pacific Beach to enjoy their "petite" raw platter, which overflows with oysters, prawns, green lip mussels, and king crab; finish with grilled swordfish with jasmine rice or Alaskan halibut with a purple potato hash.
- Head to nearby **Moondoggies** to shoot pool, sip a microbrew (look for the Strawberry Blond ale from Belmont Brewing Company, a Southern California brewery), and enjoy televised sports action and a convivial atmosphere.

- Set up camp at the chic, ultramodern ocean-side **Tower 23 Hotel**; if you're looking to splurge, book the Sweet Suite, which offers enormous space, a fabulous view of the Pacific, and a spalike bathroom with a huge chro-matherapy whirlpool tub.

Saturday

- Fuel up at **The Eggery** in Pacific Beach with a Veggie Veggie Inter-esting omelet with broccoli, mush-rooms, and bell peppers, which is hearty enough to get you going but light enough that it won't slow you down.
- Then grab your boards and head to the world-famous **Windansea** beach for a morning of surfing or, if you're new to board sports, schedule a les-son with the pros at **Surf Diva**.
- Switch out the board shorts for land-lubber attire and migrate north to **Bubba's Smokehouse BBQ** for a surprisingly light Smokehouse Cobb salad with pulled chicken—or go for an awesome baked yam with cinna-mon butter.
- Get in an afternoon round at the world-renowned **Torrey Pines Golf Course**; schedule well in advance and request the North course, which offers the best views of the Pacific Ocean.
- It's hard to leave this beautiful resort, so plan for dinner here, too, at the clubby **A.R. Valentien**, which uses organic, local ingredients to create clean, bright dishes; menus change regularly, but if it's on offer, don't miss the crispy-skin Petaluma chicken served with fried ricotta.
- After a day in the sun, kick back under the stars with a pint by the outdoor patio fire pit at the nearby **La Jolla Brewhouse** and catch up on sports action on the 55-inch-screen TV.

Sunday

- Take advantage of your hotel's proximity to the beach and go for a morning run (or take a long walk) along the stretch of boardwalk that extends just beyond the doors of Tower 23 Hotel in Pacific Beach, southward to Mission Beach.
- Calories be damned: feast on a Mediterranean brunch at the picturesque **Trattoria Acqua**, overlooking the La Jolla Cove nearby and La Jolla Shores in the distance.
- Go scuba diving or snorkeling off the **San Diego–La Jolla Underwater Park** preserve; look for the California state fish, the bright orange Garibaldi, and bring along an underwater camera to get photos of the impressive kelp forests.

ITINERARY FOR CULTURE ENTHUSIASTS

Friday Night

- Kick off the weekend with a gourmet meal of exquisite braised short ribs at **Nine-Ten**, in the heart of La Jolla village; don't miss the chance to peruse the restaurant's extensive wine list.
- Stroll down the street to the sophisticated **Whaling Bar**; order up the house specialty, The Whaler, a creamy, potent libation that is bound to stimulate conversation.

Tower 23 Hotel

Courtesy of Tower 23 Hotel

- Cross the street to overnight at the ecofriendly **Hotel Parisi**, which offers an upscale blend of European style and Asian ambiance; if there's time, indulge in an in-room Zentouch shiatsu massage.

Saturday

- Start the day with breakfast at the bistro-style **Zanzibar Café** in Pacific Beach with Greek eggs served with feta, tomatoes, and basil, or order up one of the delectable pastries; don't miss the cappuccino.
- Head back to La Jolla village to browse the many galleries; stop by the iconic **Warwicks** bookstore on Girard Ave. to shop for hard-to-find volumes and especially fine stationery supplies.
- Dive into a candied pecan salad with grilled free-range chicken at the high-style **Museum Café**, adjacent to the Museum of Contemporary Art San Diego.
- Spend the afternoon exploring the modern and contemporary works at the **Museum of Contemporary Art**; make sure to visit the outdoor sculpture exhibit, which also boasts a lovely garden and astounding views of the ocean.
- Dine at celebrity chef Wolfgang Puck's Asian restaurant **Jai**, next to the La Jolla Playhouse, on the campus of UCSD; try the crispy roasted quail with vanilla-roasted pineapple or the miso-glazed black cod with baby bok choy.
- Catch a performance at the **La Jolla Playhouse** at UCSD.

Sunday

- Before leaving the vicinity of your hotel, purchase fixings for a picnic lunch at **Girard Gourmet** in La Jolla. Then on to breakfast of Florentine crêpes with ham, creamed spinach, and hollandaise at the **French Gourmet** in Pacific Beach; don't miss the gooey pastries as well.
- Stroll through the **Stuart Collection**, the eclectic outdoor sculpture garden that is scattered throughout the campus of UCSD in La Jolla; be sure to pick up a map at the campus entry kiosk, because the university is huge, and it's easy to get lost.
- Settle in to enjoy your picnic in the shadows of *The La Jolla Project*, a large-scale piece installed on the lawn south of Galbraith Hall; students affectionately call this collection of 71 blocks of granite "Stonehenge."
- Drive to the top of scenic **Mount Soledad** in La Jolla to view the war memorial and to take in the breathtaking views over the water.

ITINERARY FOR TIGHT BUDGETS

Friday Night

- Settle in to a cozy booth at **The Spot** in La Jolla and build your own burger with a variety of toppings, breads, and proteins; come during happy hour and purchase a discounted glass of beer or wine to accompany your meal.
- Grab a flashlight and a bucket and go grunion hunting at **La Jolla Shores**; if the grunion aren't running, spend the whole evening at The Spot, which turns into a lively (reasonably priced) bar after traditional dinner hours.
- Check into the **La Jolla Cove Suites**; although the ocean-view rooms are a little pricey (but still a value, given the awesome proximity to the Cove and the extremely upscale neighborhood), garden suites are moderately priced and offer lots of room (as well as kitch-

enettes, in case you'd like to save cash and cook some of your own meals).

Saturday
- Enjoy the complimentary continental breakfast at the hotel, which is served in a rooftop venue that offers some of the best views available in any hotel, regardless of price point.
- Spend the morning snorkeling and exploring the caves of the beautiful **La Jolla Cove**—or just relax on the tiny beach with a good book.
- Chow down at **Harry's Coffee Shop** on a turkey and avocado sandwich with bacon and cheddar, served with a mound of French fries; a plateful of food will set you back less than $10—and it's easily enough to split.
- Head back to the beach at low tide to go tidepooling off **Shell Beach,**

Enjoying a Pesky Combo at Rubio's

south of La Jolla Cove. (Tip: wear slip-resistant shoes, and pay attention to the waves.)
- Grab burgers and beer—done well and done cheaply—at **Rocky's Crown Pub** in Pacific Beach; this is a 21-and-older establishment, so if you have children in tow, go instead to **Smashburger** in La Jolla.
- Take in an evening cruise on the *Bahia Belle,* a surprisingly affordable way to see the city from the water; a sunset sail is especially nice.

Sunday
- Take advantage of another complimentary breakfast at the hotel—the spread is generous, and, as noted above, the view can't be beat.
- Head across the street for a morning stroll along the walkway that runs from **La Jolla Cove** in the north and south past **Children's Pool** to the south; watch for cormorants drying their wings on the rocks just offshore.
- Head to the original **Rubio's,** one of the most beloved little taco shacks in Mission Beach, and order a Pesky Combo (two fish tacos, beans, and chips); be sure to load up at the self-serve salsa bar.
- Stake out a spot at the **Ellen Browning Scripps Park,** just above La Jolla Cove, for a summertime free concert by the sea, or just spend the afternoon soaking up the sun and watching the weekend crowd roll by.

3

North County San Diego

FROM RANCHOS TO REAL ESTATE MECCA

A drive through parts of coastal North County 20-some years ago would take you through stretches of open area, a few agricultural fields, and alongside the remains of some of the county's largest remaining ranchos—large cattle ranches that blanketed Southern California a century ago. Although today you'll still pass by small patches of strawberry and flower fields in Carlsbad and Encinitas, anything else along the coast resembling farmland has been replaced with upscale tract homes and the infrastructure that goes along with them. This is now one of the fastest growing residential areas in the county, and new suburbs seem to appear overnight.

Visitors will find great variety in coastal North County, which runs from Del Mar north to Oceanside, from tony residential neighborhoods to laid-back beach towns with plenty of cafés and boutique shopping. In general these areas are much less congested than their coastal counterparts to the south—although the freeways required to reach them have among the worst traffic in the city.

Del Mar in the south, and its tiny neighbor, Solana Beach, are expensive beach towns, with the Del Mar Race Track at the heart of the neighborhood and fine dining and extraordinary shopping in upscale malls in Del Mar and in the Cedros Design District in Solana Beach. To the east is Carmel Valley, home to polo fields and expensive suburbs. Slightly up the coast is Encinitas (which incorporates Cardiff-by-the-Sea and Leucadia), the capital of surf culture, with popular beaches, numerous friendly cafés, and board shops everywhere. Tiny Leucadia is an artsy, casual neighborhood, famous for funky Mexican cafés and for quirky, bargain shopping. Charming Cardiff is another small surfing enclave and home to the ecological reserve at the San Elijo Lagoon. Downtown Encinitas offers fine dining at pretty cafés, with plenty of small stores to explore and a pedestrian-friendly layout. Farther north still, stretching along the coast is expansive Carlsbad, which has two distinct regions: Southern Carlsbad is home to several internationally known spas and golf courses, set amid pricey suburbs and alongside the lovely Batiguitos Lagoon; northern Carlsbad offers small-town appeal in its resortlike downtown and family-friendly destinations like Legoland and the Museum of Making Music. To the far north, Oceanside has the feel of a small fishing community on the harbor. Although once known primarily as a military town (the large marine base, Camp Pendleton, is next door), Oceanside is another favorite with surfers and with suburbanites looking to beat the real estate inflation found in most other beach cities.

Although many natives will tell you "there is no life east of I-5" (the major north–south freeway that runs near the coastline), don't believe it: in North County there are vibrant inland communities that have much to offer, including exclusive Rancho Santa Fe, named by *Fortune 500* as the wealthiest zip code in America; Rancho Bernardo and Poway, favorites with golfers; Escondido, home to the San Diego Zoo Safari Park and popular with equestrians; and Julian, a delightful small town in the mountains.

Pick Your Spot

Best places to stay in North County, and what you'll find nearby . . .

Best Picks for Lodging

Best Family Friendly: Sheraton Carlsbad

Best Romantic: Cardiff-by-the-Sea Lodge

Best Spa Resort: La Costa Resort and Spa

Best Luxurious: The Grand Del Mar

Best Views: L'Auberge Del Mar Resort and Spa

Best Trendy: Grand Pacific Palisades

Best Service: Park Hyatt Aviara

Best Value: Moonlight Beach Motel

Lodging options in coastal North County tend toward small, no-frills motels and expensive upscale resorts—there isn't much middle ground, with the exception of northern Carlsbad, which has a handful of larger, moderately priced hotels and a few small bed and breakfasts scattered along the coast. Be aware, when choosing any neighborhood in North County, that the north–south freeway corridors are the most congested in the city, and if you plan to spend most of your time in downtown San Diego, these options will probably not be the best choice for you. However, if you're looking to enjoy all of San Diego County, or if you want to concentrate on the northern beaches and attractions like Legoland and the San Diego Zoo Safari Park, you'll find friendly folks and a little more breathing room in this area.

CARLSBAD

Why choose Carlsbad as your vacation home base? This family-friendly city has lovely beaches, a plethora of kid-pleasing activities, and a charming downtown "village." You'll also find that Carlsbad, although increasingly expensive for those of us who call it home, is quaint rather than upscale, so you never have to worry about the hotels or restaurants being stuffy.

Beach Terrace Inn (760-729-5951; www.beachterraceinn.com), 2775 Ocean St. This is one of the few moderately priced hotels in North County that is located

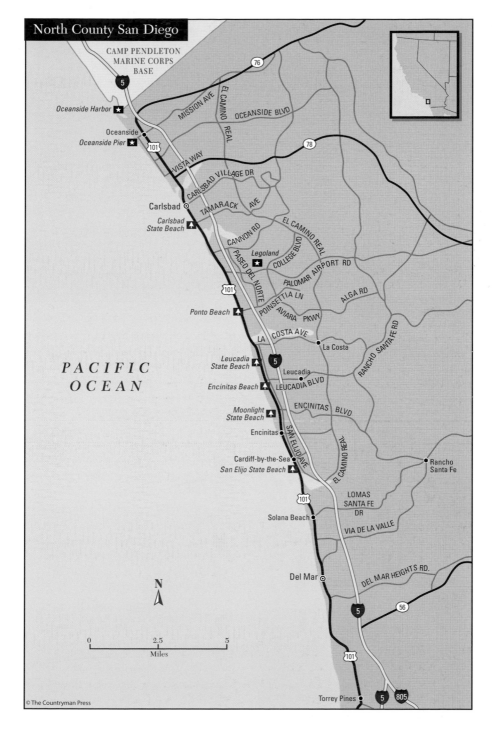

North County San Diego

CAMP PENDLETON
MARINE CORPS
BASE

Oceanside Harbor ★

Oceanside
Oceanside Pier ★

MISSION AVE

EL CAMINO REAL

OCEANSIDE BLVD

VISTA WAY

CARLSBAD VILLAGE DR

Carlsbad

TAMARACK   AVE

Carlsbad
State Beach

CANNON RD

EL CAMINO REAL

PASEO DEL NORTE

Legoland ★

COLLEGE BLVD

PALOMAR AIRPORT RD

POINSETTIA LN

Ponto Beach

AVIARA   PKWY

ALGA RD

LA   COSTA AVE

La Costa

RANCHO SANTA FE RD

Leucadia
State Beach

Leucadia

Encinitas Beach

LEUCADIA BLVD

ENCINITAS   BLVD

Moonlight
State Beach

Encinitas

SAN ELIJO AVE

Cardiff-by-the-Sea
San Elijo State Beach

EL CAMINO REAL

Rancho
Santa Fe

LOMAS
SANTA FE
DR

VIA DE LA VALLE

Solana Beach

Del Mar

DEL MAR HEIGHTS RD.

PACIFIC
OCEAN

N

0   2.5   5
Miles

Torrey Pines

© The Countryman Press

directly on the beach. With only 49 guest rooms, the inn can't offer the amenities of many larger hotels (no room service, no luxurious fixtures in the bathrooms), but it does boast a spacious ocean-view pool and Jacuzzi. The property is located in downtown Carlsbad, within a few miles of Legoland and minutes from the quaint downtown restaurants and shops. Most of the rooms have large balconies, although guest rooms are small. Moderate.

Carlsbad Inn (760-434-7020; www.carlsbadinn.com), 3075 Carlsbad Blvd. You'll find old-fashioned European charm at the Carlsbad Inn, which is also located right on the beach—steps from the ocean and close to several fine dining options and the charming downtown Carlsbad shopping district. The exterior of the hotel fits in with the Scandinavian-themed architecture throughout downtown Carlsbad. Accommodations vary, from standard rooms—some with kitchenettes, fireplaces, and private spas—to more luxurious ocean-view rooms and condominiums. Expensive.

La Costa Resort and Spa
Courtesy of La Costa Resort and Spa

Grand Pacific Palisades (760-827-3200; www.grandpacificpalisades.com), 5805 Armada Dr. A family resort located close to **Legoland** (the hotel offers a private entrance to the park), the Grand Pacific Palisades overlooks the **Carlsbad Flower Fields,** an explosion of rainbow-colored ranunculus during the blooming months of Mar. and Apr. This large property has everything to make a family comfortable, including a spacious pool, outdoor playground area, and a mini water park for young children. This hotel does more than cater to the little ones, however: the **Karl Strauss Brewery** (760-431-BREW) and restaurant is on-site, offering a lively happy hour and eight different microbrews every evening. The resort has planned activities for its guests throughout the week, including Ping-Pong tournaments, jazz nights, and wine tastings. Expensive.

La Costa Resort and Spa (760-438-9111; www.lacosta.com), 2100 Costa Del Mar Rd. This venerable resort is internationally known as a premier spa and the site of several important golfing and tennis events throughout the year. Guests can enjoy four sparkling pools (one with a water slide worthy of a theme park), world-class golf on two PGA 18-hole courses, innovative spa treatments, four-star restaurants, and boutique shopping. At the fabulous spa visitors can indulge in deep-tissue massages, skin-revitalizing facials, and full-body salt scrubs. In addition, the resort is home to the **Chopra Center for Well Being,** founded by famed Deepak Chopra, which promotes health of the total person: mind, body, and spirit. You needn't stray off the property to eat in exceptional restaurants, including the **Legends Bistro** and the **BlueFire Grill.** If you're traveling with little ones, they'll love the new Kid's Club at La Costa, with a 7-foot tree house, a 600-gallon saltwater aquarium, computer and video games, and a teen lounge that offers music and dancing, billiards, and an Xbox gaming lounge. Very expensive.

Park Hyatt Aviara (760-448-1234; www.parkaviara.hyatt.com/hyatt/hotels), 7100 Four Seasons Pt. Formerly known as the Four Seasons Aviara, this gorgeous property is perched on a hill overlooking its own golf course, the Batiguitos Lagoon (a protected wildlife sanctuary), and the Pacific Ocean in the near distance. The property is a masterpiece in understated elegance, with lush public rooms and sprawling flower- and citrus-filled gardens suggestive of a stately mansion by the sea. The five-star resort features an incomparable spa that offers more than 20 kinds of massages, facials, and body scrubs. Golfers will fall for the Arnold Palmer–designed course, which is one of the most challenging—and stunning—in a city of top-notch golf courses. There is also a tennis center with lighted clay and hard courts, outstanding on-site restaurants, and a complimentary children's program. Very expensive.

Sheraton Carlsbad (760-827-2400; www.sheratoncarlsbad.com), 5480 Grand Pacific Dr. This Mediterranean beauty atop a cliff overlooking Legoland is one of the newest luxury resorts in North County and offers something for everyone. The clean-lined guest rooms are designed with business travelers in mind, offering oversized work desks and wireless Internet access. The grounds, however, are all

Sheraton Carlsbad

about families—especially those with tiny children. The expansive, tropical pool is preequipped with floating toys. There is a Ping-Pong table, a bean-bag-toss area, and a huge play lawn in front, perfect for a breakfast picnic or just letting the kids run off some energy. The biggest draw for children, of course, is the proximity to **Legoland;** this property offers discount tickets for the park, as well as a private entrance. For adult indulgences, try the **Ocean Pearl Spa** on-site. The hotel also offers one of the finest restaurants in Carlsbad: the **Twenty/20 Grill and Bar.** Expensive.

West Inn and Suites (866-431-WEST; www.westinnandsuites.com), 4970 Avenida Encinas. Location is key at this bargain lodging option: guests are within a half mile of the ocean, and no more than 10 minutes by car to downtown Carlsbad and Legoland. The Craftsman-style lobby is rich with wood details, and manage-ment pipes in seasonal scents to offer a homey feel. A stay includes a full hot breakfast, served in a charming, clubby library setting, as well as free wine and beer in the evenings and cookies and milk before bedtime. There are two fine-dining options (**Bistro West** and **West Steakhouse**) on the property; free (and plentiful) parking; and even a gas station and minimart. The management provides a complimentary shuttle to within 5 miles, free Wi-Fi, and upscale bath products. Rooms are small but luxurious and include a refrigerator and microwave. Cats and dogs are welcome, but smokers are not (the place is 100 percent smoke free). Be aware that the property is sandwiched between the freeway and the train tracks, and across the street from a large (unsightly) power plant, so this isn't the place to come if you're looking for views. It is, however, a fabulous bargain for deluxe accommodations near the beach. Inexpensive.

DEL MAR

Del Mar Inn (800-451-4515; www.delmarinn.com), 720 Camino Del Mar. This country-style inn offers large, somewhat dated rooms, many with a distant ocean view. Some accommodations include a kitchenette. The property features a small heated pool, a whirlpool, and tropical landscaping. A light breakfast is included, as well as afternoon tea and cookies. The property is close to the restaurants and shopping of downtown Del Mar, and it is one of only a handful of lodging values in the area: the low cost is its main selling point. Inexpensive to moderate.

Del Mar Motel (858-755-1534; www.delmarmotelonthebeach.com), 1702 Coast Blvd. This small motel on the Del Mar cliffs has exceptional views of the ocean and beach below, and easy beach access—in fact, it is the only beachfront hotel in Del Mar. Outdoor public spaces come with picnic tables, lounge chairs, barbecue grills, and an outdoor beach shower. The small rooms are simply decorat-ed and bright; the basic rooms are furnished with a small desk, table and chairs, and a coffeemaker. All rooms open to the outside on wraparound porches, which are equipped with patio furniture. Guests can borrow beach chairs and boogie boards at no cost from the front desk. Moderate.

The Grand Del Mar (858-314-2000; www.thegranddelmar.com), 5300 Grand Del Mar Way. This landmark property in east Del Mar debuted its five-star accom-modations in late 2007. The luxurious resort combines Spanish, Portuguese, Moroccan, and Venetian design elements, all of which reflect the indigenous archi-tecture of San Diego. Guest rooms are spacious, elegant, and intended to pamper.

The Grand Del Mar

Courtesy of the Grand Del Mar Resort

The resort offers a kids' club and a fun teen lounge, so that busy parents can indulge their offspring while they visit the fabulous spa or get in a round of golf at the on-site, 18-hole Tom Fazio–designed course. The hotel restaurant, **Addison**, is making waves, thanks to renowned chef William Bradley's Mediterranean interpretation of fresh, local ingredients. Very expensive.

   L'Auberge Del Mar Resort and Spa (858-259-1515; www.laubergedelmar .com), 1540 Camino Del Mar. This luxurious resort and full-service spa in the heart of downtown Del Mar pampers guests with superior service and immaculate attention to detail. The richly appointed lobby has a clubby feeling, thanks to elegant appointments and a stellar ocean view. The guest rooms are bright and light, decorated with cottage-style furnishings in sunny colors; some include fireplaces. The hotel has two lighted tennis courts and a professional on staff for private or group instruction; there is also a pool, an outdoor hot tub, and a lap pool. The tranquil on-site spa offers a full array of massages, facial treatments, and body purification treatments. Dining is at the romantic **Kitchen 1540** (858-793-6460), featuring Chef Paul McCabe's inspirational contemporary American cuisine, and at the classy **Bleu Bar**, a relaxing poolside venue that offers casual food and cocktails. Expensive.

ENCINITAS

Cardiff-by-the-Sea Lodge (760-944-6474; www.cardifflodge.com), 142 Chesterfield St. This romantic bed and breakfast is centrally located in Cardiff-by-the-Sea, a charming incorporated village within Encinitas that time seems to have forgotten. The cedar clapboard siding and stone walkways suggest a Tudor influence to the otherwise neo–Spanish Colonial building, which looks as if it's been here since the 1900s. This isn't a historical property, but the stately structure suggests an era of bygone elegance. The lodge is surrounded by lush gardens, and each of the 17 guest rooms is furnished individually, with styles ranging from serene contemporary to over-the-top Victorian. Breakfasts feature fresh fruit and locally prepared pastries. Expensive.

Moonlight Beach Motel (760-753-0623; www.moonlightbeachmotel.com), 233 Second St. With only 24 rooms, this small motel has a premium location just three blocks away from Moonlight Beach in Encinitas. (Some rooms have ocean views.) This is a family-oriented motel, and each unit comes with a kitchenette as well as a full-sized balcony. A lighted tennis court is accessible to guests. Weeklong and monthlong rates are available. These aren't luxury accommodations, and the inexpensive prices reflect the bare-bones quality, but the location in North County is central, rooms are clean and comfortable, and you won't feel guilty if your little ones drag back some of the beach in their shoes. Inexpensive.

Local Flavors

Taste of the town . . . local restaurants, cafés, bars, bistros, etc.

Along the north coast of San Diego you'll find numerous upscale restaurants overlooking the Pacific, as well as plenty of mom-and-pop cafés and a few dives—perfect places to get a traditional Mexican plate or one of the innumerable variations on fish tacos you'll find throughout the county. Although

Best Picks for Dining

Best Bet All Around: Twenty/20 Grill and Bar

Best Family Friendly: 101 Café

Best Romantic: Trattoria I Trulli

Best Splurge: Addison

Best Waterside View: Jake's Del Mar

Best Hidden Gem: Beach Break Café

Best Longtime Favorite: Tony's Jacal

Best Value: Smokin' Joey's Barbeque

Del Mar can be pricey, especially if your table has a water view, fine dining is generally a little less expensive in North County than it is in downtown (chapter 1) and in La Jolla (chapter 2).

FINE DINING

Carlsbad

Casa di Bandini (760-634-3443; www.bazaardelmundo.com/bandini), 1901 Calle Barcelona. Open daily for lunch and dinner. This beloved San Diego institution was a favorite in Old Town for more than 30 years and widely regarded as one of the finest Mexican restaurants in the city. The owner lost her lease several years back, however, and it seemed as if Casa di Bandini was gone for good. A few years ago, much to my delight, the restaurant was resurrected in The Forum, an upscale outdoor mall in south Carlsbad. This reincarnation is surprisingly similar to the former Old Town site, with a large, flower- and fountain-filled patio dining space, a lively bar, and a cavernous indoor dining room with authentic Mexican décor. Specialties include the chile relleno (a stuffed pepper) and the luscious carne asada tacos. Do not miss anything that comes on flour tortillas: they are made fresh to order and are paper thin, delicate, and divine. Moderate.

Fish House Vera Cruz (760-434-6777; www.fishhouseveracruz.com), 417 Carlsbad Village Dr. Open daily for lunch and dinner. The menu at this restaurant/seafood store changes daily, but count on mahimahi, salmon, and halibut straight off the boat. All fish is mesquite grilled, which gives it a light smoky flavor. Start out with the oysters Rockefeller or a bowl of the Boston clam chowder. Each meal comes with a crisp salad and two generous sides. You'll also be served a loaf of piping hot sourdough bread, which would suffice as a meal. The portions are really too big to allow for dessert, but if you're looking to be a hero, the pecan apple cheesecake or the rocky road cake are among the many gut-busting options. Moderate.

La Passage French Bistro (760-729-7097; www.lapassagefrenchbistro.net), 2961 State St. Open Tues.–Fri. for lunch, Tues.–Sun. for dinner. This tiny bistro in downtown Carlsbad has a cadre of loyal followers—it is difficult to get a table on weekends. Start with the marinated olives, an inexpensive treat. Then if you're ready to throw caution—and cholesterol—to the wind, try the grilled filet mignon smothered in melted Roquefort cheese sauce and served with potatoes dauphine. For dessert there are apples poached in white wine and served with vanilla ice cream and caramel sauce, or a dense and rich chocolate cake served with in-season berries. Moderate.

Norte (760-729-0903; http://nortemexicanrestaurantmenu.info), 3003 Carlsbad Blvd. Open daily for lunch and dinner. Located in the accessible tourist destination of Carlsbad Village, Norte (known for 30 years previously as Fidel's) is a family-run restaurant that is beloved by locals and tourists. Consider the soups—*albóndigas,* a spicy meatball soup, or for the more adventurous, menudo, a tripe and hominy soup (an acquired taste!). Entrées include carne asada, a buttery, thinly sliced flank steak served with onions and peppers; *pescado ranchero,* grilled mahimahi smothered in a mild red sauce; or nopales, cactus cooked in a spicy tomato and serrano chile sauce and topped with cheese. If you somehow manage to have room for dessert, try the *buñuelos,* a deep-fried flour tortilla covered with sugar and cinnamon, along with a cup of Mexican hot chocolate flavored with cinnamon. Request seating in the large outdoor patio beneath colorful umbrellas. Moderate.

Twenty/20 Grill and Bar (760-827-2400; www.twenty20grill.com), 5480 Grand Pacific Dr. Open daily for breakfast, lunch, and dinner. This restaurant on the property of the **Sheraton Carlsbad** offers whimsical delights like deep-fried lemon slices mixed amid exceptional fried calamari; creamy tempura avocado heady with lime juice in the *fritti;* and day-boat bisque that can feature either catch of the day or locally grown produce. Specialties include shrimp panzanella, a refreshing bread salad laced with ocean prawns, lima beans, and baby tomatoes; local growers' risotto with squash, eggplant, and grilled tomatoes; and classic steak au poivre, served over a bed of wilted spinach and alongside a creamy and cheesy *gratin pommes Anna.* Also available are small plates of gourmet macaroni and cheese, and roasted potatoes with chive olive oil, as well as hearth-baked pizzas. Moderate to expensive.

West Steak and Seafood (760-930-9100; www.weststeakandseafood.com), 4980 Avenida Encinas. Open

Insider Tip: Request a table at the bar at West Steak and Seafood, and you can order from a less-expensive menu that offers smaller bites, all the while enjoying the same upscale experience.

daily for dinner. This restaurant offers romantic ambiance, thanks to theatrical lighting that includes a wall of light animated by multicolor fiber optics and stunning chandeliers, a combination that makes for a space that feels like a cross between a high-end eatery in Las Vegas and an upscale cruise ship dining room. Specialties include prime filet steaks and comfort-food sides such as mashed potatoes, creamed spinach, and mac and cheese with truffles—and every portion is supersized. If you have room after the enormous entrées, don't miss the mousselike bread pudding, served hot; studded with cherries, figs, and raisins; and topped with a Tahitian vanilla ice cream. On Sun. West features a family-style dinner that includes your choice of soup or salad, entrée, two sides, and a dessert at the very reasonable price of $32 per person. Expensive.

Del Mar
Addison (858-314-1900; www.addison delmar.com), 5200 Grand Del Mar Way. Open daily for dinner. The signature restaurant of **The Grand Del Mar** resort, this impressive fine-dining venue has been racking up the awards since its debut: *Mobile Travel Guide* awarded the restaurant five stars, and the **AAA** bestowed five diamonds. Culinary superstar chef William Bradley routinely creates masterful dishes, plated artistically and prepared with the freshest ingredients available. Guests can enjoy a three-course meal for $80

Wine room at Addison

or a four-course meal for $98. The seasonal menu changes frequently, but expect gems like risotto with preserved lemon and butternut squash, butter-baked salmon, and black-fig brûlée. Very expensive.

Arterra (858-369-6032; www .arterrarestaurant.com), 11966 El Camino Real. Open daily for breakfast, lunch, and dinner. Arterra, which translates to "art of the earth," specializes in contemporary cuisine that highlights the freshest, best quality regional food available. The imaginative menu changes according to the availability of produce and meats—and with the seasons and the chef's moods—so you never know what to expect. There is also an extensive sushi menu. There is no better way to celebrate a special occasion—or a really good day at the nearby Del Mar Race Track—than to indulge in Arterra's seven-course chef-inspired "grand tasting," which highlights the best of the best. Expensive.

Jake's Del Mar (858-755-2002; www.hulapie.com), 1660 Coast Blvd. Open Tues.–Sat. for dinner, Sun. for brunch. Jake's is right on the beach, and the views are no less than breathtaking. The relaxed atmosphere and friendly service attract crowds of all ages, and the food manages to live up to the beautiful surroundings. The roasted beet salad is a winner, served with arugula, endive, and smoky bacon in champagne vinaigrette. Fresh fish is always featured on the daily specials, and Jake's will prepare it however you like. Look for mahimahi with a mirin glaze and rare wok-seared ahi prepared with a tomato ginger sauce. Jake's bar packs them in at sunset, so even if you don't have an appetite, grab a cocktail and enjoy the ocean view. Expensive.

Pacifica Del Mar (858-792-0476; www.pacificadelmar.com), 1555 Camino Del Mar. Open daily for lunch and dinner, weekends for breakfast. Part of the upscale Del Mar Plaza and overlooking both downtown Del Mar and the ocean beyond, Pacifica Del Mar is a casual, elegant restaurant that specializes in seafood. Dine inside or, better yet, grab a table on the extensive upper-story patio. (Even on breezy evenings, heat lamps keep the patio comfortable.) Try the local steamed Carlsbad mussels, or for a refreshing treat try Japanese hamachi served with frozen grapes and toasted almonds. The popular on-site vodka bar offers 75 varieties from more than 20 countries. Every Wed., all martinis are only $5. Moderate to expensive.

Poseidon's (858-755-9345; www .poseidonrestaurant.com), 1670 Coast Blvd. Open daily for lunch and dinner, weekends for breakfast. This restaurant, with an extensive bar inside, is all about the views; located right on the sand, Poseidon's has a large outdoor dining patio with billion-dollar views of the surf and sunsets, and is extremely popular with locals, especially on weekend evenings. An eclectic menu specializes in seafood, but you can also get a good steak here, and there are a few vegetarian options. Starters include a supersized shrimp cocktail, ceviche, and sake-steamed black mussels. The catch of the day generally includes oven-roasted sea bass served with couscous and tender grilled swordfish served with a mango salsa. Expensive.

Sbicca (858-481-1001; www.sbicca bistro.com), 215 15th St. Open daily for lunch and dinner. Local culinary star Susan Sbicca has attracted a lot of attention to her Del Mar restaurant, which offers an expansive patio that takes full advantage of the Pacific Ocean views, just as Sbicca's menu takes full advantage of the bounty of fresh ingredients available in San Diego. The appetizer menu offers too many good options, like shiitake–blue crab egg rolls, and grilled portobello mushrooms served with creamy blue cheese, crunchy walnuts, and chewy dried currants. Inventive entrées include the prosciutto-wrapped sea scallops served with chard and truffle aioli; the hearty grilled lamb loin served with a rich, creamy butternut risotto with a hazelnut glaze; and the maple-roasted pork prime rib served with sweet potatoes, a spicy pecan butter, and a bourbon chantilly sauce. Moderate to expensive.

Taste of Thai (858-793-9695; www.tasteofthaidelmar.com), 15770 San Andreas Dr. Open daily for lunch and dinner. Located in the east end of Flower Hill Mall, just east of I-5 and conveniently located near the Del Mar Race Track, Taste of Thai serves up flavor-packed meals that you can customize on a spiciness scale of 1–10. To start, try the beef or chicken satay skewers with rich peanut sauce, or the shrimp sa-rong, wrapped with egg noodles and fried golden and crispy. You'll also find creamy Thai curries perfumed with coconut milk and a wide selection of noodle dishes, including the ever-popular pad thai— rice noodles with dried shrimp, bean sprouts, scallions, eggs, and ground nuts. Moderate.

Tony's Jacal (858-755-2274; www .tonysjacal.com), 621 Valley Ave. Open Mon., Wed.–Sat. for lunch; Wed.–Sun. for dinner (hours increase during Del Mar race season). This San Diego insti- tution, located in a residential neigh- borhood in Solana Beach, has been serving homestyle Mexican food to locals since 1947, when Tony and

> **Insider Tip:** On warm days, request a patio table in the front courtyard of Tony's Jacal, the favorite seating of most longtime patrons, and enjoy a bottomless basket of fresh tortilla chips.

Catalina Gonzalez opened the Jacal (loosely translated as "shack") out of the front of what was the family's home. The restaurant has grown in size considerably in the past 60 years, and the menu has expanded. But current managers and waitstaff are still Gonza- lez family members—and a very gra- cious, welcoming bunch. Chiles rellenos—a mild poblano chile that is stuffed with tangy *antijo* cheese, lightly breaded and fried in a fluffy egg batter, and then covered in a mild red sauce— is a specialty. A trip to Tony's is not complete without an order of sopapillas for dessert, a fried pillow of pastry, the hollow center of which is perfect for filling with honey. Moderate.

Encinitas

El Callejon (760-634-2793; www.el- callejon.com), 345 S. Coast Hwy. 101. Open daily for lunch and dinner. This colorful patio restaurant tucked in front of the train tracks and near Moonlight Beach has an added bonus: the bar boasts a selection of more than 75 kinds of tequila, and the bartenders make a mean margarita. You'll find the usual combination plates, but consider the *medallones al cilantro,* filet mignon served with melted cheese and topped with a piquant cilantro sauce, or *ceviche valentin,* raw red snapper marinated in lemon juice and spices, and served with crackers. This is a pop- ular choice for young families and tends to be noisy in the early evenings. Moderate.

Passage to India (760-753-1309; www.passagetoindiasd.com), 257 N. El Camino Real #K. Open daily for lunch and dinner, Sun. for brunch. This small Indian restaurant secreted away in a strip mall in suburban Encinitas serves authentic Indian cuisine—most notably tandoori meats and a huge selection of vegetarian items. The restaurant also serves more than a dozen traditional Indian breads, including delicious onion *kulcha* and chile-flavored naan. If you've never tried Indian cuisine and aren't sure what to order—or if you're watching your budget—consider the well-priced combination dinners for two, which include soup, several meat or vegetari- an items, *raita* (a yogurt salad), and bread for $30. Moderate.

Sage Grill (760-943-7243; www .sagegrill.com), 1506 Encinitas Blvd. Open daily for lunch and dinner. In suburban Encinitas, Sage Grill is an unpretentious wine bar and grill that caters to a local clientele. Favorites include mushroom risotto served with aged Asiago, pan-fried buttermilk catfish, and grilled salmon with maple glaze. Entrées pair well with wines, and the house list is extensive. Sage also sells wines by the bottle to take home and adds only a $5 corkage fee to bottles purchased to be consumed in the restaurant, which means good wine at a reasonable price. Moderate.

Trattoria I Trulli (760-943-6800; www.itrulli.signonsandiego.com), 830 S. Coast Hwy. Open daily for lunch and dinner. In downtown Encinitas, this tiny Italian bistro has a rustic dining room and wine bar, as well as a tiny, romantic sidewalk patio. The caprese salad with beefsteak tomatoes and fresh mozzarella is as beautiful as it is tasty. Other specialties include *Orecchiette alla Barese,* pasta with broccoli rabe and Italian sausage; roasted chicken stuffed with cheese, spinach, and artichokes; and homemade ravioli. The wine list is extensive, and the offerings are well priced. The intimate atmosphere and twinkling lights make this restaurant especially appealing in the evenings. Moderate.

Vigilucci's Trattoria Italiano (760-942-7332; www.vigiluccis.com), 505 S. Coast Hwy. Open daily for lunch and dinner. The Vigilucci family has more than a half dozen restaurants throughout the county, and this small trattoria in downtown Encinitas is particularly popular thanks to a charming candlelit

interior and a lively sidewalk dining patio. Pastas are fresh and substantial; especially good is the *Penne alla Vodka con Porcini*, with mushrooms, fresh tomatoes, and basil in a creamy vodka sauce, and the yummy spaghetti carbonara. Moderate.

Oceanside

Monterey Bay Canners Restaurant (760-722-3474; www.montereybay canners.com), 1325 N. Harbor Dr. Open daily for lunch and dinner. A casual, fun restaurant, Monterey Bay on the Oceanside harbor offers just about every traditional seafood dish you could want, including coconut shrimp, crabcakes, steamed mussels, ceviche, clam chowder (served in a sourdough bowl), mesquite-broiled halibut, traditional fish and chips, and cioppino. For the popular happy hour (4–7), this restaurant serves inexpensive nibbles like fish tacos, fried clams, and Irish nachos. Moderate.

Robin's Nest Café (760-722-7837), 280 South Harbor Dr. Open daily for breakfast, lunch, and dinner. The marina in Oceanside is a quaint walking-only collection of shops and restaurants, frequented by local fishermen who moor their boats here, marines from nearby Camp Pendleton, and families. This small café offers an expansive outdoor patio to view the lovely marina and is an especially good place to enjoy a quiet breakfast or lunch. In addition to seafood specialties, Robin's Nest has a nice selection of Mexican breakfasts. (You shouldn't leave San Diego without trying huevos rancheros—corn tortillas topped with eggs cooked any style and served with beans and salsa.) Moderate.

333 Pacific (760-433-3333; www .cohnrestaurants.com/restaurants/333 pacific), 333 N. Pacific St. Open daily

Ahi stack from 333 Pacific

Courtesy of the Cohn Restaurant Group

for dinner, Fri.–Sun. for lunch. The owners of 333 Pacific filled the need for an upscale, elegant restaurant along the pretty coastline of Oceanside. The restaurant capitalizes on the ocean views, which are especially enticing at night, when the Oceanside Pier twinkles with lights. 333 Pacific boasts a raw bar, a large selection of sushi, and an eclectic menu that is heavy on seafood. I'm a sucker for the sweet chile calamari; other favorites include the shrimp masala and eggplant curry, the saffron-infused seafood stew, and the signature blue-cheese-crusted Kobe beef meat loaf. The bar serves $7 cocktails like the Sour Kiss, with grapefruit-infused vodka, white cranberry juice, and pomegranate; and the indulgent White Chocolate Zebra, with vanilla vodka and chocolate liquor served in a glass lined with chocolate. Moderate to expensive.

CASUAL DINING

Carlsbad

Allen's New York Pizza (760-918-9999), 6943 El Camino Real. Open daily for lunch and dinner. You know you're getting the real deal in this La Costa neighborhood gem in south Carlsbad when you hear Allen's New York accent: it's a dead giveaway. Thin, crunchy crust is lightly sauced and heavily topped with good-quality mozzarella; pepperoni is always a safe bet, but the vegetarian and sausage pizzas also deliver the goods. Moderate.

Bistro West (760-930-8008; www.bistrowest.com), 4960 Avenida Encinas. Open daily for lunch and dinner, Sun. for brunch. This restaurant is oddly sited next to a power plant and across from the train tracks, but what it lacks in location it makes up for in value. Look for oversized gourmet burgers, pizzas, enormous salads, and weekday specials that include Mexican "street tacos" and chicken cordon bleu. Don't miss the sweet potato fries. Moderate.

Daily News Café (760-729-1023; www.dailynewscafe.com), 3001-A Carlsbad Blvd. Open daily for breakfast and lunch. The Daily News in downtown Carlsbad has a good selection of omelets and salads—but the pièce de résistance is the popular Belly Bomber Burger. As the name suggests, this isn't for petite appetites. Inexpensive.

Hennessey's Tavern (760-729-6951; www.hennesseystavern.com), 2777 Roosevelt St. Open daily for breakfast, lunch, and dinner. Although the pub grub is especially good, Hennessey's is better known as a nightspot that sometimes hosts live music. Although the tavern isn't likely to get big names, there is never a shortage of amplitude. Inexpensive.

Knock Out Burgers (760-729-8478), 2971 Carlsbad Blvd. Open daily for lunch and dinner. Don't let the crowd of teenage surfers and skaters dissuade you from trying this hole-in-the-wall. For about $4 you can get a made-while-you-wait 0.25-pound cheeseburger that is as good as a burger has a right to be. You can also buy a bag of tasty miniburgers by the dozen or half dozen. Inexpensive.

La Especial Norte (760-942-1040), 664 N. Coast Hwy. 101. Open daily for dinner. This longtime local favorite offers little curb appeal, but don't let the exterior scare you away. The pleasant interior is almost always full at dinnertime, and the Mexican food is authentic and fresh. Rolled chicken tacos are crispy and flavorful, and the *molcajete*—strips of beef and cactus served with a piquant sauce inside a boiling hot stone bowl—is something you won't soon forget. Moderate.

Los Olas (760-942-1860; www.lasolasmex.com/cardiff.php), 2655 S. Coast Hwy. 101. Open daily for dinner. Off the San Elijo Lagoon, Los Olas is a funky, always crowded, and usually noisy Mexican joint that serves up great fish tacos, as well as a pile of nachos at their artery-clogging best. They also feature Puerto Nuevo–style lobster (boiled in oil and split down the middle). The moderately priced food and full bar attract a young happy-hour crowd. Moderate.

Roberto's (760 634-2909), 1900 Coast Hwy. 101. Open daily for lunch and dinner. Roberto's, in Leucadia, just south of the Carlsbad State Beach, cranks out hundreds of inexpensive, authentic tacos a day, made with thick, crispy corn tortillas and stuffed generously with shredded beef or chicken. (You'll want to pass on the fish tacos here.) This local chain has been serving addictive, slightly greasy food to surfers and others for years. The lines can be long during mealtime rush, but for about $6, it's worth the wait. Inexpensive.

Sammy's Woodfired Pizza (760-438-1212; www.sammyspizza.com), 5970 Avenida Encinas. Open daily for lunch and dinner. Sami Ladeki opened the first Sammy's Woodfired Pizza in North County nearly 20 years ago, and locals liked the smoky flavors and crisp crust so much that it wasn't long before Sammy's expanded to locations throughout San Diego. The LaDou's Barbeque Chicken Pizza is a signature dish featuring sweet barbecue sauce topped with chunks of chicken breast, smoked Gouda, red onion, and fresh cilantro. But the real star of the show is Sammy's famous dessert, the trademarked Messy Sundae—vanilla ice cream served in an enormous wine glass and literally overflowing with caramel sauce, walnuts, fudge, and whipped cream. Moderate.

Smokin' Joey's Barbeque (760-929-1396; www.joeyssmokinbbq.com), 6955 El Camino Real. Open daily for lunch and dinner. Tucked into a barely

Messy Sundaes at Sammy's Woodfired Pizza

noticeable corner of a suburban strip mall and all but hidden from everyone except locals and those in the know, this outpost of Smokin' Joey's (a small San Diego chain) offers up reliably good barbecue, with the right amount of smoke and a delicious homemade sauce with a little spice and a little sweet. Specialties include spoon-tender baby back ribs, served wet or dry; moist pulled pork and chicken; and—according to my Texan relatives—the best brisket outside of the Lone Star State. Inexpensive.

Del Mar

Café Secret (858-792-0821; www.cafe secret.com), 1140 Camino Del Mar. Open daily for breakfast and lunch. This small café is run by a Peruvian couple and offers fantastic omelets and good coffee, which makes it one of the best places to grab a delicious, inexpensive breakfast in Del Mar. The empanadas (savory meat pies) are fantastic. Service can be slow, so this is not the best bet if you're in a hurry. Moderate.

Crepes and Corks Café (858-847-3382; www.crepesandcorks.com), 1328 Camino Del Mar. Open Tues.–Sat. for breakfast, lunch, and dinner; Sun. for breakfast and lunch. This hole-in-the-wall specializes in French crêpes and Italian panini, and also offers an extensive wine list. (You can bring your own bottle, for a small corkage fee.) Don't miss the Blue Crumble, a crêpe with grilled chicken, blue cheese, walnuts, and baby spinach. Moderate.

Pizza Port and Brewery (858-481-7332; www.pizzaport.com), 135 N. Hwy. 101. Open daily for dinner. Since there's an additional location in Carlsbad, you'd think this pizza and beer pub wouldn't get so crowded—but expect lines out the door with folks angling to get a cold, wet Sharkbite Red or seasonal specialties like Blonde

Bombshell Barleywine and McHale's Irish Stout. The pizza is pretty tasty, too; you'll need plenty of brew to wash down the fiery Pizza Vallarta, with Canadian bacon, olives, onions, and jalapeños. Moderate.

Encinitas

E Street Café (760-230-2038; www .estreetcafe.com), 130 W. E St. Open daily 7 AM–10 PM. E Street specializes in fair-trade organic coffees and also offers a huge selection of teas and vegetarian snacks and sweets. The comfortable and eclectically decorated café has free high-speed Internet access, and there are regular poetry readings and occasional live music. Inexpensive.

KC's Tandoor (760-753-7452; www.kcstandoor.com), 1070 N. El Camino Real. Open daily for lunch and dinner. A friend from Mumbai turned me on to this tiny place in a big-box mall in suburban Encinitas, recommending it as one of the most authentic Indian eateries in the area—and although I can't vouch for this, I can promise that the food is *good* (and well priced). Don't miss the *dosa,* a paper-thin pancake made with a lentil batter and stuffed with veggies. Inexpensive.

Oggi's Pizza and Brewery Company (760-944-8170), 305 Encinitas Blvd. Open daily for lunch and dinner. Pronounced "oh-gees," this outlet of a local pizza and brewery chain is hopping every night of the week. Wedge your way inside and get a pie with the works, with pepperoni, sausage, mushrooms, red onions, bell peppers, and fresh tomatoes. Moderate.

Pannikin Coffee and Tea (760-436-5824; http://pannikincoffeeand tea.com), 510 N. Hwy. 101. Open daily 6–6. Housed in what looks like a big yellow house with white picket railing (actually it's a converted 19th-century train station), Pannikin feels like

Pannikin Coffee and Tea

you're visiting a favorite auntie's place. You'll be welcomed with comfortable surroundings, friendly people, and on-the-premises freshly baked cookies, muffins, breads, pies, and quiches, as well as a fine collection of gourmet coffees and teas. The small Pannikin chain has been a San Diego institution since 1968 (there are locations in La Jolla and Del Mar), well before the idea of coffeehouses became chic, and they have a loyal local clientele. Inexpensive.

Swami's Café (760-944-0612), 1163 S. Coast Hwy. 101. Open daily for breakfast and lunch. Catering to the health-conscious surfing crowd and local vegans, Swami's Café (across from Swami's Beach) features fresh whole foods. Hearty breakfast options include the black egg burrito, a concoction of scrambled eggs, black

beans, avocado, and cheddar wrapped in a wheat tortilla and served with homestyle potatoes (ingeniously mixed with zucchini); organic multigrain pancakes; and a wide variety of made-to-order omelets. The outdoor seating in front of the café is tight and a little noisy from Hwy. 101 just steps away, and weekends are crowded, but the folks are friendly, and the prices are unbeatable. Inexpensive.

Oceanside

Angelo's Burgers (760-967-9911), 2035 S. Coast Hwy. Open daily for breakfast, lunch, and dinner. Despite what the name implies, this joint offers Mexican food, Greek sandwiches, chili dogs, omelets, deli sandwiches, and salads in addition to a good choice of hamburgers. House-made onion rings are huge and amazing. Inexpensive.

Beach Break Café (760-439-6355), 1902 S. Coast Hwy. Open daily for breakfast and lunch. If a friend hadn't taken me to this tiny neighborhood favorite tucked next to a Laundromat, I would never have tried it—or probably even noticed it; I'm grateful she did. There aren't many tables inside, so be prepared to wait on weekends. Put your name in, grab a cup of coffee from the honor bar outside, and relax: Service is *fast,* so you won't have to wait as long as you might think—and portions are

> **Insider Tip:** Serve yourself at the honor coffee bar while waiting for a table at the Beach Break Café, and keep your eyes open for local skating and surfing celebrities, who are known to patronize this establishment.

huge. The spicy and delicious Santa Fe omelet comes bursting with chorizo sausage, cheese, onions, and fresh slices of avocado, and it's topped with a mountain of sour cream. Sides include your choice of a monster portion of homemade hash browns or home fries, and tortillas or a yummy hunk of glazed coffee cake. Inexpensive.

Longboarder Café (760-721-6776), 400 Mission Ave. Open daily for breakfast, lunch, and dinner. Recently relocated but still on the main drag of downtown Ocean-side, a pretty, nostalgic area full of vintage movie theaters and midcentury-modern architecture, the café is unpretentious and comfortable. Food is basic as well—hamburgers, grilled sandwiches, salads—but the portions are huge, and as the name implies, this eatery is a favorite with the local surf community. Moderate.

101 Café (760-722-5220; www.101cafe.net), 631 S. Coast Hwy. Open for breakfast, lunch, and dinner. The oldest restaurant in Oceanside (perhaps the oldest in the county—it opened in 1928), the relaxed 101 Café is a comfort-food diner that has a devoted local following. Burgers are a good bet, as are familiar dinner specials like meat loaf and gravy, fried chicken, and liver and onions. Don't miss the butterscotch malt. Inexpensive.

SNACKS

Carlsbad

Carlsbad Danish Bakery (760-729-6186; http://carlsbaddanish.com/carls baddanish2/Welcome.html), 2805 Roosevelt St. Open Mon.–Sat. 7–4. This bakery's authentic Danish pastries are about as good as you'll get outside of Copenhagen; don't miss the cinnamon custard bun and the lemon-filled pastry. You'll also find an array of crusty home-baked breads. Inexpensive.

Swirlicious (760-720-2888; www.swirliciousyogurt.com), 2992 State St. Open daily 11–10. Make your own healthy and delicious frozen yogurt treats with flavors like cheesecake, green tea, and pumpkin pie eggnog, and toppings that include candies, sprinkles, and fresh fruit. Inexpensive.

Vinaka Café (760-720-7890), 300 Carlsbad Village Dr. Open daily 7 AM–10 PM. Upstairs in downtown Carlsbad's Village Faire shopping center, Vinaka is a welcoming, homey coffeehouse with overstuffed sofas and chairs, stacks of board games, a pretty outdoor patio, and free Wi-Fi. While you're here, try one of the dozen flavors of homemade ice cream. Inexpensive.

Del Mar

Champagne French Bakery and Café
(858-792-2222; www.champagnebakery
.com), 12955 El Camino Real. Open
for breakfast, lunch, and dinner. This
Parisian-style bakery in a small shopping mall in Carmel Valley serves fragrant pastries like chocolate croissants,
cinnamon elephant ears, and dark
chocolate tortes. Inexpensive.

Cupcake Love (858-755-5506;
www.cupcake-love.com), 437 S. Hwy.
101. Open daily 11–5. This tiny shop is
a little hard to find in a strip mall off
101, but it's well worth the effort. Daily
specials rotate, but the fudgy, not-too-
sweet Chocolate Sin dusted lightly
with edible gold glitter is a crowd-
pleaser. Inexpensive.

Seaside Yogurt (858-720-1168),
1231 Camino Del Mar. Open daily
noon–9:30. A self-serve frozen yogurt
parlor, Seaside offers unusual flavors

Cupcake Love

like mango tart and pomegranate-
raspberry. Inexpensive.

Encinitas

Bubby's (760-436-3563), 937 S. Hwy.
101. Open daily 11–9. Bubby's sells
authentic Italian gelato and offers a
rotating menu with intriguing flavors
like vanilla rosewater and lemon
cheesecake. It is pricier than ice cream
and served in tiny portions, but the flavors are so concentrated that a little
goes a long way. Moderate.

Elizabethan Desserts (760-230-
6780; www.elizabethandesserts.com),

> **Insider Tip:** The increasingly popu-
> lar Elizabethan Desserts bakes cup-
> cakes fresh each morning, and
> some flavors sell out before noon.
> Call ahead to have your favorites
> set aside—or come first thing in
> the morning.

155 Quail Gardens Dr. Open
Tues.–Sat. 10–5. This *very* hidden local
gem is tucked into the corner of a
nursery, and it's easy to miss. Do yourself a favor: look for it! This place has
the best cupcakes in town (and yes, I
believe I've tried them all), including a
blackberry chocolate concoction that
melts my heart. The all-natural bakery
also sells awesome cherry pies and
caramel-apple cheesecake bites. Moderate.

St. Tropez Bakery (760-633-0084;
www.sttropezbistro.com), 947 S. Coast
Hwy. 101. Open daily 7 AM–8 PM. This
cozy bakery and bistro is decorated in
the bright yellows and blues of
Provence, and murals of French scenes
remind visitors of a sidewalk café
almost anywhere in France. The

numerous dessert pastries, such as the tiny raspberry and chocolate tarts or the crème brûlée, are winners. This is a wildly popular place on weekends, and it is a nice atmosphere to while away an hour with a café au lait. Moderate.

Oceanside

Hill Street Donuts (760-439-7741), 1926 S. Coast Hwy. 101. Open daily. This old-fashioned donut shop offers a wide selection of fresh, homemade donuts; they also sell made-to-order smoothies and a handful of yummy breakfast sandwiches. Inexpensive.

Petite Madeline Bakery (760-722-1222; www.petitemadelinebakery.com), 3776 Mission Ave., Ste. 137. Open daily for breakfast and lunch. You'd never expect a bakery hidden away in a shopping center next to a major grocery store to be this good—but it is. Petite Madeline has an enormous selection of exquisite sweet treats, like the luscious raspberry chocolate mousse domes, mile-high éclairs, and especially good croissants (plain and chocolate). For locals, this is a great place for special-order cakes, which are both delicious and gorgeous. Inexpensive.

Strawberry crêpes at Petite Madeline

Don't Miss

Must-see attractions, in North County and nearby . . .

North County isn't just for surfers anymore. Laid-back Leucadia, for example, has long attracted artists, and charming Encinitas is a mecca for gourmets. Carlsbad has expansive flower fields that rival those in Holland. And the Cedros Avenue design district in Solana Beach offers some of the best furniture and accessories in the county.

Best Picks for Local Attractions

Best Cultural Attraction: Museum of Making Music

Best Historical Place: Mission San Luis Rey de Francia

Best Beach: Del Mar City Beach

Best Garden: San Diego Botanical Gardens

Best Outdoor Activity: Hiking Batiguitos Lagoon

Best Family Fun: Legoland

Best Shopping: Cedros Design District

Best Nightlife: The Belly Up Tavern

BEST CULTURAL ATTRACTIONS

California Surf Museum (760-721-6876; www.surfmuseum.org), 312 Pier Way, Oceanside. Open daily 10–4. This newly relocated museum, dedicated to all things that pertain to the surfing lifestyle, sponsors a new exhibit each year highlighting surfing equipment, sports photography, or a surfing legend. You'll also find a small gift shop featuring surfing books, DVDs, and an amusing collection of bumper stickers (GOT SURF?). Adults $3, children $1.

Lux Art Institute (760-436-6611; www.luxartinstitute.org), 1550 S. El Camino Real, Encinitas. Open Thurs. and Fri. 1–5, Sat. 11–5. The Lux Art Institute is an exhibit venue that highlights the work of contemporary artists—and it's also a place where visitors can go to watch art-making in progress. The artist-in-residence program allows guests to observe artists painting, sculpting, and so forth, and at the same time experience their finished works in a vibrant museum setting. Adults $10, visitors under 21 free.

Museum of Making Music (760-438-5996; www.museumofmaking music.org), 5790 Armada Dr., Carlsbad. Open Tues.–Sun. 10–5. You'll find more than five hundred instruments on display, as well as traveling exhibits, at this small museum near Legoland. You can see the inner workings of a grand piano, pick and then listen to selections on a Victrola, or examine a replica of Ringo Starr's drum set. Guests can also arrange for private tours of the museum, and the facility is available to rent out for special events in the evenings. Adults $7; seniors, active military, and students $5.

North Coast Repertory Theater (858-481-1055; www.northcoastrep .org), 987 Lomas Santa Fe Dr., Solana Beach. With year-round performances in an intimate two-hundred-seat theater in Solana Beach, the North Coast Repertory Theater is one of the best small theaters in San Diego. The NCRT is known for the diversity of performances it presents, from the classics to contemporary theater.

Mission San Luis Rey de Francia (760-757-3651; www.sanluisrey.org), 4050 Mission Ave., Oceanside. Open daily 9:30–4. Known as the King of the Missions, the Mission San Luis Rey was founded in 1798 by Padre Fermín de Lasuén as the 18th in a line of 21 Spanish missions established in California. This is the largest of all the missions, and there is a lot to explore. The museum displays mission-era artifacts like Native American handwoven baskets and pottery, Roman Catholic vestments, and 18th-century liturgical vessels. Visitors can stroll through re-creations of mission living quarters, including the kitchen, a padre's bedchamber, and workshops for weaving and handicrafts. Visitors can also explore a small garden courtyard before stepping into the large church, which has hand-painted ceilings and walls, a bright cupola highlighted with skylights, and carved and painted wooden religious statues. An audio tour narrates continually during visiting hours. Outside, visitors can hike through trails that explore the Lavandaria—the Native American laundry and site of the sunken gardens. Note that this is a working church, and the grounds and on-site accommodations are used for religious retreats, as well as by the Franciscan monks who still live and work here. Adults $6, students $4, children under seven free.

BEST GREEN SPACES

North County San Diego is known throughout the world for some of the widest, sandiest beaches around— and some of the biggest surf as well— and this has long been a draw for sun-seeking visitors. In addition, the North

Original arch at the Mission San Luis Rey de Francia

County offers a handful of unique gardens that are open to the public.

Beaches

Carlsbad State Beach, off Hwy. 101, north of La Costa Blvd., Carlsbad. South Carlsbad Beach, known to locals as Ponto, has a paid parking lot ($12 for a weekend day, with seasonal passes available) and a long expanse of free street parking (although this can be hard to find, especially in the early morning hours, when surfers arrive before dawn). The crowds are generally manageable, and the beach is popular with families and local surfers alike.

Del Mar City Beach, via 15th St. and Coast Blvd., Del Mar. Del Mar City Beach is one of the loveliest stretches of sand in Southern California, with bottle-glass green waves backed by ragged red cliffs and blanketed with miles of uninterrupted sand. Except during high tides, visitors can walk down the coast from the northernmost stretch to Torrey Pines State Beach to the south. Several reefs off the coast make for good surf breaks, especially at 15th St. and 11th St. (the "neighborhoods" within the beach are named for the numbered streets that run perpendicular to the shoreline). From Oct. through May, dogs are allowed to run at Rivermouth, the northernmost beach.

Moonlight State Beach, off Encinitas Blvd., Encinitas. This beach lives up to its romantic name and is an excellent spot to watch the sunset (and wait for the moonlight). The waves can be huge, so this is quite popular with surfers and those who like to watch them. There are fire rings and volleyball courts just beneath the elevated parking lot.

Oceanside City Beach, off N. Coast Hwy., Oceanside. Just north of the Oceanside Pier, near the harbor,

Oceanside City Beach has a nice covered picnic area with a dozen tables. The beach is wide and long, and waves are good—this is the site of several surfing championships throughout the year. The sands aren't always as clean as you'll find to the south, but if you're willing to walk a bit beyond the parking, this is a good place to find a little seclusion.

Swami's Beach, off Hwy. 101, next to the Self-Realization Fellowship Temple, Encinitas. Made famous by the Beach Boys' unofficial California anthem, "Surfin' USA," the breaks off Swami's are world renowned. The secluded beach has a tiny off-street parking lot that fills up quickly, but roadside parking is generally available if you aren't shy about walking. You'll need good legs anyhow to tackle the steep staircase that leads from the top of the cliffs down to the shores, but your aerobic undertaking will be rewarded with a quiet beach, interest-ing cliff caves (a byproduct of coastal erosion), and good tidepooling (especially in Jan. and Feb., when the tides are at their lowest).

Gardens and Parks

Flower Fields of Carlsbad (760-431-0352; www.theflowerfields.com), corner of Palomar Airport Rd. and Paseo del Norte, Carlsbad. Hours vary. In the spring these 50 acres become a dazzling mosaic of brilliantly colored flowers, planted in rainbow ribbons. This spectacular field grows more than 8 million Tecolote giant ranunculus, mainly to harvest for bulbs. For a price, starting in Mar. and through early May, visitors can stroll through the fields, take photographs, and enjoy other garden-related attractions, including a sweet pea maze, hayride, and activities for children. The fields overlook the ocean and a nearby decorative windmill. Admission varies.

Del Mar City Beach

Leo Carrillo Park (760-476-1042), 6200 Flying LC Lane, Carlsbad. Open Tues.–Sun. 10–5. This small neighborhood historical park gives visitors a taste of old North County, with an expansive ranch and restored original adobe buildings. Leo Carrillo, a one-time reporter for Randolph Hearst and— later in his life—an actor best known for his role as Pancho in the 1950s *Cisco Kid* series, bought the ranch in 1937 and restored the buildings. Today

> **Insider Tip:** Look for historical graffiti preserved in the side of the little adobe building Mrs. Carrillo used as an art studio at Leo Carrillo Park; these days this structure is sometimes used as a gallery for artwork by local schoolchildren.

visitors can stroll the trails, on weekends take an informative guided tour through the handful of buildings (including stables and an art studio), and observe native vegetation in the extensive gardens. Throughout the year there are community festivals that fea-

Peacock at Leo Carrillo Park

Courtesy of Jon Preimesberger

ture native crafts and demonstrations of how life on the old rancho might have been. A unique feature of the park are the wild peacocks, descended from a flock Carrillo kept, that roam the grounds. Admission is free.

San Diego Botanical Gardens (760-436-3036; www.sdbgarden.org), 230 Quail Gardens Dr., Encinitas. Open daily 9–5. Formerly known as the Quail Gardens, this beautiful botanical garden's 35 acres of exhibits include a bamboo orchard, a Mediterranean landscapes garden, and a subtropical fruit garden. The miles of trails that crisscross the property wind by a gingerbread-style gazebo. You'll also find a lily pond (that blooms most prodigiously in Aug.) and a peaceful, secluded waterfall. A small on-site nursery sells exotic plant specimens. Adults $12, seniors and active military $8, children 12 and younger $6.

Self-Realization Fellowship Temple and Ashram Center (760-753-2888), 215 K St., Encinitas. Open Tues.–Sat. 9–5, Sun. 11–5. You can't miss the temple driving along the Coast Hwy. in Encinitas: the large cream-colored structure is topped with several gold-leafed onion domes, and the temple itself is surrounded by a high stucco wall. Along the side entrance on K St., you can access the small meditation gardens, which are open to the public. Stroll through a well-manicured shade garden and enjoy a koi pond and small waterfall. At the summit of the garden there is a panoramic view of the ocean and several benches. Admission is free.

BEST OUTDOOR ACTIVITIES

Boating
Boaters can launch their own boats from the Oceanside Marina or rent

watercraft by the hour from **Helgren's** (see *Deep-Sea Fishing*). An alternative to the somewhat choppy waters of North County is the secluded Carlsbad Lagoon, a quiet body of water just east of I-5. Rent aqua cycles, paddleboats, kayaks, and Wave Runners at **California Watersports** (760-434-3089; 4215 Harrison Street, Carlsbad).

Diving and Snorkeling

North County Scuba Center (760-753-0036; www.ncscubacenter.com), 122 Encinitas Blvd., Encinitas. This organization has monthly boat trips to prime dive spots such as Wreck Alley, the Coronado Islands, and the La Jolla kelp beds. Instruction is available, from beginning certification to a refresher academic course.

USA Dive Shop Oceanside (760-722-7826; www.usascuba.com), 225 Brooks St., Oceanside. Purchase dive equipment, or take scuba classes, from beginning certification to master diver programs. Also on-site is an adaptive scuba course for individuals with physical disabilities.

Fishing

The pretty Oceanside marina is the starting point for deep-sea fishing in the North County. Although there are fewer trips heading out than from Point Loma in the south (see chapter 1), it's often easier to book trips from here at the last minute. You'll also find several peaceful, protected lagoons in the north coastal region that allow fishing in limited areas.

Deep-Sea Fishing

Catch deep-sea fishing trips from Oceanside Harbor via **Helgren's Oceanside Sportfishing** (760-722-2133; 315 Harbor Drive S., Oceanside), which offers day trips to local kelp beds up to 3 miles out and multiple-day trips (up to six days) to Guadalupe and islands off the coast of Mexico, depending on where the fish are running.

Oceanside Harbor

Pier and Surf Fishing

Oceanside Pier, off Pier View Way, Oceanside, is the longest municipal wooden pier on the U.S. west coast— so long that a golf cart is used to take visitors to the end! This is a popular spot for fishing, as well as a picturesque place to spend an afternoon. The crowds are generally smaller than at piers to the south. As with all piers in San Diego, you won't need a fishing license, but catch limits are enforced.

Lagoons and Bays

The calm waters of **Agua Hedionda Lagoon** (north of Cannon Road, Carlsbad) is a beautiful 400-acre saltwater lagoon that is popular for fishing croaker, halibut, and sea bass. Fishing is only allowed in the 50-acre passive-use portion of the lagoon, in the southeast section. **Batiquitos Lagoon** (off Batiquitos Drive, Carlsbad) can only be fished from the rock jetties at the mouth of the lagoon and from the rocks under I-5 (east or west of the freeway, but

only on the north side). Avoid the marsh areas to protect waterfowl nesting sites. Fishing licenses are required at both lagoons.

Golfing

In addition to a plethora of stunning coastal courses, North County inland also offers several premier golf courses. Be sure to call ahead for tee times, especially on weekends.

Arrowood Golf Course (760-967-8400; www.arrowoodgolf.com), 5201A Village Dr., Oceanside. This relatively new course designed by Ted Robinson Jr. is located next to a protected wildlife refuge, which makes a round here a serene experience. The open course will please golfers with a range of skill levels. Green fee: $85–110.

The Crossings at Carlsbad (760-444-1800; www.thecrossingsatcarlsbad.com), 5800 The Crossings Dr., Carlsbad. This new municipal course in south Carlsbad takes its design inspiration from the canyons and surrounding

Where the Turf Meets the Surf

Hollywood legend Bing Crosby, along with pals Pat O'Brien, Jimmy Durante, and other Tinseltown luminaries, founded Del Mar Thoroughbred racing in 1937, in what was then a sleepy seaside community, so that they could while away the summer hours betting on horses in a casual atmosphere. Thanks to the seaside breezes and the charm of the Spanish Colonial architecture at what is now called the **Del Mar Race Track and Fairgrounds** (858-755-1161; 2260 Jimmy Durante Boulevard), Del Mar quickly became the place to be in August. In the early days it wasn't uncommon to see Lucille Ball and Desi Arnaz, W. C. Fields, Ava Gardner, Bob Hope, and other stars of the golden era of cinema.

Hollywood glitterati still make the Del Mar race scene, and in recent years Rod Stewart, Leonardo DiCaprio, and Jessica Simpson, among others, have dropped by. But it isn't a casual affair anymore. These days it has grown into one of the best racing venues in the world and one of the biggest parties on the West Coast. Del Mar consistently posts record-breaking pari-mutuel exchanges, and track attendance has grown consistently over the past several decades. Races run six days a week (the track is closed on Tuesday) in August through early September, with post times generally at 2 PM.

Batiguitos Lagoon

wetlands. You'll find five bridges that link the course and several expansive water features. Note that this course is directly in the flight path of small Palomar Airport, which is just down the road, and the air traffic—and noise—from small commercial jets and recreational planes is especially heavy on weekends. Green fee: $60–110.

Encinitas Ranch Golf Course (760-944-1936; www.jcgolf.com), 1275 Quail Gardens Dr., Encinitas. With 18 championship holes carved into the bluffs of Encinitas, overlooking the ocean, Encinitas Ranch provides a scenic golfing experience on a par 72 course. The first nine holes are relatively straightforward, but the back nine provide a greater challenge. Green fee: $81–103.

Grand Golf Course (858-314-2000; www.thegranddelmar.com/golf), 5300 Grand Del Mar Ct., Del Mar.

Grand Golf Course

Courtesy of the Grand Del Mar Resort

Located on the property of the exquisite new **Grand Del Mar Resort**, this par 71 course designed by Tom Fazio offers more than 7,000 yards of greens and deceptive bunkers, making this one of the most challenging courses in the city. Green fee: $195–215.

Maderas Golf Course (858-451-8100; www.maderasgolf.com), 17750 Old Coach Rd., Poway. This beautiful inland course (about 15 miles east of Del Mar) winds through natural creeks, forests, and cliffs—as well as three human-made lakes and five landscaped waterfalls. This is a challenging and exciting course. Green fee: $170–210.

Park Hyatt Aviara Golf Club (760-603-6900; www.golfsd.com/aviara .html), 7447 Batiguitos Dr., Carlsbad. Formerly the Aviara Four Seasons, this pricey, gorgeous 18-hole course in the suburbs of south Carlsbad was designed by Arnold Palmer to take advantage of the lovely views of the adjacent Batiguitos Lagoon. The course has great variety and some especially difficult holes. Carts, included in the cost of the green fee, come with GPS systems that will pinpoint the exact distance from your cart to the pin. Green fee: $215–235.

Rancho Bernardo Inn (858-385-8733; www.ranchobernardoinn.com), 17550 Bernardo Oaks Rd., Rancho Bernardo. A San Diego favorite for more than 40 years, this old-style course has deceptively sloped greens, a well-maintained course, and plenty of serenity. Green fee: $100–135.

Hiking

Batiguitos Lagoon Trail, trailhead off Gabbiano Lane, Carlsbad. A flat 3-mile out-and-back trail takes you along the waterline through coastal salt marshes and mudflats—one of the few remaining tidal wetlands in Southern California. You'll see native scrub, abundant water birds, and plenty of locals getting some exercise. Information panels flank the trail, and benches are placed along the way so you can stop and enjoy the lagoon views. The Batiguitos Lagoon Foundation maintains a nature center at the west end of the hike, which offers guided walks.

San Elijo Lagoon, off La Orvilla, Encinitas. An ecological preserve, the lagoon and surrounding marshland is a birder's paradise: you'll likely see herons, egrets, and sandpipers. The trail is a flat 4 miles out and back, with water views most of the way. No biking is allowed, but you may share the trail with a few horses.

Surfing

Surfing and pristine waves put coastal North County on the map, and even though the beach communities have grown and evolved, at the heart of many young and old residents alike is the search for the perfect wave. Swami's is a world-famous surfing beach in Encinitas, chosen by *Surfing* magazine as one of the 10 best surfing sites in the country. Also check out 15th Street Beach in Del Mar and Cardiff Reef, and farther north Leucadia State Beach, Carlsbad State Beach, and Tamarack Surf Beach in Carlsbad. Oceanside Beach at the Strand and Sixth Street are also popular. Die-hard locals can be territorial, but the waves are open to anyone who dares.

Good surf schools include **Kahuna Bob's Surf School** (760-721-7700; 2526 Woodlands Way, Oceanside) and **Surfin' Fire** (760-473-2281; 6714 Lemon Leaf Drive, Carlsbad).

BEST FAMILY FUN

Legoland (760-918-5346; www.lego .com/legoland), 1 Legoland Dr., Carlsbad. Open Thurs.–Mon. (Sept.–May) and daily June–Aug.; opens 10 AM; closing varies seasonally. Sprawling across more than 120 acres in south Carlsbad, Legoland California is a triumph of engineering. Once you pass through the entrance gates (themselves designed to look like giant Legos), you enter a world of impressive building on a tiny scale. The park is divided into several zones, including Dino Island, Fun Town, Pirate Shores, Explore Village, Knights Kingdom, and Imagination Zone, each with attractions to match. At the heart of the park is Miniland USA, featuring scale models of a dozen U.S. cities. More than 20 million Legos were used to design Minitown alone. Check out the miniature New Orleans featuring a Mardi Gras parade and a miniature Washington, D.C., with a changing of the honor guard in front of a model of the U.S. Capitol. In addition to a staggering display of Lego building, the park boasts more than 50 rides and attractions,

many of which are kid powered via rope pulling, pedal pushing, and water squirting. The lines are manageable throughout most of the year—with the exception of summer and holiday weekends, when the waits can build up later in the afternoon. Children past 10–12 will probably not be excited by the park, unless they are huge Lego fans—although Minitown is an impressive sight for just about anyone. Adults $69, children $59. Note that significant discounts apply when purchasing bundled tickets for **Legoland Water Park** and **Sealife Aquarium**.

Insider Tip: Beware of height restrictions at Legoland, which range from 34 to 48 inches for even the tamest rides. Waiting in a hot line only to be told your little one is *too* little could be the trigger for a memorable tantrum.

Legoland

Courtesy of Legoland

Legoland Water Park (760-918-5346; www.legoland.com), 1 Legoland Dr., Carlsbad. Open Thurs.–Mon. (Sept.–May) and daily June–Aug.; opens 10 AM; closing is seasonal. Opened in the summer of 2010, the more than 5-acre Legoland Water Park extends the appeal of the adjacent **Legoland** by including attractions that will amuse a wider range of ages. Attractions include six-person raft slides, single-person tube slides, and extensive water play areas for toddlers and young children. The Lego branding is never out of sight, as the new park is adorned with Lego statues and decked out in Lego colors. This is unlike other water parks in Southern California in that families can interact with hands-on projects, like a build-your-own raft you can then ride on the lazy river. A separate entry fee is required, but significant discounts apply when purchased as a package with either Legoland or **Sealife Aquarium** or both. Adults $79, children under 13 $69 (purchased with admission to Legoland).

San Diego Zoo Safari Park (760-747-8702; www.sandiegozoo.org/wap), 15500 San Pasqual Valley Rd., Escondido. Open daily at 9 AM; closing varies seasonally. The famous San Diego Zoo's east county site (formerly known as the Wild Animal Park) is a 2,200-acre wildlife preserve located 30 miles northeast of San Diego. It's designed to give visitors a chance to observe animals in their native habitats, so enclosures are kept as natural as possible, and animals in expansive field exhibits roam freely and mingle with other animals they would encounter naturally. More than three thousand animals call the park home, including almost 50 species that are endangered. There are miles of trails winding through the beautifully landscaped grounds—which include approximately 4,000 species of

Insider Tip: For an additional charge, at the San Diego Zoo Safari Park you can take part in adventures like the Photo Caravan Safaris, where you'll board a small off-road vehicle and drive even deeper into the enclosures to take close-up photos of animals, and the Balloon Safari, where you'll ride a tethered hot-air balloon to get an unbeatable view of the park from 400 feet up.

plants, more than 250 of which are also endangered—and dozens of exhibits and guided hikes. The highlight of a park visit is a trip aboard the African Express, a vehicle that drives right into the wide-open enclosures, bringing guests close to the animals. Other not-to-be-missed exhibits in the park include the Lion Camp, where visitors view lions through a glass wall at exhibits designed to allow the animals to come closer than they otherwise could in a traditional enclosure; Condor Ridge, a trail that leads visitors through a habitat created for animals indigenous to North America, including the California condor, whose recovery from near extinction has been one of the great success stories of animal conservation; an exciting ⅝-mile zipline that runs high above the park; and the children's petting zoo, filled with docile deer and small animals. Adults $37, children $27.

Sealife Aquarium (760-918-LEGO; www.sealifeus.com), 1 Legoland Dr., Carlsbad. Open daily; hours vary by season. In 2008, this aquarium and ocean-themed park opened right next door to Legoland. (Sealife Aquarium has a secondary entrance that allows guests to walk in directly from Legoland.) Although there are tanks of

San Diego Zoo Safari Park

sea life to observe and plenty of ocean-themed exhibits and attractions, guests never get far from the Lego theme: expect to see Lego buildings underwater, too! The highlight is the Lost City of Atlantis exhibit, which offers enormous fish tanks and whimsical faux Lego reefs. There's also a handful of small-scale rides, a petting pool, and gift shops. The Legoland parent company has plans to expand this park, but for now it is very small, and even for the most curious children it can be seen in fewer than two hours. Note, also, that this is themed to very young children. Anyone over seven or eight is

Roar and Snore

Even if you think you're not the camping type, falling asleep to the sounds of lions roaring and waking to the sun rising over a savanna full of giraffes and gazelles will make a convert out of you. Bring your own sleeping bag, and the San Diego Zoo Safari Park will set you up with a premier camping spot on grassy Kilima Point, overlooking the park's Africa Field Exhibit. You'll be assigned a pre-assembled tent, ranging from a basic model that sleeps up to six or an upgraded premium model with a queen-sized platform bed and safari-themed décor. This is a pricey adventure and doesn't include the cost of admission to the park—which is required—but you'll be treated to a campfire program; an exclusive tour of the park at night; and dinner, snacks, drinks, and a hot breakfast in the morning. Book well in advance.

likely to be bored. Adults $20, children $13. (Combination Legoland/Sealife Aquarium tickets offer substantial discounts.)

Surfbowl in Oceanside (760-722-1371; www.surfbowloceanside.com), 1401 S. Coast Hwy., Oceanside. Open daily noon–11. Glow-in-the-dark lanes, strobe lights, and throbbing party music make bowling at Surfbowl an experience kids won't soon forget. There's also laser tag, and—believe it or not—a fairly good snack bar.

BEST SHOPPING

Hands down my favorite place to window-shop is in Solana Beach, just north of Del Mar, in the expansive **Cedros Design District** (www.cedros designdistrict.net), along S. Cedros Avenue, just south of Lomas Santa Fe Drive. This is *the* place for designers and decorating divas to find unusual furniture and accessories, and the showroom displays are inspirational. Nearby are **The Carlsbad Company Stores** (5600 Paseo del Norte, Carlsbad), an upscale outlet mall in south Carlsbad featuring bargains on such name brands as Waterford, Coach, and Wedgwood. In addition, the small, European-style **Del Mar Plaza** (1555 Camino del Mar, Del Mar) has eclectic boutiques in a storybook outdoor setting. Hundreds of small independent boutiques can also be found throughout downtown Del Mar, downtown Encinitas, and the village of Carlsbad.

Bon Bon (858-792-1668; www .bonbonhome.com), 301 Coast Hwy., Solana Beach. This Solana Beach antiques store literally overflows with tempting items from Europe; the owners specialize in British and French wares, and the collection is always eclectic and fun. You'll find one-of-a-kind chandeliers, salvaged wrought-

Del Mar Plaza

iron gates, and smaller accessories to give your home and garden a Continental flair.

Gardenology (760-753-5500; www.gardenology.com), 587 S. Coast Hwy., Encinitas. In the heart of downtown Encinitas, this quaint store is a great place for gardeners and design fans. Look for upscale outdoor furniture and accessories, with especially lovely European urns and whimsical garden statuary.

Jolie Femme (858-792-1222; www.joliefemmeboutique.com), 2690 Via de la Valle, D250, Del Mar. In the Flower Hill Promenade shopping mall, this lovely store sells delicate lingerie that is upscale, tasteful, and sexy.

Leaping Lotus (858-720-8283; www.leapinglotus.com), 240 S. Cedros Ave., Solana Beach. This rambling department store in the Cedros Design District sells just about everything, from handmade clothing and dramatic costume jewelry to eclectic designs for the home. Look for charming accent pieces for the patio and garden, one-of-a-kind tableware, and fine small furnishings.

Longboard Grotto (760-634-1920), 978 N. Coast Hwy. 101, Encinitas. The Longboard Grotto's motto is "not quite a museum but more than a surf shop," which speaks to its extensive collective of vintage boards on display. You can buy new and used boards here as well.

Lou's Records (760-753-1382; www.lousrecords.com), 434 N. Coast Hwy. 101, Encinitas. This independent music store draws people from throughout California, thanks to an impressive collection of new and used records, CDs, tapes, DVDs, and laser discs, representing almost any music genre you can imagine, including a large selection of local artists. The staff is friendly and knowledgeable, and if you can't find what you're looking for, chances are Lou's can order it for you.

BEST NIGHTLIFE

Coastal North County has a relaxed, hip vibe that you won't find downtown (which tends to the upscale) or farther inland (which tends to the rustic). Nevertheless, the proximity to the ocean (and the resultant higher rents) attracts a well-heeled crowd, although there are plenty of funky surf dives sprinkled in for flavor. Look for casual neighborhood bars, relaxed wine bars, swanky beachside bistros, and larger venues that offer world-class live music.

Bar Leucadian (760-753-2094), 1542 N. Coast Hwy., Encinitas. Leucadians proudly proclaim that their hometown is "funky," and this tiny, out-of-the-way bar proves the point. There's often live music, and when there's not, there's a jukebox. There are also pool tables and a host of regulars.

The Belly Up Tavern (858-481-8140; www.bellyup.com), 143 S. Cedros Ave., Solana Beach. Locals have been rocking at the Belly Up since 1974, and it is still the premier nightclub for live music in North County. The warehouse space has enough room for a huge bar, a handful of billiards tables, and a cavernous dance floor. The large nightclub features eclectic live music from local bands as well as nationally recognized artists. There are regular theme nights, often with dance instruction before 8 PM.

Gaffney's Wine Bar (760-633-1011; www.gaffneyswinebar.com), 166B El Camino Real, Encinitas. Newly relocated in the midst of strip malls and medical buildings in inland Encinitas, this mom-and-pop establishment likes to bill itself as "like home, but with a better wine collection." The friendly place specializes in small-production wines from around the world, and the list changes daily.

Hensley's Flying Elephant Pub and Grill (760-434-2660; www.hensleyspub.com), 850 Tamarack, Carlsbad. Owned by a local skating celebrity (Matthew Hensley), the Flying Elephant Pub is a large, lively bar in quiet Carlsbad with billiards, live music, food, and plenty of space. Look for two-for-one pizza night on Thurs., and expect weekend crowds.

Karl Strauss Brewery (760-431-2739; www.karlstrauss.com), 5801 Armada Dr., Carlsbad. This chain of microbreweries started right here in San Diego, and there are several outlets in town (including downtown and La Jolla). All brews are on tap, and you can buy sampler glasses to get the full range of beers. Try a pint of the easy-going Red Trolley Ale, brewed with caramel malts, or the rich, nutty Black's Beach Extra Dark lager.

La Paloma Theatre (760-436-7469; www.lapalomatheatre.com), 471 S. Coast Hwy., Encinitas. This grand old movie theater in downtown Encinitas was one of the first theaters to show "talkies" and has been a local favorite since its opening in 1928. Today the beautiful old venue hosts both films and live concerts (as well as midnight showings of *The Rocky Horror Picture Show*).

O'Sullivan's Irish Pub (760-729-7234; www.osullivanscarlsbad.com), 640 Grand Ave., Carlsbad. In downtown Carlsbad, this adorable, rustic pub is a cozy, friendly place to grab a pint and a hearty shepherd's pie, listen to live music, or just catch up with friends. The pub hosts a monthly Irish dance night where local Irish dance schools show off their skills.

Wine Steals (760-230-2657; www.winestealssd.com), 1953 San Elijo Ave., Cardiff-by-the-Sea. This combination wine store/wine bar offers a retail outlet that stocks more than three hundred varieties, a small outdoor patio space that faces the ocean, and a wine grotto lounge with a wine barrel bar and an old-world feel. Come here to relax with friends and to score some real bargains on wine.

48 Hours

ITINERARY FOR COUPLES

Friday Night

- Savor rack of lamb followed by creamy panna cotta at the luxurious five-diamond **Addison** restaurant in The Grand Del Mar, where you'll be overnighting.

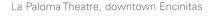

La Paloma Theatre, downtown Encinitas

- Before departing the restaurant, choose a bottle of wine (or better yet, a bottle of champagne) from Addison's extensive collection and have it sent to your guest room with two glasses and a plate of strawberries.
- Lodge in impeccable style at **The Grand Del Mar**; run a bubble bath in the European-style soaking tub (big enough for two) and enjoy your nightcap.

Saturday
- Begin the day with luscious berry and cream crêpes at the **Champagne French Bakery and Café** in Del Mar.
- Beat the crowds and go early (before 10 AM) to claim a prime spot on the gorgeous **Del Mar City Beach**; spend the morning frolicking in the waves or just relaxing in the sun.
- Dust off the sand from your flip-flops and head for a long, late lunch at the casual **Café Secret** in Del Mar; you won't go wrong with the beef empanadas.
- Prepare for an afternoon of total pampering at **The Spa** at The Grand Del Mar; schedule a couples massage, and afterward be sure to check out the Relaxation Pool, an adults-only retreat just outside the treatment rooms.
- Arrive for dinner at **Jake's Del Mar** in time to watch the sunset from the expansive outdoor patio; feast on fresh fish, sip pink grapefruit martinis, and save room enough to share Jake's signature Hula Pie.
- Rock the night away to live music at **The Belly Up Tavern** in nearby Solana Beach; dance, shoot pool, or just sit back and observe the melee.

Sunday
- Feast on the lush All-American Buffet at upscale **Arterra** in Del Mar; grab a Bellini, and don't miss the house-made chicken-apple sausage.
- Spend the morning shopping for antiques and imported furnishings at **Bon Bon** in Solana Beach.
- Refuel with a portobello mushroom sandwich with handmade mozzarella and balsamic onions at the casually elegant **Pacifica Del Mar**, upstairs at the Del Mar Plaza.
- Travel a few miles north to the small, picturesque **Swami's Beach** in Encinitas to explore the rocky cliffs and tide pools; if the surf is up, watch for some of the city's finest surfers here.

ITINERARY FOR FAMILIES
Friday Night
- Treat the kids to an oversized gourmet burger or a meaty chicken pot-pie at **Bistro West** in Carlsbad. Be sure to save room for the cherry cobbler for dessert.
- Head to the **Sheraton Carlsbad**, next door to Legoland, to overnight in a spacious, stylish guest room.
- Spend the evening playing Ping-Pong at the outdoor table; swimming at the well-heated, expansive hotel pool; or soaking in the oversized Jacuzzi.

Saturday
- Grab a table on the outdoor patio of the highly regarded **Twenty/20 Grill and Bar** on-site at the hotel; enjoy a Southwestern omelet with house-made chorizo, a healthy bowl of Irish steel-cut oatmeal with berries, or a fluffy Belgian waffle with cream and real Vermont maple syrup.

- Take advantage of the hotel's private entrance to **Legoland**, as well as the discounts to the park offered by the Sheraton; once inside the park, check out the Dragon roller coaster for the park's biggest thrills—or if you're traveling with younger children, go straight for the Storybook Canal boat ride.
- Maximize your time by dining in the park—there really are many good choices, most of which are reasonably priced. *Healthy lunch option:* A fresh salad with roasted chicken or a pint-sized peanut butter and jelly sandwich on wheat bread at the **Garden Restaurant** near Minitown.

Legoland Water Park

Courtesy of Legoland

Indulgent lunch option: Hot apple fries coated in cinnamon and sugar and served with a big dollop of vanilla whipped cream (yum!) at **Granny's Apple Fries** near the Hideaway playground.

- Once you've seen all there is to see at Legoland, grab your bathing suits and head next door to the colorful water slides at the new **Legoland Water Park**—or for toddlers, keep dry observing the creatures of the ocean at the tiny **Sealife Aquarium**.
- Refuel at **Pizza Port and Brewery** in downtown Carlsbad, which offers some of the best pies in the city as well as astonishingly tasty and varied microbrews for the parents.
- Head northward to Oceanside for glow-in-the-dark bowling at **Surfbowl**.

Sunday

- Breakfast at the nostalgic **101 Café** in Oceanside, where the children will giggle at menu options like Dicey Conditions (two eggs, two pancakes, and two pieces of bacon or sausage), Accelerate Now (French toast with eggs and bacon), and Classic SOS (toast smothered in gravy, home fries, and eggs).
- Head to family-friendly **Carlsbad State Beach** for boogie boarding and rock collecting (there's always a pile of colorful polished stones near the pathway to the parking lot).
- No need to de-sand when dining at the outdoor **El Callejon** in nearby Encinitas; kids can feast on chicken fingers, and parents can sample a variety of tequilas.
- Visit the south Carlsbad suburbs for a short, easy hike through the historic **Leo Carrillo Park;** be on the lookout for peacock feathers, shed by the noisy resident flock.

ITINERARY FOR OUTDOORS ENTHUSIASTS

Friday Night

- Dine on mesquite-grilled catch of the day at **Fish House Vera Cruz** in Carlsbad; because you plan to be extra active this weekend, don't shy away from the cheese-covered mashed potatoes.
- Play shuffleboard or billiards, or rock out to the live band at the eclectic, ever-entertaining **Hensley's Flying Elephant Pub and Grill** in Carlsbad; don't forget to top off the night with a pint of Guinness.
- Overnight at the fabulously elegant **Park Hyatt Aviara** in south Carlsbad; take time to enjoy the live piano music in the lobby or stroll the grounds by moonlight.

Saturday

- Start the day like the local surfers do: grab a veggie breakfast burrito and a power juice at the funky **Swami's Café** in Encinitas.
- Go directly to the tiny, hidden **Elizabethan Desserts** to pick up delights like passion fruit cupcakes and juicy cherry tarts on the way to the **San Diego Botanical Gardens;** while inside the gardens, be sure to check out the amazing bamboo orchard.
- Make a picnic of your sweet treats at the pretty gazebo in the center of the gardens; a nearby snack cart sells drinks, fruit, and delightful Italian ices if you're feeling extra peckish.
- If you booked a room overlooking the spectacular golf course, then you've probably been frothing at the mouth to get in a round at the **Park Hyatt Aviara Golf Course;** ask your concierge about priority tee times for guests.

- Dine outdoors on the sidewalk patio of **Trattoria I Trulli** in Encinitas; try any of the handmade raviolis or, for a real treat, check out the seafood pasta with clams, mussels, and jumbo shrimp.
- Burn off some of the evening's carbs by exploring downtown Encinitas, which is easily walkable and generally buzzing on weekend nights.

Sunday

- Elbow your way into the very popular **Beach Break Café** in Oceanside; look for local surfing and skating celebrities, and don't miss the hot coffee cake.
- Hike the meandering trail that rings the **Batiguitos Lagoon,** just beneath your hotel; keep an eye open for shorebirds like snowy egrets and the harder to spot black-necked stilts.
- Enjoy a fast lunch at **KC's Tandoor** in Encinitas; try the hara masala lamb or shrimp, a spicy but light concoction with cilantro, garlic, and green onions.
- Join in a pickup game of beach volleyball at **Moonlight Beach;** the diehard regulars are friendly, but be prepared for competitive play.

ITINERARY FOR CULTURE ENTHUSIASTS

Friday Night

- Start the weekend with an exotic meal of Bangkok seafood with scallops, squid, shrimp, and crab, or spicy panang curry with chicken and green beans, at **Taste of Thai** in Del Mar.
- Head to the swanky **Bleu Bar** in the L'Auberge Del Mar resort to enjoy ocean views while sipping their signature Coconut Bikini martini, with vodka, pineapple juice, and fresh coconut.

Moonlight Beach

- Overnight at the elegant **L'Auberge Del Mar Resort and Spa,** which offers European style and spectacular ocean views.

Saturday
- Grab a quick breakfast of croissants and café au lait at the casual **St. Tropez Bakery** in Encinitas; grab a table in the outdoor courtyard.
- Explore the unusual **Museum of Making Music** in Carlsbad; surprise yourself with your musical talent by getting some hands-on time with a Bob McNally Strumstick, which is designed to make even beginners sound like they've taken years of lessons.
- Take a vacation within a vacation by lunching at the authentic Mexican restaurant **Norte** in Carlsbad; if you're really adventurous, try the menudo (tripe soup) or go for a

tamer combo plate with tacos and enchiladas.
- Check out home décor and clothing wares from around the world at the eclectic world market known as **Leaping Lotus,** in the Cedros Design District in Solana Beach; this is a great place to pick up an unusual souvenir like sandals from Guatemala or a scarf from Pakistan.
- Although it is located in a nondescript strip mall in Encinitas, **Passage to India** *can* be transporting— especially if you order the palak paneer (spicy creamed spinach with milk curds) or the ever-popular chicken tikka masala.
- Enjoy an evening performance by the **North Coast Repertory Theater** or take in an independent film at the historic **La Paloma** movie theater in Encinitas.

Sunday

- Wake up with an eminently civilized breakfast of tea and scones (or coffee and Danish) at the quaint **Pannikin Coffee and Tea** house in Encinitas; try to score a table on the big front porch.
- Take in the exhibits at the **California Surf Museum** in Oceanside.
- Stick with the surfing genre and grab a burger and fries at the **Longboarder Café** nearby.
- Spend the afternoon exploring the historic **Mission San Luis Rey de Francia**; toss a coin into the fountain in front for prosperity, and be sure to hike through the gardens.

ITINERARY FOR TIGHT BUDGETS

Friday Night

- Fight any anxieties the exterior of **La Especial Norte** in Leucadia might inspire and head inside for a generously portioned, exceptionally well-priced Mexican feast served by friendly waitstaff.
- Grab a fire ring and some wood, and enjoy a toasty bonfire by the sea at **Moonlight Beach** in Encinitas; don't forget the marshmallows (but leave the alcohol behind—it's not allowed on the sands).
- Overnight at the **Moonlight Beach Motel**, which is modest in every way except location—which is primo.

Saturday

- Grab a coffee and some pastries at the **E Street Café** in Encinitas, and while you're here, check your e-mail using their free high-speed Internet access.
- Take a contemplative stroll through the ocean-view gardens of the **Self-Realization Fellowship Temple and Ashram Center** in Encinitas; be sure to walk to the top of the garden to get the best views of the Pacific.
- Split a Belly Bomber burger with side salad or pasta at the **Daily News Café** in Carlsbad, where the portions for just about every menu item are ideal for sharing.
- Observe artists-in-residence at work at the **Lux Art Institute** in Encinitas; visitors 21 and younger are admitted for free.
- Hunt for the tiny **Smokin' Joey's Barbeque** in Carlsbad, and then dive into mile-high pulled pork sandwiches, hot links, and—for a less-thrifty investment—sticky pork and beef ribs; don't miss the sweet potato fries.
- Soak up the casual atmosphere at **Wine Steals** in Cardiff-by-the-Sea; order a half glass of your favorite vintage or explore the daily offerings with a $10 tasting (pours are generous).

Sunday

- Breakfast on *divine* ham and cheese croissants, coffee, and jelly-filled donuts at the no-frills **Hill Street Donuts** in Oceanside; split an apple fritter for a sweet treat.
- Stroll through the picturesque **Oceanside Harborfront**; bring along a pole and fish off the **Oceanside Pier**, no license required.
- Munch on beef taquitos or crispy chicken tacos at the tiny local takeout **Roberto's**, near Carlsbad State Beach.
- Try your hand at body surfing at **Carlsbad State Beach** or hike southward along the cliffs to find a quiet place for a nap.

Half a Dozen Side Trips

EXTEND YOUR STAY BEYOND THE SAN DIEGO COUNTY BORDER

One of the real joys of San Diego is the variety of experiences available. We have a cosmopolitan city, a handful of quaint beach towns, oceans, mountains, and deserts all within the county limits—and many would argue that there's no reason to leave this bounty. But if you *are* interested in expanding your trip, there are some excellent options just beyond the county lines, including one of the world's most beloved family theme parks (The Disneyland Resort®); a postcard-perfect beach town with fine-art opportunities disproportionate to its diminutive size (Laguna Beach); the second-largest city in the country and the entertainment capital of the world (Los Angeles); a lovely desert resort town with championship golf and myriad spas (Palm Springs); a small, glamorous island that is three parts nature reserve and one part upscale resort (Santa Catalina); and a surprising patch of lush wine country just over the Riverside County border (Temecula).

THE DISNEYLAND® RESORT

Ninety miles north of San Diego, Anaheim is the town that Mickey Mouse built. Actually, Anaheim was home to thriving citrus groves before Walt Disney came along, but it was **Disneyland** (714-781-4400; http://disneyland.disney.go.com, 1313 Harbor Boulevard, Anaheim) that put the city on the tourist map. Today more than 15 million people visit Anaheim annually, and more than 13 million of them come to Disneyland. To help draw off the crowds from the main park, the resort added **Disney's California Adventure** (714-781-4400; http://disneyland.disney.go .com, 1313 S. Harbor Boulevard, Anaheim) in 2001, a Golden State–themed amusement park that features a miniaturized San Francisco cityscape, a Holly-wood-themed street, Napa-esque vineyards, a beachfront-style boardwalk with carnival games, and gushing rapids that circle a mountain carved into the likeness of a growling grizzly. Through 2012, Disney's California Adventure is undergoing a major renovation, revamping existing attractions and adding many more to the park; the additions promise to bring more excitement, more attractions, and technologically amazing nightlife entertainment. Admission for either park is $76 for guests 10 and older and $68 for guests three to nine (two and under are free); for a little more ($101 for 10 and older and $91 for guests three to nine) you can purchase a Park Hopper Pass that allows you to go to both parks on the same day. There are also multiple-day passes that offer significant savings and specially priced packages for Southern California residents. Buy these at either park or online at http://disney land.disney.go.com. Both parks are open every day of the year. Adjacent **Downtown Disney** (714-781-4400; http://disneyland.disney.go.com), a spectacularly designed shopping, entertainment, and dining complex, is conveniently located between the two theme parks. The pedestrian-only thoroughfare is stunning, with eclectic and entertaining storefronts and whimsical landscaping, which is transformed by hundreds of thousands of glittering lights once the sun sets. Admission to the shopping area does not require a ticket.

Insider Tip: To avoid the worst crowds at Disneyland on weekends and holidays, come early: gates sometimes open as much as a half hour earlier than advertised. Once the crowds thicken, be sure to take advantage of FASTPASS tickets, which allow guests to bypass the standby lines. Find the FASTPASS machines near the front of designated rides, and insert your park ticket. You'll be issued a timed pass that allows you to come back during a given 60-minute window, at which point you present the pass and get into a significantly shorter line than you would otherwise. You can get additional FASTPASS tickets as soon as the designated time period of the previous ones expire.

Top 10 Don't-Miss Attractions in The Disneyland® Resort

- **California Screamin,'** at Paradise Pier, California Adventure. This *fast* roller coaster, which features an inverted loop and plenty of hair-raising drops, takes off like a rocket and doesn't let up for a second. This is arguably the most thrilling of all rides in either theme park and a hands-down favorite with most teenagers.
- **Dumbo,** in Fantasyland, Disneyland. This sweet attraction is original to the 1955 park. Guests climb into brightly colored Dumbo look-alikes for a (brief) flight aboard a flying elephant. Kids can control the height by moving a joystick that will make Dumbo climb or descend; it is amusing enough for older kids and adults, and gentle enough for toddlers.
- **Finding Nemo Voyage,** in Tomorrowland, Disneyland. Recently reopened (the ride used to be the old submarine attraction), this ride includes scenes from *Finding Nemo,* and it is a huge draw, especially with fans of the movie. Come early (or within an hour of the park closing) to avoid the worst of the crowds.
- **Fireworks Show,** over the Sleeping Beauty Castle in Fantasyland, Disneyland. Hours and days vary by season, but expect pyrotechnics every weekend evening, throughout the two-week traditional school winter holiday break, and throughout the summertime. Look for an explosion toward the end of the show that looks suspiciously like mouse ears.
- *Indiana Jones* **Adventure,**™ in Adventureland, Disneyland. Disney is legend at creating a total experience, and nowhere is the company's creativity on better display than in the queue for this ride, which winds through authentic ruins and

a forbidden temple, in this case making getting there half the fun. The ride itself is brilliant: thrilling, unexpected, and with stunning special effects.

- **"it's a small world,"** in Fantasyland, Disneyland. Although it is true that the music for this classic attraction is mind-numbingly unforgettable, the nearly 10-minute boat ride through the expansive collection of internationally costumed Audio-Animatronics dolls is not to be missed. The ride is even more impressive during the holidays, when the interior of the ride is transformed with Christmas and Hanukkah decorations and thousands of lights.
- **Soarin' Over California,** in the Golden State, California Adventure. This attraction is part movie, part moving attraction, set to mimic soaring in a hang glider over inspiring filmed scenes taken throughout the state of California, and it's one of my all-time favorite rides, appropriate for young children and elderly grandparents. (Hint: try to smell the orange blossoms when flying over the citrus groves.)
- **Space Mountain,** in Tomorrowland, Disneyland. A high-speed indoor roller coaster cruising through darkened passageways mimics hurtling through space, all to the accompaniment of a high-decibel soundtrack. This is another ride that makes the most of the queue, which is convincingly staged to look like a space station.
- **Toy Story Mania!** at Paradise Pier, California Adventure. One of the newest attractions to come out of the ongoing renovations at Disney's California Adventure, this impressive 4-D attraction is interactive and wildly popular (i.e., expect a *long* wait in line). After donning 3-D glasses, guests use spring-action shooters to launch rings at aliens, darts at balloons, and paint balls at various targets—which when hit result in special effects. The ride changes every time, and patrons can compete for the highest score.
- **World of Color,** at Paradise Pier, California Adventure. New to the park, the World of Color is a water, music, and lights spectacular staged on the Paradise Bay in California Adventure. Computer choreography coordinates nearly 1,200 water fountains, familiar Disney music, audio and visual effects, and projections of new animation on massive "screens" of water, offering perhaps the biggest nighttime draw of the Disney resort.

Five Best Bets for Lodging and Dining near The Disneyland® Resort
Lodging
To maximize your time in the parks—and to take advantage of perks like early admission and hotel-delivery for packages purchased in the parks—I recommend staying in one of the resort hotels. They are pricier, to be sure, but worth the splurge.

- **The Anabella** (714-905-1050; www.anabellahotel.com), 1030 W. Katella Ave., Anaheim. Within walking distance of the Disney theme parks and the Anaheim Convention Center, this ecofriendly property offers suite configurations designed with separate sleeping areas, making this ideal for families traveling with children. Parents will appreciate that this property is a true bargain. Inexpensive.
- **Disneyland Hotel** (714-778-6600; www.disneyland.com), 1150 Magic Way, Anaheim. This is the oldest property, and my sentimental favorite, thanks to kid-friendly extras like the Never Land–themed pool and the on-site character dining at **Goofy's Kitchen**. Expensive.

- **Disney's Grand Californian** (714-635-2300; www.disneyland.com), 1600 S. Disneyland Dr., Anaheim. The priciest, most elegant option at The Disneyland Resort®, Disney's Grand Californian is located at the epicenter of the action, in the heart of Downtown Disney and just a short walk from the entrance of both Disneyland and Disney's California Adventure. Very expensive.
- **Disney's Paradise Pier Hotel** (714-999-0990; www.disneyland.com), 1717 S. Disneyland Dr., Anaheim. Although hardly a bargain, Paradise Pier offers the best in-park lodging choice for budget travelers, and there are often significant online discounts available during the off-season for this hotel. The

Hilton Anaheim

Courtesy of Hilton Hotels

property is the farthest from the parks, although it is still walkable. Moderate to expensive.
- **Hilton Anaheim** (714-750-4321; www1.hilton.com/en_US/hi/hotel/SNAAHHH -Hilton-Anaheim-California/index.do), 777 Convention Way, Anaheim. The expansive Hilton Anaheim is immediately next door to the Anaheim Convention Center and connected to the theme parks via shuttle. Some rooms offer a view to watch the evening fireworks over Disneyland. Moderate.

Disney Dining

For priority seating at any park restaurant, call 714-774-4442. Priority seating isn't *quite* a reservation—but it does ensure that your party will be seated before anyone who arrives without their names on the eatery list.

- **Blue Bayou**, in New Orleans Square, Disneyland. Open daily for lunch and dinner. Waterside tables at this indoor fine-dining establishment overlook the start of the **Pirates of the Caribbean** attraction. This is one of the most popular eateries in The Disneyland® Resort, and thus it is vital to secure priority seating well in advance. Very expensive.
- **Catal Restaurant and Uva Bar**, Downtown Disney. Open daily for lunch and dinner. Upstairs in a tower dining room, Catal serves multicourse Mediterranean meals. Downstairs at the outdoor Uva Bar, guests can grab tapas, coffee, or dozens of tempting desserts. Expensive.
- **Goofy's Kitchen**, on the ground floor of the Disneyland Hotel. Open daily for breakfast, lunch, and dinner. The beloved Goofy's Kitchen offers buffet-style meals hosted by Goofy, Mickey, and a handful of other costumed characters that roam the dining hall to pose for photographs and to sign autographs. Moderate.
- **House of Blues** (714-778-2583; www.houseofblues.com/venues/clubvenues/ anaheim), 1530 S. Disneyland Dr. Open daily for lunch and dinner, Sun. for

House of Blues, Anaheim   Courtesy of House of Blues

brunch. Located in Downtown Disney, this House of Blues outlet is always packed, thanks to hearty Southern food and nightly live music. Don't miss the chicken-fried chicken. Moderate.

- **Napa Rose,** Downtown Disney. Open daily for dinner. By far the finest dining experience on the Disneyland property, Napa Rose's sophisticated Arts and Crafts décor, seasonal wine-country cuisine, and extensive wine cellar have drawn rave reviews since it opened in 2002. Very expensive.

LAGUNA BEACH

Just a short hour and a half drive up the Pacific Coast Highway is Laguna Beach, which is stunning in just about every way—with natural beauty from pristine beaches, rolling hills that rise up close to the shoreline, and cultural opportunities that are disproportionate to the size of the city. Laguna Beach was founded at the turn of the 20th century as an artists' colony and today comprises hundreds of art galleries, quaint clothing boutiques, seafood and ethnic bistros, and a handful of idyllic beaches with some of the whitest sand and clearest aquamarine water in California. Every year the city hosts several well-attended arts festivals, including the Pageant of the Masters and the Sawdust Festival. The city also includes world-class resorts and a seemingly endless supply of outdoor sporting options.

Top 10 Don't-Miss Attractions in Laguna Beach

- **Crescent Bay Beach,** off Viejo and North Coast Hwy. The northernmost beach in Laguna, the small Crescent Bay is postcard perfect, with white sand, crystalline waters, and a gently curving shoreline. Because of the generally calm waters and the reefs offshore, the beach is popular with scuba divers and snorkelers.

- **Crystal Cove State Park** (949-497-7647; www.crystalcovestatepark.com), off Los Trancos. This surprisingly pristine bit of wilderness falls just north of Laguna Beach. The 2,400 acres include open sand dunes and grassland, and more than 3 miles of scenic coastline. The offshore waters are designated as an underwater park. Parking $15.
- **Goff Island Cove**, south Laguna Beach, below **Montage Laguna Beach.** This gorgeous cove beach is part of a protected marine park; there's great tidepooling here, and the water is the color of bottle glass. Look for the pretty Keyhole Rock.
- **The Laguna Playhouse** (949-497-2787; www.lagunaplayhouse.com), 606 Laguna Canyon Rd. Since the 1920s, the Laguna Playhouse has been an active community theater that has earned critical acclaim for professional excellence.
- **Main Beach**, at Pacific Coast Hwy. and Ocean. This downtown beach is at the heart of the action and offers numerous beach volleyball courts, a small boardwalk, and an idyllic stretch of shoreline.
- **Marine Park**, above Goff Island Cove. This perfectly manicured park has curving walkways that showcase breathtaking views of the ocean, overflowing native flower gardens, lush lawn, and intimate benches overlooking the cliffs and the Pacific Ocean beyond.
- **Monarch Beach Golf Course** (949-240-82471; www.monarchbeachgolf.com), 50 Monarch Beach Dr., Dana Point. Emerald greens and jaw-dropping ocean views make this course south of Laguna one of the most beautiful in Orange

Goff Island Cove, Laguna Beach

County. Well-manicured and challenging holes make it one of the locals' favorite courses as well. Green fee: $115–195.

- **Pageant of the Masters** (949-494-1145). Running from early July through the end of Aug. is the world-famous Pageant of the Masters, in which classical and contemporary art comes to life in living, breathing creations: live models pose in an outdoor amphitheater, with the accompaniment of an orchestra and live narration.
- **Sawdust Art Festival** (949-494-3030; www.sawdustartfestival.org). Beginning late in July and running through the end of Aug., this well-attended art festival offers workshops, exhibits, and a chance to meet artists.
- **Spa Montage** (949-715-6010; www.spamontage.com), 30801 S. Coast Hwy. Part of the beautiful **Montage Laguna Beach,** this upscale oceanfront spa is one of the finest in the area, and quintessentially "OC." Look for sea-inspired treatments like the Marine Wrap, which uses exfoliating and detoxifying seaweed and aromatic sea salt scrubs.

Five Best Bets for Lodging and Dining in Laguna Beach
Lodging
- **Hotel Laguna** (949-494-1151; www.hotellaguna.com), 425 S. Coast Hwy. The historic "Grand Old Lady" has been in Laguna for more than one hundred years and has hosted countless dignitaries and celebrities; it remains one of the most recognizable landmarks in Laguna Beach, conveniently located smack downtown, fronting the wildly popular Main Beach. Expensive.
- **Inn at Laguna Beach** (949-497-9722; www.innatlagunabeach.com), 211 N. Coast Hwy. Perched at the top of a small bluff that overlooks the ocean and the hillsides beyond, the intimate Inn at Laguna Beach in downtown has incomparable views and elegant service. Moderate.
- **La Casa del Camino** (949-497-2446; www.lacasadelcamino.com), 1289 S. Coast Hwy. Built in 1929 as a retreat for Hollywood movie stars, this eclectic hotel has personality to spare—with suites individually designed to be part accommodation/part art gallery. Moderate to expensive.
- **Montage Laguna Beach** (949-715-6000; www.montagelagunabeach.com), 30801 S. Coast Hwy. This oasis of calm elegance is the epitome of Southern California chic, and it manages to be welcoming and comfortable at the same time that it is opulent and exclusive. Very expensive.

Montage Laguna Beach

- **Surf and Sand Resort and Spa** (949-497-4477; www.surfandsandresort.com), 1555 S. Coast Hwy. Surf and Sand is built right on the shore. The ocean views from the guest room balconies are second to none—in fact, the experience of staying at this resort is very much like being on a boat, because the water is *that* close. Expensive.

Dining

- **Brussels Bistro** (949-376-7955; www.brusselsbistro.com), 222 Forest Ave. Open daily for lunch and dinner. This adorable European brasserie serves authentic Belgian fare and offers live jazz concerts Tues.–Thurs., starting at 7 PM. Moderate.
- **C'est la Vie** (949-497-5100; www.cestlavierestaurant.com), 373 S. Coast Hwy. Open daily for breakfast, lunch, and dinner. Romantic C'est la Vie offers a little bit of Paris, combined with premier views of the Pacific Ocean. Moderate.
- **Crab Zone** (949-376-7035), 217 Broadway. Open daily for lunch and dinner. This casual eatery a block off Main Beach is an intriguing blend of Vietnamese, Chinese, and French cuisine, specializing in jumbo crab legs, crabcakes, and Dungeness crab. Moderate.
- **The Loft** (949-715-6010; www.montagelagunabeach.com), 30801 S. Coast Hwy. Open daily for dinner. At the **Montage Laguna Beach,** The Loft showcases an upscale organic farm-to-table approach. The in-house fromagier features more than 150 cheeses and 100 different honeys every night. Very expensive.
- **Watermarc** (949-376-6272; www.watermarcrestaurant.com), 448 S. Coast Hwy. Open daily for dinner. In the heart of downtown Laguna, this restaurant offers a bewilderingly extensive menu, and for lighter appetites includes two-for-$10 grazing plates (served after 9 PM). Order wine by the half glass, glass, half carafe, or bottle. Moderate.

LOS ANGELES

LA is one of the most eclectic, exciting places in the world, and even with the infamous gridlock, smog, and sprawling layout, the city has attractions and rewards like no other. The geography is almost incomprehensible in size: the city is 467 square miles, and Los Angeles County comprises more than 4,000 square miles. There are 88 incorporated cities within LA County, including LA City, with a population of its own of nearly 4 million, making the city the second largest in the nation. The county includes more than 10 million residents—more than most states. *Don't try to see it all.* Focus instead on a couple of the most popular areas, including lovely Santa Monica, a longtime favorite of mine because of its relatively slower pace and its astonishing collection of world-class restaurants; incomparable Malibu, an ultrapricey beach community that is favored by Hollywood celebrities; downtown LA, awash with dazzling skyscrapers and a revitalized attitude that is attracting young adults by the droves; Hollywood, West Hollywood, and Beverly Hills, the renowned playgrounds of some of the most famous people in the world and the site of stunning nightlife, dining, and shopping; and Pasadena, famous for being home to the Rose Bowl and the Rose Parade. These regions offer the biggest bang for the tourist buck in terms of attractions, natural beauty, abundance of hotels and dining, and ease of access.

- **Getty Center** (310-440-7300; www.getty.edu), 1200 Getty Center Dr., Los Angeles. Open Tues.–Sun.; hours vary by season. This miraculous arts center in Malibu is an architectural treasure as well as home to world-class art exhibits and a stunning garden. Admission is free.
- **Hollywood Sign** (www.hollywoodsign.org). You can't come to LA without seeing it: the Hollywood Sign is best viewed from afar via the courtyard of the Hollywood and Highland retail complex.
- **The Huntington Library, Art Collection, and Botanical Gardens** (626-405-2100; www.huntington.org), 1151 Oxford Rd., San Marino. Open Mon., Wed.–Fri. noon–4:30; Sat. and Sun. 10:30–4:30. The 120 lavish acres of gardens that boast more than 14,000 kinds of plants would be reason enough to visit this magnificent estate, which once belonged to railroad titan Henry Huntington. But beyond the gardens, the Huntington, near Pasadena, also offers four art galleries and arguably the most extensive collection of rare books on the West Coast. Weekend admissions: adults $20, seniors $15, students $10, children 5–11 $6, under five free. Discounts apply on weekdays and for group rates.
- **LA Live's Grammy Museum** (213-765-6803; www.grammymuseum.org), 800 W. Olympic Blvd., downtown Los Angeles. Open Sun.–Fri. 11:30–7:30, Sat. 10–7:30. The 30,000-square-foot Grammy Museum at **LA Live**, a sports and entertainment complex downtown, features exhibits on the art and technology of the recording process, as well as thematic collections of memorabilia once owned by famous musicians like Michael Jackson and Madonna. Adults $13, children $11.

Huntington Library and Gardens, near Pasadena

- **Olvera Street** (213-628-1274; www.olvera-street.com), downtown Los Angeles. This open-air marketplace is overflowing with Mexican restaurants and strolling mariachis, and is home to the city's old town, with 27 historic buildings, including the Avila Adobe, LA's oldest building (dating to 1818).
- **Pacific Park** (www.pacpark.com), on Santa Monica Pier, Santa Monica. Open daily; hours vary seasonally. This small amusement park is perched on the iconic Santa Monica Pier and offers spectacular views to Malibu and beyond from the Pacific Wheel, the world's only solar-powered Ferris wheel. There are a dozen other rides, including a small roller coaster.
- **Sunset Strip,** 2 miles of Sunset Blvd. between Doheny Dr. and Crescent Heights Blvd., West Hollywood. Look for music venues that are legend, as well as a bewildering display of billboards and hellish traffic on weekend nights.
- **Universal Studios Hollywood** (800-UNIVERSAL; www.universalstudioshollywood.com), 1000 Universal Center Dr., Universal City. Open daily; hours vary by season. Just north of downtown LA, Universal Studios Hollywood is a fascinating mix of movie-themed thrill park and real working studio. Admission to the park includes a full studio tour, admission to live-action shows, and unlimited passes to the many thrill rides. Adjacent CityWalk comprises 65 entertainment-themed restaurants, nightclubs, shops, and entertainment options. Adults $74, children $64.
- **Whisky a Go Go** (310-652-4202; www.whiskyagogo.com), 8901 W. Sunset Blvd., West Hollywood. This iconic music club was the epicenter of the rock scene in the late 1960s and into the 1970s. Jim Morrison and the Doors were once the house band.
- **Zuma Beach Park,** 30000 block of Pacific Coast Hwy., Malibu. This very wide, very long sandy beach is arguably the most beautiful in Los Angeles. It offers stunning wide-angle views; good sunbathing, wading, and swimming; and volleyball courts; and is appropriate for families and singles alike.

Five Best Bets for Lodging and Dining in Los Angeles
Lodging

- **Andaz WeHo** (323-656-1234; http://westhollywood.hyatt.com/hyatt/hotels/index.jsp), 8401 Sunset Blvd., West Hollywood. This sleek, sexy property reflects the youthful energy of the rock and roll crowd that still cruises the portion of the Sunset Strip on which this property is sited. Moderate.
- **Beverly Hills Hotel and Bungalows** (800-283-8885; www.beverlyhillshotel.com), 9641 Sunset Blvd., Beverly Hills. The historic "pink palace" has been the home away from home for Golden Age Hollywood A-listers like Marilyn Monroe, Elizabeth Taylor, and Warren Beatty. Despite the rarified status of most guests today and all the Hollywood history, don't worry that this upscale icon will be stuffy: service is surprisingly friendly and personalized. Very expensive.
- **The Langham Huntington Hotel and Spa** (626-568-3900; www.langhamhotels.com), 1401 S. Oak Knoll Ave., Pasadena. The palatial Langham is the finest accommodation in Pasadena and offers the look and feel of a residential mansion. Dating to 1865, the hotel is sited on 23 immaculately landscaped acres overlooking the tony San Marino suburb. Expensive.
- **Shutters on the Beach** (310-458-0030; www.shuttersonthebeach.com), 1 Pico Blvd., Santa Monica. This exclusive property offers light, breezy luxury, with

Andaz WeHo, on the Sunset Strip

spalike bathrooms, large guest rooms, and numerous inviting public spaces. The property sits on the beach, so views from most guest rooms are top-shelf. Very expensive.

- **Westin Bonaventure** (213-624-1000; www.thebonaventure.com), 404 S. Figueroa St., downtown Los Angeles. The huge, centrally located Bonaventure offers 1,400-plus guest rooms and suites, which are spacious and recently refurbished, and top floors offer stellar views of the city (and on those rare smog-free LA days, vistas all the way to the ocean). Inexpensive.

Dining
- **Ciudad** (213-486-5171; www.ciudad-la.com), 445 S. Figueroa St., downtown Los Angeles. Open Mon.–Fri. for lunch and dinner, Sat.–Sun. for dinner. Owned by celebrity chefs Mary Sue Milliken and Susan Feniger (*Too Hot Tamales*), this downtown restaurant combines Mexican cuisine with influences from Honduras, Argentina, Cuba, Spain, and Brazil. Moderate.
- **The Ivy** (310-274-8303), 113 N. Robertson Blvd., Beverly Hills. Open daily for lunch and dinner. A current favorite with the Hollywood crowd, The Ivy has a surprisingly homey, country-chic aesthetic, with rustic antiques and fat fragrant roses blooming on the brick patio (the favored seating for the biggest stars). Very expensive.
- **Pink's Hot Dogs** (323-931-4223; www.pinkshollywood.com), 709 N. La Brea Ave., La Brea. Open daily 9:30 AM–2:30 AM. Since 1939, anyone who's anyone in

Los Angeles has lined up at this hot dog stand near West Hollywood—and do expect to stand in line at this ever-popular joint, where Orson Welles once downed 18 dogs at one sitting. Inexpensive.

- **Polo Lounge** (310-276-2251; www.beverlyhillshotel.com), 9641 Sunset Blvd., Beverly Hills. Open daily for breakfast, lunch, and dinner. Part of the world-renowned **Beverly Hills Hotel,** the Polo Lounge is equally as legendary as the one-time hangout of the Rat Pack—and continues to be a favorite with current A-listers. Expensive.
- **Reel Inn** (310-456-8221), 18661 Pacific Coast Hwy., Malibu. Open daily for lunch and dinner. This fish shack across the street from the ocean is the least-expensive (and arguably the best) seafood restaurant you'll find in Malibu. Order from a take-out window and seat yourself at picnic tables—some of which are likely to be populated by celebrities. Moderate.

PALM SPRINGS

The diversions of the desert resort of Palm Springs, which is a two-hour drive from downtown San Diego, have morphed over the past few decades to reflect the new, broader appeal of the valley, and in addition to plenty of sun-drenched pools and hip lounge spaces, today's Palm Springs and the other desert cities nearby offer even more world-class dining, four-star resorts, and a fair share of culture to balance out the otherwise overwhelmingly hedonistic pleasures. There are numerous outdoor activities, including an embarrassment of riches when it comes to golf courses, hiking in some of the loveliest high-desert scenery any-where in the world, and plenty of flat terrain for biking. Especially in the family-friendly resorts to the east of Palm Springs, such as La Quinta and Indian Wells, families will find lots to entertain themselves, from outrageous resort pools and educational zoos and museums to fun accommodation options designed with kids in mind. TV and movie A-listers continue to flock to the desert to chill out—as do couples and families who live in Southern California. In addition, the area is extremely welcoming to (and popular with) the LGBT community. In late spring through early fall, temperatures can top out at 120 degrees Fahrenheit, and although locals will assure you that because it is a "dry heat" it is more bearable than more humid climes, hot is hot. To ameliorate the worst of the season, most businesses have installed misters that will spray you with cool vapors as you walk by on the sidewalks in front, and all major resorts employ similar misters to make sitting by the pool bearable. Of course, a frozen cocktail in hand doesn't hurt, either.

Top 10 Don't-Miss Attractions in Palm Springs
- **Agua Caliente Casino Resort and Spa** (866-923-7244; www.hotwatercasino .com), 32250 Bob Hope Dr., Rancho Mirage. With nearly two thousand slot machines and video poker, high-limit gaming, and many wining and dining venues, this resort near Palm Springs offers a true Vegas-style experience.
- **Agua Caliente Cultural Museum** (760-778-1079), 219–223 S. Palm Canyon Dr., Palm Springs. Open Wed.–Sat. 10–5, Sun. noon–5. This tiny museum in downtown Palm Springs offers rotating exhibits highlighting the history and culture of the Agua Caliente band of Cahuilla Indians. Admission is free.

- **Big Wheel Bike Tours** (760-779-1837; www.bwbtours.com), P.O. Box 4185, Palm Springs, CA 92261. A tour with this group include bikes, helmets, snacks, and a Palm Springs specialty: a date shake. One tour option is the Earthquake Canyon Express, which is a 20-mile trip through the San Andreas fault zone amid typical desert scenery.
- **The Living Desert** (760-346-5694; www.livingdesert.org), 47900 Portola Ave., Palm Springs. Open daily 9–5. This combination zoo and botanical garden is home to more than 450 animals indigenous to the deserts of North America and Africa. Also on display are hundreds of species of cacti and other plants native to the desert. Adults $14.25, children $7.75.
- **Palm Springs Aerial Tramway** (760-325-1391; www.pstramway.com), off CA 111, Palm Springs. Open daily 8–5 (last tram up is at 4). One of the magical aspects of Southern California is the spectacular variety of scenery and terrain, and nowhere is this more striking than in Palm Springs, where you can move from the desert floor to the top of Mount San Jacinto at 8,500 feet in less than 10 minutes via the world's largest rotating suspended tram. Adults $22.95, children $16.25.
- **Palm Springs Air Museum** (760-778-6262; www.palmspringsairmuseum.org), 745 N. Gene Autry Trail, Palm Springs. Open daily 10–5. Check out the extensive collection of World War II combat aircraft, as well as photographs and other memorabilia of the era. Adults $12, children $10.
- **Parker Palm Springs Spa** (760-770-5000; www.theparkerpalmsprings.com), 4200 E. Palm Canyon Dr., Palm Springs. Rated by *Condé Nast Traveler* as one of the 10 best spas in the country, this spa in the **Parker** hotel offers the kind of upscale beauty and health treatments that have been drawing the rich and famous to Palm Springs for decades.
- **Plaza Theater** (760-327-0225; www.psfollies.com), 128 S. Palm Canyon Dr., Palm Springs. The historic Plaza in downtown Palm Springs is home to the infamous **Palm Springs Follies,** a Las Vegas–style music, dance, and comedy review that features showgirls well into their golden years.
- **Spa Resort Casino** (888-999-1995; www.sparesortcasino.com), 100 N. Indian Canyon Dr., Palm Springs. Located in downtown Palm Springs, this casino offers baccarat, poker, and high-stakes gaming tables.
- **The Trilogy at La Quinta** (760-771-0707; http://trilogycountryclub.com/golf .htm), 60-151 Trilogy Pkwy., La Quinta. A good percentage of visitors to Palm Springs come to golf, and there is arguably no better place to do so in town than The Trilogy at La Quinta, just outside of the city, which has been awarded four stars by *Golf Digest.* Green fee: $50–150.

Five Best Bets for Lodging and Dining in Palm Springs
Lodging
- **Hyatt Grand Champions** (760-341-1000; www.grandchampions.hyatt.com), 44-600 Indian Wells Lane, Indian Wells. Just outside of Palm Springs proper, this resort (adjacent to the magnificent 36-hole Indian Wells Golf Resort) is the epitome of desert relaxation. The extensive grounds are beautifully landscaped with drought-resistant native plants and a generous helping of towering palm trees, and is punctuated by seven pools, including a kids pool with a water slide and an adults-only pool lined with private cabanas. Moderate.

- **Hotel Zoso** (760-325-9676; www.hotelzoso.com), 150 S. Indian Canyon Dr., Palm Springs. This edgy boutique hotel in the heart of downtown Palm Springs is all about clean lines, sensual pleasures, and high-style décor. The on-site **Zlounge Supper Club and Cabaret** is a hot nightspot for locals and visitors. Expensive.
- **Parker** (760-770-5000; www.theparkerpalmsprings.com), 4200 E. Palm Canyon Dr., Palm Springs. This chic property was once film star Gene Autry's private estate, and it retains an air of residential comfort in its overflowing gardens and private bungalows. Famed designer Jonathan Adler is responsible for the eclectic midcentury modern chic aesthetic. Very expensive.
- **Riviera Resort and Spa** (760-327-8311; www.psriviera.com), 1600 N. Indian Canyon Dr., Palm Springs. Located in downtown Palm Springs, this revitalized, rambling 1950s-era resort is the very definition of fabulosity. Public spaces are flamboyant, and private spaces are just this side of overdone—although the effect is stylish. Moderate.
- **Westin Mission Hills Resort and Spa** (760-328-5955; www.starwoodhotels.com /westin), 21333 Dinah Shore Dr., Rancho Mirage. This all-inclusive resort just outside of Palm Springs offers enough amenities to keep guests on the property throughout their visit (including two spectacular golf courses), and the sophisticated, vaguely Asian-influenced design ensures that a stay of any length will be restful. Moderate to expensive.

Riviera Resort and Spa, Palm Springs

- **Big Mama's Soul Food** (760-324-8116), 68510 E. Palm Canyon Dr., Cathedral City. Open daily for lunch and dinner. Tucked into a strip mall amid car dealerships and fast-food chains, this small restaurant serves authentic Southern-style food at modest prices. Inexpensive.
- **Circa 59** (760-778-6659; www.psriviera.com), 1600 N. Indian Canyon Dr., Palm Springs). Open daily for breakfast, lunch, and dinner. Part of the **Riviera Resort**, this glamorous restaurant offers an outside space overlooking the sparkling pool, a romantic covered patio with gauzy curtains, and the over-the-top retro-chic interior space that boasts red walls and black chandeliers. Cuisine is classic steakhouse. Expensive.
- **Las Casuelas Terraza** (760-778-6744; www.lascasuelas.com), 222 S. Palm Canyon Dr., Palm Springs. Open daily for lunch and dinner. This festive family-owned restaurant has been serving up authentic and inventive Mexican specialties for more than 30 years. Large portions ensure that no one goes home hungry, and live nightly entertainment makes dinner here an event. Moderate.
- **Norma's** (760-321-4630; www.theparkerpalmsprings.com), 4200 E. Palm Canyon Dr., Palm Springs. Open daily for breakfast and lunch. Located at the exclusive **Parker** hotel, Norma's is stylish, relaxed, and offers possibly the coolest breakfast menu ever. Expensive.
- **Pomme Frite** (760-778-3727; www.pomme-frite.com), 256 S. Palm Canyon Rd., Palm Springs. Open daily for lunch and dinner. This friendly café on the main drag of Palm Springs serves French and Belgian bistro food. When the weather is temperate, eat outside on the sidewalk café and watch the world drive by. Moderate.

SANTA CATALINA ISLAND

A rocky, hilly island northwest of San Diego, Santa Catalina belongs to the Channel Islands chain off the coast of Long Beach. Catalina's crescent-shaped harbor has startlingly clear blue water and is perennially studded with sailboats and yachts (and sometimes cruise ships). The island has long been a favorite getaway for well-heeled Southern Californians and is popular with the Hollywood glitterati—and this is all thanks to a chewing gum magnate. In 1919, William Wrigley Jr. (also one-time owner of the Chicago Cubs) purchased the island and developed it into a resort destination. Wrigley liked the serenity and pristine beauty of the place so much that he built himself a mansion in the hills and brought the Cubs to the island for spring training for nearly 30 years. In 1975, Wrigley's heir turned over 88 percent of the island to the Catalina Island Conservancy, which now acts as steward to the wilderness reserve and runs most of the island's concessions.

To get here, take the **Catalina Express** (310-519-1212 or 877-358-6363; www.catalinaexpress.com; 34675 Golden Lantern, Dana Point), departing from Dana Point. Costs for a round-trip ticket are $68.50 for adults and $53 for children, and the trip takes approximately one hour. Be prepared for a rough ride; windy conditions can make for stomach-churning swells. If you aren't prone to seasickness, the trip over can be half the fun; expect to see schools of dolphins swimming alongside the boat, especially as it nears the Catalina harbor. To preserve the ecosystem and to cut down on road congestion, even locals have to wait at least 10

Santa Catalina Harbor and Casino

years to obtain the right to drive a car on the island, so plan to see Catalina by foot or aboard a tour bus. You can also rent bikes and golf carts by the hour. Note that Avalon, the only real city on the island, is within a few minutes' walk from the ferry landing.

Top 10 Don't-Miss Attractions on Santa Catalina Island

- **Adventure Rafting/Catalina Ocean Rafting** (310-510-0211; www.catalina oceanrafting.com), on the harbor. Tour the Avalon waterfront or Two Harbors aboard motor-powered inflatables, or book snorkeling trips to explore sea caves or frolic with dolphins.
- **Afishinado Charters** (310-510-2440; www.fishcatalina.com), on the harbor. Charter fishing trips for families or expert anglers, and expect to catch yellowtail tuna.
- **Avalon Theater** (310-510-0179), Santa Catalina Casino. This large restored art deco theater on the ground floor of the iconic Casino shows first-run movies in a stylish setting; the colorful wall murals are worth the price of admission.
- **Casino Building** (310-510-2414). At the northeastern end of the bay, the eye-catching Casino Building, a circular art deco structure, is the jewel of Avalon Harbor. Don't bring your bucket of coins to gamble the night away: in this instance, *casino* refers to the Italian word meaning "gathering place."
- **Catalina Adventure Tours** (877-510-2888; www.catalinaadventuretours.com), on the harbor. If you don't want to get wet, book a trip aboard a real-life yellow submarine, or board a glass bottom boat, for a peek into the clear Catalina waters.
- **Descanso Beach**, on the far end of Avalon Casino. This small, scenic private beach offers prime swimming and snorkeling. Part of the Descanso Beach Club, it has ample facilities, including outdoor showers, dressing rooms, and chair and umbrella rentals.
- **Green Pleasure Pier.** At the center of Crescent Ave., this historic pier dates to 1910 and is the jumping-off point for fishing trips and glass-bottom boat and submarine tours, and home to a handful of local fast-food outlets.
- **Luau Larry's** (310-510-1919), 509 Crescent Ave. This tropical tiki bar is adjacent to the beach and offers rowdy nightlife that attracts locals and tourists.
- **South Beach**, just right of the Green Pleasure Pier. This beach is at the heart of the action, near the many eateries in downtown Avalon and on the pier. The water is calm and deepens very gradually, which makes it ideal for children.
- **Wrigley Memorial and Botanical Gardens** (310-510-2595; www.catalina.com /memorial.html), Avalon Canyon Rd. Just 2 miles from Avalon Bay, the Wrigley Memorial and Botanical Gardens features a Spanish mausoleum inlaid with Catalina tiles.

Lodging

- **Avalon Hotel** (310-510-7070; www.theavalonhotel.com), 124 Whittley Ave. This small, historic hotel off Avalon Harbor showcases the famous Catalina tile and fine wooden details in Craftsman style, with individually decorated rooms that are comfortable and plush, and nice views of the harbor. Moderate.
- **Hotel St. Lauren** (310-510-2299; www.stlauren.com), P.O. Box 2166, Avalon, CA 90704. This romantic Victorian-style hotel is a block from the beach and the main drag of Avalon—and frankly it is a bit of a hike from the ferry landing—but it offers some real bargains, depending on room choice, view, and season. Inexpensive.
- **The Inn on Mt. Ada** (310-510-2030; www.innonmtada.com), P.O. Box 2560, Avalon, CA 90704. Listed on the National Register of Historic Places and dating to 1921, this Georgian Colonial mansion (former home to William Wrigley) is perched high on a hill overlooking Avalon Bay. A stay at this pricey lodging feels very much like a visit with a well-heeled friend, thanks to the luxurious yet comfortable surroundings and the impeccable hospitality of the innkeepers. Very expensive.
- **Snug Harbor Inn** (310-510-8400; www.snugharbor-inn.com), 108 Sumner Ave. This tiny inn is across from the beachfront and overlooks the bay. The small property manages to be quaint without being overly precious and offers the unparalleled convenience of being right in town. Expensive.
- **Zane Grey Pueblo Hotel** (310-510-0996; www.zanegreypueblohotel.com), 199 Chimes Tower Rd. High on a cliff overlooking the Casino, with lovely views of

Two Harbors, Santa Catalina

Courtesy of the Catalina CVB

the ocean and the mountains, this former home to Western novelist Zane Grey is a pueblo-style structure decorated with Southwestern flair. There are no clocks, no TVs, and no phones in the rooms—and children are not allowed. Moderate.

Dining

- **Antonio's Pizzeria** (310-510-0060), 114 Sumner Ave. Open daily for breakfast, lunch, and dinner. This longtime island favorite offers tasty Neapolitan pizza, antipasto, salads, pasta, and huge subs, to eat outside on the patio overlooking the harbor. Inexpensive.
- **Armstrong's Fish Market and Seafood Restaurant** (310-510-0133; www.armstrongseafood.com), 306 Crescent Ave. Open daily for lunch and dinner. The outdoor patio right off the water of this seafood restaurant offers great views of the harbor and the iconic Casino—and reliably good cuisine. Expensive.
- **Eric's on the Pier** (310-510-0894), Green Pier No. 2. Open daily for lunch and dinner. This snack shack on the water has been family run for more than 75 years and couldn't be more casual: don't be surprised to see guests pull up a stool in their bathing suits. Inexpensive.
- **Lobster Trap** (310-510-8585; www.catalinalobstertrap.com), 128 Catalina St. Open daily for lunch and dinner. This seafood joint is a bit of a dive, but the cuisine is top-notch, even if the ambiance is a little rough around the edges. Moderate.
- **Steve's Steakhouse** (310-510-0333; www.stevessteakhouse.com), 417 Crescent Ave. Open daily for dinner. This pricey yet casual steakhouse is sure to please carnivores with a wide variety of red meat, a smattering of seafood, and a full bar. Expensive.

Ballooning over vineyards in Temecula

TEMECULA WINE COUNTRY

The Temecula wine country—just northeast of the San Diego County line in Riverside—has grown up in the past decade, and now world-class wines are being produced at many of the valley wineries. The rolling hills, granitic soils, and 1,500-foot elevation provide ideal conditions for growing grapes, and vintners are taking advantage of this bounty. The wine country of Temecula is a 60-mile drive from downtown San Diego; many of the wineries are situated on a strip of Rancho California Road, about 6 miles east of the I-15, and the rest are nearby, just outside the suburban sprawl that is Temecula city. Although the highway through the vineyards gets congested on weekends, the wineries, restaurants, and resorts are still largely underappreciated by San Diegans—and therefore present a great opportunity to discover a hidden treasure. The winery zone boasts rolling vineyards and magnificent views of the mountains, and the charming wineries and quaint restaurants give Napa a run for its money. There are more than 50 wineries, most of which have daily tastings (usually beginning at 10 AM and running until 4 or 5 PM). Tastings generally cost $5 to $10 for five or six wines—although most wineries will pour a complimentary taste of one or two wines if you are serious about purchasing.

Top 10 Don't-Miss Attractions in Temecula Wine Country

- **Callaway Vineyard and Winery** (951-676-4001; www.callawaywinery.com), 32720 Rancho California Rd., Temecula. Founded by Ely Callaway, of golfing fame, this vineyard is one of the oldest in the valley and produces a large selection of wines, including the big reds for which Temecula is famous as well as dessert wines.
- **Falkner Winery** (951-676-8231; www.falknerwinery.com), 40620 Calle Contento, Temecula. With rolling vineyards and a stunning tasting room that is a popular site for weddings, Falkner Winery is generally abuzz with activity, offering free jazz concerts on Sun. and special wine and food events at critically acclaimed **The Pinnacle** restaurant.
- **Longshadow Ranch Vineyards** (951-587-6221; www.longshadowranchwinery .com), 39847 Calle Contento, Temecula. Offering horse-drawn carriage wine tours through the vineyards, Longshadow Ranch celebrates the old West heritage of Temecula and features award-winning merlots.
- **Old Town Temecula**, west of I-15, off Old California Rd., Temecula. Old Town Temecula (about 10 miles from the winery region) offers a Wild West–themed shoppers paradise, where you can pick up ostrich jerky from **The House of Jerky** (951-308-9232), authentic muffuletta from the **Temecula Olive Oil Company** (951-693-0607), and sample root beers and other vintage sodas from **Old Town Rootbeer Company** (951-676-5088).
- **Ponte Winery** (951-694-8855; www.pontewinery.com), 35053 Rancho California Rd., Temecula. A favorite with locals, the Ponte tasting room is relaxed and friendly, with some of the most helpful pourers in the area. The evocative barrel room is the site of special food and wine events throughout the year.
- **Robert Renzoni Vineyards** (951-302-8466; http://robertrenzonivineyards.com), 37350 Rancho California Rd., Temecula. Well-priced pinot grigio and chardonnay (available for about $20 per bottle) are the stars of this new vineyard, which boasts a stunning Tuscan villa tasting room.
- **South Coast Winery** (951-587-9463; www.wineresort.com), 34843 Rancho California Rd., Temecula. This elegant property boasts a lovely resort, fine restaurant, and a large tasting room, and is a favorite with 20-something wine lovers.
- **Tesoro Winery** (951-308-0000; www.tesorowinery.com), 28475 Old Town Front St., Temecula. The tasting room for this new winery is located in Old Town Temecula, convenient for shoppers. Every fall, Tesoro Winery hosts an *I Love Lucy*–style grape stomping, featuring live music and, of course, plenty of wine.
- **Thornton Winery** (951-699-0099; www.thorntonwine.com), 32575 Rancho California Rd., Temecula. An old-timer in the valley and one of the most respected wine destinations, thanks to premier vintner Don Reha, who specializes in big

reds and champagnes, Thornton also boasts a pretty herb garden and an especially good winemaking tour.

- **Wilson Creek Winery** (951-699-9463; www.wilsoncreekwinery.com), 35960
  Rancho California Rd., Temecula. A family-owned facility that doesn't take itself
  too seriously, Wilson Creek's owner/manager Bill Wilson jokes, "We will release
  no wine before its time. But when you're out of wine, it's time." Look for the
  unusual almond champagne.

Five Best Bets for Lodging and Dining in Temecula Wine Country
Lodging

- **Inn at Churon Winery** (951-694-9070; www.innatchuronwinery.com), 33233
  Rancho California Rd., Temecula. A quaint B&B that is part of the Churon
  Winery, this small inn offers a little bit of the French countryside in Temecula.
  The château-style inn is lavishly furnished and offers huge marble bathrooms,
  ornate European style, and spectacular views of the vineyard. Expensive.
- **Loma Vista Bed and Breakfast** (877-676-7047; www.lomavistabb.com), 33350
  La Serena Way, Temecula. Housed in a rambling mission-style home, the Loma
  Vista B&B offers serenity and views near the wineries. A stay includes a hot
  breakfast; don't miss the authentic scones. Moderate.
- **South Coast Winery Resort and Spa** (951-587-9463; www.wineresort.com),
  34843 Rancho California Rd., Temecula. Sited in the middle of the vineyards
  and wineries, South Coast is a luxurious and pricey collection of nearly 80 private villas designed to feel like individual vacation homes. The on-site restaurant and spa are extremely upscale. Expensive.

South Coast Winery, Temecula

- **Springhill Suites** (951-699-4477; www.marriott.com/hotels/travel/ontst-spring hill-suites-temecula-valley-wine-country), 28220 Jefferson Ave., Temecula. This conveniently located Marriott outlet offers large, bright suites and includes a pool, spa, and complimentary breakfast. Inexpensive to moderate.
- **Temecula Creek Inn** (951-694-1000; www.temeculacreekinn.com), 44501 Rainbow Canyon Rd., Temecula. Temecula Creek Inn is a relaxed, less-expensive option south of the winery region, on a beautiful golf course and surrounded by lush grounds overflowing with rosebushes. Moderate.

Dining

- **Café Champagne** (951-699-0099; www.thorntonwine.com), 32575 Rancho California Rd., Temecula. Open daily for lunch and dinner. My favorite restaurant choice close to the wineries (and on-site at the **Thornton Winery**), this small dining room offers finely prepared cuisine that, not surprisingly, pairs exceedingly well with Thornton wines. Expensive.
- **Meritage Restaurant** (951-676-4001; www.callawaywinery.com/callaway -restaurant.html), 32720 Rancho California Rd., Temecula. Open daily for dinner. At the **Callaway Winery**, this restaurant offers an enclosed terrace dining room with views of the vineyard and specializes in tapas. Expensive.
- **Smokehouse Restaurant** (951-694-8855; www.pontewinery.com/Temecula -Winery-Ponte-Smokehouse-Restaurant/4081.html), 35053 Rancho California Rd., Temecula. Open daily for dinner. At the **Ponte Winery**, the Smokehouse offers a covered outdoor patio surrounded by vineyards. Look for the chicken and potato pizza and the roasted portobello sandwiches. Moderate to expensive.
- **Temet Grill** (877-517-1823; www.temeculacreekinn.com), 44501 Rainbow Canyon Rd., Temecula. Open daily for breakfast, lunch, and dinner; Sun. for brunch. On-site at the **Temecula Creek Inn,** the Temet Grill offers a relaxing atmosphere and nice views of the links and the mountains beyond, as well as a stellar the Sun. champagne brunch. Moderate.
- **Vineyard Rose** (951-587-9463; www.wineresort.com), 34843 Rancho California Rd., Temecula. Open daily for breakfast, lunch, and dinner. Part of the beautiful **South Coast Winery Resort,** this expansive restaurant (with a lovely outdoor patio overlooking the vineyards) serves one of the best breakfasts in the area. Do not miss the bananas Foster pancake. Expensive.

Planning Your Trip

KNOW BEFORE YOU GO

Surprises can be the most memorable parts of a vacation. But it never hurts to be prepared, in case one of these unexpected adventures turns unpleasant. What follows is a brief guide that may help you resolve problems or answer questions once you arrive in town. I've also included a list of seasonal events at the end of the chapter, to help you take advantage of all the area has to offer.

Use this page to find what you need:

AMBULANCE, FIRE, AND POLICE

As with any U.S. locale, the only number you need to remember in an emergency in San Diego is 911. You'll instantly reach an operator who will put you through to the correct agency. To reach the police in nonemergency situations, call 619-531-2000. For the Poison Control Center, call 800-876-4766.

AREA CODES AND ZIP CODES

Area Codes

You must dial 1 plus the area code to make any local call in San Diego—even if you are calling another number in the same area code. Local long-distance rates apply when phoning local areas with different area codes, and additional long-distance service fees may be tacked on when dialing from a hotel phone.

Downtown San Diego, Uptown San Diego, Mission Valley, Coronado, Ocean Beach, and Point Loma: **619**
Mission Beach, Pacific Beach, La Jolla, Del Mar, Solana Beach: **858**
Encinitas, Carlsbad, Oceanside, Escondido: **760**

Zip Codes

Carlsbad	92008, 92009	La Jolla	92037
Coronado	92118	Ocean Beach	92107
Del Mar	92014	Oceanside	92054, 92057
Downtown San Diego	92101	Pacific Beach	92109
Encinitas	92024, 92027	Point Loma	92016

The Lily Pond and Botanical Building in Balboa Park

Although major earthquakes are extremely rare in San Diego, we live near several seismic hot spots, including the San Jacinto and the Rose Canyon faults, which produce tremblers every now and then and have the potential for catastrophic quakes. Small earthquakes usually last only a minute or so and do little more than rattle the windows—although it is always wise to take precautions even in what appears to be an insignificant episode, in case the trembler turns into something more serious. The U.S. Federal Emergency Management Agency (FEMA) recommends that in an earthquake you "drop, cover, and hold on"—in other words, drop to the ground, take cover under a sturdy table or desk, and hold on to it until the earthquake subsides.

Should you find yourself in the aftermath of a major earthquake, the American Red Cross counsels that you check yourself and others in your party for injuries, locate and then put out any small fires that may have been triggered by the episode, and inspect your dwelling for damage—and get out if you have any concerns about the structural integrity of the building. Note, however, that if your accommodation remains safe, you are better off remaining indoors. If you're inside, check for gas leaks, watch out for loose and broken plaster that could fall, and avoid broken windows and mirrors. If you're outside, stay away from fallen power lines, which can be deadly, and avoid spilled chemicals. Use telephones (both land lines and cell phones) only in emergencies; as other recent natural disasters have shown us, the communications infrastructure can become overloaded quickly, and tying up lines unnecessarily may prevent emergency and rescue workers from doing their jobs. Use a portable radio to tune in to safety advisories and to get more information. And expect aftershocks from major quakes. These can be almost as strong as the original earthquakes and can cause already compromised structures to fail completely.

It's wise to carry emergency supplies with you, even while traveling in your vehicle, including a first-aid kit, a flashlight, water and food, a portable radio, extra batteries, and a whistle. For more information on earthquake safety, download and read the online booklet *Steps to Safety*, published by the Southern California Earthquake Center, at www.scec.org/education/public/safetysteps.html.

HANDICAP SERVICES

Public transportation is barrier-free in San Diego, and fares on San Diego buses and trolleys are discounted for all those with disabilities. City buses are equipped with wheelchair lifts, and drivers will provide assistance as necessary. Many of the rental car agencies in town offer hand-controlled cars, although most companies require between 48 to 72 hours advance notice to ensure that an accessible vehicle will be available.

All major attractions and most restaurants and hotels in San Diego are wheelchair accessible. For specific questions about accessibility and to obtain up-to-date information on services in the city, call or check the Web site of **Access Center of San Diego** (619-293-3500; http://accesstoindependence.org) or **Accessible San Diego** (858-279-0704; www.asd.travel).

HOSPITALS

The following hospitals have 24-hour emergency room care, with physicians on duty.

Scripps Memorial Hospital (Encinitas)
760-633-6501
354 Santa Fe Dr.

Scripps Memorial Hospital (La Jolla)
858-626-4123
9888 Genesee Ave.

Sharp Coronado Hospital (Coronado)
619-522-3600
250 Prospect Pl.

Sharp Memorial Hospital (San Diego)
858-939-3400
7901 Frost St.

UCSD Medical Center (Hillcrest)
619-543-6222
200 W. Arbor Dr.

MEDIA

Major Newspapers and Magazines
La Prensa San Diego (newspaper)
North County Times (newspaper)
San Diego (magazine)
San Diego Business Journal (newspaper)
San Diego Daily Transcript (newspaper)
San Diego Reader (newspaper)
San Diego Union Tribune (newspaper)

San Diego Radio Stations
FM Stations

KBZT, 94.9	KIOZ, 105.3	KSON, 97.3
KFMB, 100.7	KMYI, 94.1	KUSS, 95.7
KHRM, 92.5	KPBS, 88.3	KYXY, 96.5
KHTS, 90.3	KPLN, 103.7	XHTS, 93.3
KIFM, 98.1	KSDS, 88.3	XTRA, 91.1

AM Stations

KFMB 760	KLSD 1360	KOGO 600

San Diego Television

KBNT, Channel 17 (Spanish)	KGTV, Channel 10	KUSI, Channel 9
KFMB, Channel 8	KSND, Channels 7, 39	XETV, Channel 6

Most visitors to Southern California are shocked by housing prices, which are among the most costly in the country. Although prices in some neighborhoods have taken as much as a 50 percent dive in the recent recession, in 2010 the median home cost in San Diego County was still more than $400,000. This translates to between $200 to $250 a square foot for suburbs that have no immediate access to the beach, and as much as $1,000 a square foot for beachfront or ocean-view properties.

If you come to San Diego and find yourself yearning to own a piece of paradise, like so many people do, call the **San Diego Association of Realtors** (858-715-8000), which will refer you to licensed agents. You can also check out real estate Web sites for photographs and other specifics on current listings (a good source is www.realtor.com) or peruse the *San Diego Union Tribune*, the Sunday real estate section of which is helpful in tracking new construction and finding existing properties for sale.

RELIGIOUS SERVICES

All major religions are represented in San Diego, and many services are offered in languages other than English. To find particular religious services, check the *San Diego Reader* Web site at www.sandiegoreader.com/places/places-worship/.

San Diego Convention Center

ROAD SERVICE

Nothing can ruin a vacation faster than getting stranded on the freeway or stuck in a beach parking lot. For emergency road service, members can call the American Automobile Association at 800-222-4357. Numerous local tow companies offer 24-hour assistance as well. Beware of tow trucks that come without being called first; such trucks troll the freeways for stranded motorists and often charge exorbitant towing rates. Get a quote in writing before you allow any company to move your vehicle.

SMOKING PROHIBITIONS

Many San Diego residents are not sympathetic to smokers, and California state law is becoming increasingly prohibitive. It is illegal to smoke inside restaurants or bars, as well as outdoor patio dining establishments. You may not smoke in outdoor stadiums (although there are designated smoking areas well away from the crowds), and it is illegal to smoke within 50 feet of an entrance to any public building. Many hotels ban smoking altogether. Smoking is also banned on public beaches throughout the county. Interestingly, the casinos run by Native American tribes are an exception, because they are not subject to state regulations.

TOURIST INFORMATION AND ONLINE ADDRESSES

Information Center	Description	Telephone	Web site
Coronado	visitors center	619-437-8788	www.coronadovisitor center.com
San Diego Arts	online visual and arts information	NA	www.sandiego.org/nav/ Visitors/WhatToDo/ ArtsCulture
Travelers Aid Society	travelers aid	619-295-8393	www.travelersaidsan diego.org
Union Tribune SignOn San Diego online information	online events	NA	www.signonsan diego.com

WEATHER, WHAT TO WEAR, AND WHEN TO VISIT

Weather

There is rarely cause for complaint about the weather in San Diego: temperatures generally stay comfortable all year long, with a daytime average of 70 degrees Fahrenheit (21 degrees Celsius), and there is usually low humidity. Neighborhoods close to the coast are cooler in the summer, often with heavy morning and evening fog during late summer and early fall, and these same neighborhoods are subject to year-round morning clouds. In late spring and early summer, the prevailing weather is so gray at the beaches that the phrases "May Gray" and "June Gloom" were coined to describe the ubiquitous clouds. Inland neighborhoods, which tend

Boats at Mission Bay

to be sunnier, can reach temperatures of more than 100 in the middle of summer and drop to the 40s and even 30s in winter evenings—although it rarely dips below freezing in the valleys. Even during summer months, it can get chilly at night, especially if you're near the ocean.

The area gets very little precipitation (an average of about 10 inches a year), and this almost always comes

Average Temperatures (in degrees Fahrenheit)		
	Low	*High*
January	50	66
April	56	69
July	66	76
October	61	74

during our "rainy season," between December and March. We average nearly 325 clear days a year. The mountains sometimes get snow in high elevations, but we don't see flurries in the city or along the coast. Starting in September and stretching into early December, we're subject to Santa Anas, which are strong, hot, dry winds that blow through for several days at a time. These unfortunately coincide with fire season, and although in past years populated areas generally had little cause to worry, in recent years large swaths of the city have been evacuated because of threatening wildfires. During these rare episodes, air quality is significantly compromised.

Weather Reports

For up-to-date weather reports, call 619-289-1212. For beach reports and surf conditions, call 619-221-8824.

What to Wear

The stereotype of "laid-back" Californians is apt when considering dress codes. Casual clothing like jeans, shorts, and T-shirts are common at all local beaches, attractions, and most restaurants, especially those located near the shores. Downtown restaurants and clubs are more formal, as are pricier establishments throughout the area, especially in La Jolla and Del Mar. A jacket for men and a smart dress or pantsuit for women will suffice for all but the fussiest places. Be sure to pack a bathing suit, no matter the time of year you're visiting, and flip-flops or sandals for walking on the beach. Don't forget a light sweater in the summer, especially if you'll be near the beach at night. A light jacket will do for the colder months; there is no need for a heavy coat, boots, or gloves, even if you come during what ought to be the dead of winter. A good pair of sunglasses will stand you in good stead as well; the glare of the sun is stronger here than in northern locales.

Average Total Precipitation (in inches)	
January	2.28
February	2.04
March	2.26
April	0.75
May	0.20
June	0.09
July	0.03
August	0.09
September	0.21
October	0.44
November	1.07
December	1.31

Ellen Browning Scripps Park, near La Jolla Cove

La Jolla Cove

When to Visit

Thanks to the mild temperatures and low precipitation, San Diego is a year-round destination. You can beat the heat and humidity that prevails throughout most of the rest of the United States if you visit during the summer, and you can escape the deep freeze by coming here in winter—although near the beach it can get nippy enough to require a light jacket year-round. Spring is glorious—the normally olive-drab hills turn bright green after the winter rains, and the flowers explode into color. Another great time to visit is autumn, when the lodging rates are lower and crowds have thinned. Best of all, as every local knows, the ocean temperatures are usually warmer in early October than they are in early June.

SEASONAL EVENTS

January

- Ring in the new year—literally—with the Buddhist Temple of San Diego (619-239-0896) at the annual **New Year's Eve Bell-Ringing Ceremony** at Shelter Island's Friendship Bell.
- Kick off the year with **San Diego Restaurant Week** (www.sandiegorestaurant week.com), when more than one hundred of the best restaurants in the city offer three-course fixed-price menus for $35 or $40 per person.
- In midmonth, catch the **Martin Luther King Jr. Day Parade and Festival** (619-264-0542) downtown, where you'll find lively marching bands and floats and a multicultural festival of food, entertainment, and art.
- The **Buick Invitational Golf Tournament** (800-888-2842), one of the biggest golf events in the country, is held at the Torrey Pines Municipal Golf Course in La Jolla this month.

February

- Join the San Diego Chinese Center for the annual **Chinese New Year Celebration** (619-234-7844) downtown, at Third Ave. and J St., featuring food, artisans, and entertainment.
- Grab some beads at the annual **Mardi Gras** celebration in the Gaslamp Quarter downtown (619-233-5227) on Fat Tuesday, featuring New Orleans–style food and entertainment.
- Feb. is prime whale watching season; catch a two-hour tour with **Helgren's Sportfishing** (760-722-2133) and head out into the migration path as the California gray whales make their way from Alaska to the warmer waters of Baja lagoons to mate and have their babies.

March

- Don't miss the **Kiwanis Ocean Beach Kite Festival** (http://oceanbeachkiwanis .org) this month, which features contests for making and flying kites, as well as free food for participants, entertainment, and a craft show.
- The Irish Congress of Southern California sponsors the annual **Saint Patrick's Day Parade** (858-268-9111) in Mar., which lights up Fifth and Sixth avenues alongside Balboa Park with bands, floats, and dancers; be sure to stick around for the **Smilin' Irishman** contest.
- Or if you're in North County, check out the **St. Patrick's Day Parade and Festival** (760-931-8400) held in Carlsbad Village on Mar. 17, beginning at Roosevelt St. and Walnut Ave., complete with food and live music.
- Starting in early Mar. and running through mid-May, ranunculus in Carlsbad's famous **Flower Fields** in Carlsbad Ranch (760-431-0352) are blooming, and for a fee you can wander the colorful few acres.

April

- In early Apr. join the **ArtWalk Festival** (619-615-1090); self-guided tours begin in Little Italy downtown and highlight the visual and performing arts.
- Also early this month, catch the **San Diego Crew Classic** (619-225-0300) at Crown Point Shores Park in Mission Bay. The annual regatta features more than three thousand collegiate, masters, and high school rowers.
- **San Diego Botanical Gardens** (760-436-3036) in Encinitas hosts the **Flower by the Sea Show** the first weekend in Apr., showcasing professional horticulturalists and floral designers.
- Later in the month catch **Art Alive** (619-232-7931), a yearly exhibit of floral arrangements by some of the best designers in the city, inspired by the permanent art collection at the San Diego Museum of Art in Balboa Park, where the creations are displayed.

May

- The **Old Town Fiesta Cinco de Mayo** (619-220-5422) on May 5 is consistently one of the best parties in town, with historic re-creations of the Battle of Puebla (the victory Cinco de Mayo celebrates) and plenty of food, drinks, and mariachi music to celebrate the festive holiday.

- The **Carlsbad Village Street Faire** (760-931-8400) is held the first Sun. in May and is the largest single-day street fair in California. You'll find the festivities along the whole of Grand Ave., one block north of Carlsbad Village Drive.
- Get a peek into some of the most beautiful residential gardens in the city throughout this month with the **Secret Garden Tour** (858-459-5335), sponsored by the La Jolla Historical Society.

June

- Starting in June, enjoy a night under the stars at the **Summer Organ Festival** (619-702-8138), a Mon.-night free concert series at Balboa Park's outdoor Spreckels Organ Pavilion.
- Also starting in June and continuing through Labor Day, come to La Jolla Cove on Sun. afternoons for the free **La Jolla Concerts by the Sea** (www.ljconcerts bythesea.org) series, with musical offerings ranging from rock and roll oldies to big band and swing groups.
- Starting in mid-June and stretching through the Fourth of July is the **San Diego County Fair** (858-755-1161), held on the **Del Mar Fairgrounds and Racetrack**. This expansive event comprises 4-H animal displays, cooking contests, arts and crafts displays, hundreds of entertaining exhibitors hawking their gadgets, a midway with more than 50 thrill rides and nearly one hundred games, and food booths that specialize in anything fried on a stick.

Ride at the San Diego County Fair

July

- Running from July through Sept., the **San Diego Symphony Summer Pops** (619-235-0804) downtown provides outdoor nighttime musical entertainment at the Embarcadero.
- You'll find an old-fashioned Fourth of July celebration at the **Coronado Independence Day** bash (619-437-8788), with a flag-waving parade, demonstrations by the U.S. Navy (including exhilarating flybys), and fireworks over Glorietta Bay, with the San Diego skyline as a backdrop.
- Also this month, the **U.S. Open Sandcastle Competition** (http://members.cox.net/usopensandcastle), held at Imperial Beach (just south of Coronado) every summer, brings together professional sand sculptors, amateurs, and kids of all ages for one of the largest sand-castle-building competitions in the United States.
- A weekend-long celebration of diversity, the annual lesbian and gay **Pride Parade, Rally, and Festival** (619-297-7683) culminates in a parade through Hillcrest featuring more than two hundred floats, bands, and dance ensembles.
- It doesn't get bigger (or rowdier) than the **World Championship Over-the-Line Tournament** (619-688-0817) on Fiesta Island in Mission Bay, held over two weekends in July, where more than 1,200 three-member teams compete in a softball-like tourney that inevitably devolves into good-humored debauchery.
- To celebrate the founding of the first mission in California, the Mission San Diego de Alcalá, in mid-July the **Festival of the Bells** (619-281-8449) features the ringing of the Alcalá tower bells.
- **Jazz in the Parks** is a free outdoor event in Carlsbad held every Fri. evening throughout the month of July and rotates between **Stagecoach Park** (3420 Camino de los Coches) and **Calavera Hills Park** (2997 Glasgow Dr.) in Carlsbad.

August

- Aug. ushers in the La Jolla Music Society's **SummerFest** (858-459-3724), featuring more than a dozen performances of classical and new compositions performed by ensembles and world-class artists in venues throughout the city.
- Also this month, head to the Oceanside Pier and Beach to watch the **World Body Surfing Championships** (www.worldbodysurfing.org), where more than two hundred of the world's best body surfers battle it out.

September

- Check out the **Cabrillo Festival** (619-557-5450) at the Cabrillo National Monument in Point Loma, which commemorates Juan Cabrillo's explorations with a weeklong celebration that includes a historical reenactment.
- The annual **Ocean Beach Jazz Festival** (619-224-4906), sponsored by a local jazz radio station and the Ocean Beach Mainstreet Association, features dozens of musicians from around the country at the Ocean Beach Pier.
- **YachtFest** (www.yachtfest.com), in mid-Sept. at Shelter Island, celebrates the Port of San Diego, which is said to attract more yachts than any other harbor in the Pacific Rim.

- **Oktoberfest** (760-931-8400) is celebrated the first weekend in Oct. at **Holiday Park** at the corner of Chestnut St. and Pio Pico in Carlsbad. The festivities feature music, dancing, crafts, German food, and—of course—beer.
- Celebrate Italian culture at the annual **Little Italy Precious Festa** (619-233-3898) downtown, sponsored by the Little Italy community association and the Precious Cheese Company in mid-Oct.; while you're here, check out four of the best teams in the nation competing for honors in the **Festa Stickball Championship.**
- Keep your eyes on the skies in mid-Oct. for the annual **Miramar Air Show** (858-577-4099), held at the Miramar Marine Corps facility and featuring the famous Blue Angels precision flying team as well as other aeronautic acrobats.
- If you're looking for something to spook up your Halloween celebrations, look into the **Ghosts and Gravestones** tour (619-298-8687) led this month by Old Town Trolley Tours and the San Diego Historical Society; you'll visit "haunted" sites throughout the city.
- Enjoy an only-in-Southern-California event at the annual **Underwater Pumpkin Carving Contest** (858-565-6054) off La Jolla Shores, where scuba divers compete to carve the best jack-o'-lanterns while submerged. It's sponsored by a local dive shop, and proceeds from the event, which includes a barbecue, are donated to local charities.

November
- Starting in Nov. and running through Jan., strap on your ice skates and head to Horton Plaza; **The Fantasy on Ice Rink** (619-238-1596) at Horton Square downtown is a big hit with weary shoppers and children.
- East of downtown, the suburb of **El Cajon** hosts the charming **Mother Goose Parade** (619-444-8712) on the Sun. before Thanksgiving, a nationally televised parade that features more than two hundred floats, bands, and equestrian demonstrations.
- In late Nov., and running through the end of the year, enjoy the **Holiday of Lights at Del Mar** (858-755-1161), when the Del Mar Race Track is transformed with more than 350 brilliant holiday light displays that guests can view from their car while driving the infield racetrack (an interesting experience even without the festive lights).

December
- Usher in the holidays with **Balboa Park December Nights** (619-239-0512), on the first Fri. and Sat. of Dec.; you'll enjoy a candlelight procession beginning near the Spreckels Organ Pavilion, carolers, crafts, food, and an appearance by Santa Claus himself.
- Bring your holiday cheer to La Jolla for the annual **La Jolla Christmas Parade,** held in early Dec., starting on Silverado Rd. and featuring local marching bands, scout groups, floats, and classic cars. The day ends with the traditional lighting of the community Christmas tree.
- Celebrate Christmas in pure San Diego fashion at the **San Diego Bay Parade of Lights** (619-224-2240; www.sdparadeoflights.org); watch the harbor overflow with lighted and holiday-themed boats that sail in a procession beginning at

Ice-skating rink on Coronado Beach, at the Hotel del Coronado   Courtesy of the Hotel del Coronado

Shelter Island and ending at the Coronado Ferry Landing. The evenings' festivities are capped off by a rousing fireworks show.
- Throughout the month, enjoy afternoon ice skating (call for hours) with a view of the ocean at the **Hotel del Coronado** (619-435-6611), which puts up a temporary rink on the beach every Dec.
- Football fans will not want to miss the **Pacific Life Holiday Bowl** (619-283-5808), held in Qualcomm Stadium at the end of the month, a postseason football game between two college teams from the PAC 10 and the Big 12. It is preceded by the **Pacific Life Holiday Bowl Parade**, held along the downtown waterfront and featuring giant inflatable balloon characters, marching bands from across the country, and floats.

Index